ANALYSIS OF FINANCIAL DATA

ANALYSIS OF FINANCIAL DATA

by

Gary Koop

University of Strathclyde

John Wiley & Sons, Ltd

Other Wiley Editorial Offices

John Wiley & Sons Inc., 111 River Street, Hoboken, NJ 07030, USA

Jossey-Bass, 989 Market Street, San Francisco, CA 94103-1741, USA

Wiley-VCH Verlag GmbH, Boschstr. 12, D-69469 Weinheim, Germany

John Wiley & Sons Australia Ltd, 42 McDougall Street, Milton, Queensland 4064, Australia

John Wiley & Sons (Asia) Pte Ltd, 2 Clementi Loop #02-01, Jin Xing Distripark, Singapore 129809

John Wiley & Sons Canada Ltd, 22 Worcester Road, Etobicoke, Ontario, Canada M9W 1L1

Wiley also publishes its books in a variety of electronic formats. Some content that appears in print may
not be available in electronic books

Library of Congress Cataloging-in-Publication Data

Koop, Gary.
     Analysis of financial data / by Gary Koop.
       p.   cm.
     Includes bibliographical references and index.
     ISBN-13 978-0-470-01321-2 (pbk. : alk. paper)
     ISBN-10 0-470-01321-4 (pbk. : alk. paper)
   1. Finance – Mathematical models.   2. Econometrics.   I. Title.
     HG106.K67 2006
     332′.01′5195 – dc22

                                      2005017245

British Library Cataloguing in Publication Data

A catalogue record for this book is available from the British Library

ISBN-13 978-0-470-01321-2
ISBN-10 0-470-01321-4

Typeset in 11 on 13pt Garamond Monotype by SNP Best-set Typesetter Ltd., Hong Kong

Contents

Preface

This book aims to teach financial econometrics to students whose primary interest is not in econometrics. These are the students who simply want to apply financial econometric techniques sensibly in the context of real-world empirical problems. This book is aimed largely at undergraduates, for whom it can serve either as a stand-alone course in applied data analysis or as an accessible alternative to standard statistical or econometric textbooks. However, students in graduate economics and MBA programs requiring a crash-course in the basics of practical financial econometrics will also benefit from the simplicity of the book and its intuitive bent.

This book grew out of a previous book I wrote called *Analysis of Economic Data*. When writing my previous book I attempted to hold to the following principles:

1. It must cover most of the tools and models used in modern econometric research (e.g. correlation, regression and extensions for time series methods).
2. It must be largely non-mathematical, relying on verbal and graphical intuition.
3. It must contain extensive use of real data examples and involve students in hands-on computer work.
4. It must be short. After all, students in most degree programs must master a wide range of material. Students rarely have the time or the inclination to study statistics in depth.

In *Analysis of Financial Data* I have attempted to follow these principles as well but change the material so that it is of more interest for a financial audience. It aims to teach students reasonably sophisticated statistical tools, using simple non-mathematical intuition and practical examples. Its unifying themes are the related concepts of regression and correlation. These simple concepts are relatively easy to motivate using verbal and graphical intuition and underlie many of the sophisticated models (e.g. vector autoregressions and models of financial volatility such as ARCH and GARCH) and techniques (e.g. cointegration and unit root tests) in financial research today. If a student understands the concepts of correlation and regression well, then she can understand and apply the techniques used in advanced financial econometrics and statistics.

This book has been designed for use in conjunction with a computer. I am convinced that practical hands-on computer experience, supplemented by formal lectures, is the best way for students to learn practical data analysis skills. Extensive problem sets are accompanied by different data sets in order to encourage students to work as much as possible with real-world data. Every theoretical point in the book is illustrated with practical financial examples that the student can replicate and extend using the computer. It is my strong belief that every hour a student spends in front of the computer is worth several hours spent in a lecture.

This book has been designed to be accessible to a variety of students, and thus, contains minimal mathematical content. Aside from some supplementary material in appendices, it assumes no mathematics beyond the pre-university level. For students unfamiliar with these basics (e.g. the equation of a straight line, the summation operator, logarithms), appendices at the end of chapters provide sufficient background.

I would like to thank my students and colleagues at the Universities of Edinburgh, Glasgow and Leicester for their comments and reactions to the lectures that formed the foundation of this book. Many reviewers also offered numerous helpful comments. Most of these were anonymous, but Ian Marsh, Denise Young, Craig Heinicke, Kai Li and Hiroyuki Kawakatsu offered numerous invaluable suggestions that were incorporated in the book. I am grateful, in particular, to Steve Hardman at John Wiley for the enthusiasm and expert editorial advice he gave throughout this project. I would also like to express my deepest gratitude to my wife, Lise, for the support and encouragement she provided while this book was in preparation.

CHAPTER 1

Introduction

There are many types of professionals working in the world today who are interested in financial data. Academics in universities often derive and test theoretical models of behavior of financial assets. Civil servants and central bankers often study the merits of policies under consideration by government. Such policies often depend on what is happening with stock markets, interest rates, house prices and exchange rates. In the private sector, practitioners often seek to predict stock market movements or the performance of particular companies.

For all of these people, the ability to work with data is an important skill. To decide between competing theories, to predict the effect of policy changes, or to forecast what may happen in the future, it is necessary to appeal to facts. In finance, we are fortunate in having at our disposal an enormous amount of facts (in the form of "data") that we can analyze in various ways to shed light on many economic issues.

The purpose of this book is to present the basics of data analysis in a simple, non-mathematical way, emphasizing graphical and verbal intuition. It focuses on the tools used by financial practitioners (primarily regression and the extensions necessary for time series data) and develops computer skills that are necessary in virtually any career path that the student of finance may choose to follow.

To explain further what this book does, it is perhaps useful to begin by discussing what it does **not** do. Financial econometrics is the name given to the study of quantitative tools for analyzing financial data. The field of econometrics is based on probability and statistical theory; it is a fairly mathematical field. This book does not attempt to teach much probability and statistical theory. Neither does it contain much mathematical content. In both these respects, it represents a clear departure from traditional financial econometrics textbooks. Yet, it aims to teach most of the tools used by practitioners today.

Books that merely teach the student which buttons to press on a computer without providing an understanding of what the computer is doing, are commonly referred to as "cookbooks". The present book is **not** a cookbook. Some econometricians may interject at this point: "But how can a book teach the student to use the tools of financial econometrics, without teaching the basics of probability and statistics?" My answer is that much of what the financial econometrician does in practice can be understood intuitively, without resorting to probability and statistical theory. Indeed, it is a contention of this book that most of the tools econometricians use can be mastered simply through a thorough understanding of the concept of correlation, and its generalization, regression (including specialized variants of regression for time series models). If a student understands correlation and regression well, then he/she can understand most of what econometricians do. In the vast majority of cases, it can be argued that regression will reveal most of the information in a data set. Furthermore, correlation and regression are fairly simple concepts that can be understood through verbal intuition or graphical methods. They provide the basis of explanation for more difficult concepts, and can be used to analyze many types of financial data.

This book focuses on the **analysis** of financial data. That is, **it is not a book about collecting financial data**. With some exceptions, it treats the data as given, and does not explain how the data is collected or constructed. For instance, it does not explain how company accounts are created. It simply teaches the reader to make sense out of the data that has been gathered.

Statistical theory usually proceeds from the formal definition of general concepts, followed by a discussion of how these concepts are relevant to particular examples. The present book attempts to do the opposite. That is, **it attempts to motivate general concepts through particular examples**. In some cases formal definitions are not even provided. For instance, P-values and confidence intervals are important statistical concepts, providing measures relating to the accuracy of a fitted regression line (see Chapter 5). The chapter uses examples, graphs and verbal intuition to demonstrate how they might be used in practice. But no formal definition of a P-value nor derivation of a confidence interval is ever given. This would require the introduction of probability and statistical theory, which is not necessary for using these techniques sensibly in practice. For the reader wishing to learn more about the statistical theory underlying the techniques, many books are available; for instance *Introductory Statistics for Business and Economics* by Thomas Wonnacott and Ronald Wonnacott (Fourth edition, John Wiley & Sons, 1990). For those interested in how statistical theory is applied in financial econometrics, *The Econometrics of Financial Markets* by John Campbell, Andrew Lo and Craig MacKinlay (Princeton University Press, 1997) and *The Econometric Modelling of Financial Time Series* by Terrence Mills (Second edition, Cambridge University Press, 1999) are two excellent references.

This book reflects my belief that the use of concrete examples is the best way to teach data analysis. Appropriately, each chapter presents several examples as a means of illustrating key concepts. One risk with such a strategy is that some students might interpret the presence of so many examples to mean that a myriad of concepts must be mastered before they can ever hope to become adept at the practice of econometrics. This is not the case. At the heart of this book are only a few basic concepts, and they appear repeatedly in a variety of different problems and data sets. The best approach for teaching introductory financial econometrics, in other words, is to illustrate its specific concepts over and over again in a variety of contexts.

Organization of the book

In organizing the book, I have attempted to adhere to the general philosophy outlined above. Each chapter covers a topic and includes a general discussion. However, most of the chapter is devoted to empirical examples that illustrate and, in some cases, introduce important concepts. Exercises, which further illustrate these concepts, are included in the text. Data required to work through the empirical examples and exercises can be found in the website which accompanies this book **http://www.wiley.com/go/koopafd**. By including many data sets, it is hoped that students will not only replicate the examples, but will feel comfortable extending and/or experimenting with the data in a variety of ways. Exposure to real-world data sets is essential if students are to master the conceptual material and apply the techniques covered in this book.

Most of the empirical examples in this book are designed for use in conjunction with the computer package Excel. However, for the more advanced time series methods used in the latter chapters of the book, Excel is not appropriate. The computer package Stata has been used to do the empirical examples presented in these latter chapters. However, there is a wide range of other computer packages that can be used (e.g. E-views, MicroFit, Gauss, Matlab, R, etc.).

The website associated with this book contains all the data used in this book in Excel format. Excel is a simple and common software package and most other common packages (e.g. Stata) can work with Excel files. So it should be easy for the student to work with the data used in this book, even if he/she does not have Excel or Stata. Appendix B at the end of the book provides more detail about the data.

Throughout this book, mathematical material has been kept to a minimum. In some cases, a little bit of mathematics will provide additional intuition. For students familiar with mathematical techniques, appendices have been included at the end of some chapters.

The content of the book breaks logically into two parts. Chapters 1–7 cover all the basic material relating to graphing, correlation and regression. A very short course would cover only this material. Chapters 8–12 emphasize time series topics and analyze some of the more sophisticated financial econometric models in use today. The focus on the underlying intuition behind regression means that this material should be easily accessible to students. Nevertheless, students will likely find that these latter chapters are more difficult than Chapters 1–7.

Useful background

As mentioned, this book assumes very little mathematical background beyond the pre-university level. Of particular relevance are:

- Knowledge of simple equations. For instance, the equation of a straight line is used repeatedly in this book.
- Knowledge of simple graphical techniques. For instance, this book is full of graphs that plot one variable against another (i.e. standard XY-graphs).
- Familiarity with the summation operator is useful occasionally.
- In a few cases, logarithms are used.

For the reader unfamiliar with these topics, the appendix at the end of this chapter provides a short introduction. In addition, these topics are discussed elsewhere, in many introductory textbooks.

This book also has a large computer component, and much of the computer material is explained in the text. There are a myriad of computer packages that could be used to implement the procedures described in this book. In the places where I talk directly about computer programs, I will use the language of the spreadsheet and, particularly, that most common of spreadsheets, Excel. I do this largely because the average student is more likely to have knowledge of and access to a spreadsheet rather than a specialized statistics or econometrics package such as E-views, Stata or MicroFit.

I assume that the student knows the basics of Excel (or whatever computer software package he/she is using). In other words, students should understand the basics of spreadsheet terminology, be able to open data sets, cut, copy and paste data, etc. If this material is unfamiliar to the student, simple instructions can be found in Excel's on-line documentation. For computer novices (and those who simply want to learn more about the computing side of data analysis) *Computing Skills for Economists* by Guy Judge (John Wiley & Sons, 2000) is an excellent place to start.

Appendix 1.1: Concepts in mathematics used in this book

This book uses very little mathematics, relying instead on intuition and graphs to develop an understanding of key concepts (including understanding how to interpret the numbers produced by computer programs such as Excel). For most students, previous study of mathematics at the pre-university level should give you all the background knowledge you need. However, here is a list of the concepts used in this book along with a brief description of each.

The equation of a straight line

Financial analysts are often interested in the relationship between two (or more) variables. Examples of variables include stock prices, interest rates, etc. In our context a variable is something the researcher is interested in and can collect data on. I use capital letters (e.g. Y or X) to denote variables. A very general way of denoting a relationship is through the concept of a function. A common mathematical notation for a function of X is f(X). So, for instance, if the researcher is interested in the factors which explain why some stocks are worth more than others, she may think that the price of a share in a company depends on the earnings of that company. In mathematical terms, she would then let Y denote the variable "price of a share" and X denote the variable "earnings" and the fact the Y depends on X is written using the notation:

$$Y = f(X)$$

This notation should be read "Y is a function of X" and captures the idea that the value for Y depends on the value of X. There are many functions that one could use, but in this book I will usually focus on linear functions. Hence, I will not use this general "f(X)" notation in this book.

The equation of a straight line (what was called a "linear function" above) is used throughout this book. Any straight line can be written in terms of an equation:

$$Y = \alpha + \beta X$$

where α and β are *coefficients* which determine a particular line. So, for instance, setting $\alpha = 1$ and $\beta = 2$ defines one particular line while $\alpha = 4$ and $\beta = -5$ defines a different line.

It is probably easiest to understand straight lines by using a graph (and it might be worthwhile for you to sketch one at this stage). In terms of an XY graph (i.e. one which measures Y on the vertical axis and X on the horizontal axis) any line can be defined by its intercept and slope. In terms of the equation of a straight line α is the intercept and β the slope. The intercept is the value of Y when $X = 0$ (i.e. point at which the line cuts the Y-axis). The slope is a measure of how much Y changes when X is changed. Formally, it is the amount Y changes when X changes by one unit. For the student with a knowledge of calculus, the slope is the first derivative, $\dfrac{dY}{dX}$.

Summation notation

At several points in this book, subscripts are used to denote different observations of a variable. For instance, a researcher in corporate finance might be interested in the earnings of every one of 100 companies in a certain industry. If the researcher uses Y to denote this variable, then she will have a value of Y for the first company, a value of Y for the second company, etc. A compact notation for this is to use subscripts so that Y_1 is the earnings of the first company, Y_2 the earnings of the second company, etc. In some contexts, it is useful to speak of a generic company and refer to this company as the *i*-th. We can then write, Y_i for $i = 1, \ldots, 100$ to denote the earning of all companies.

With the subscript notation established, summation notation can now be introduced. In many cases we want to add up observations (e.g. when calculating an average you add up all the observations and divide by the number of observations). The Greek symbol, Σ (pronounced "sigma"), is the summation (or "adding up") operator and superscripts and subscripts on Σ indicate the observations that are being added up. So, for instance,

$$\sum_{i=1}^{100} Y_i = Y_1 + Y_2 + \ldots + Y_{100}$$

adds up the earnings for all of the 100 companies. As other examples,

$$\sum_{i=1}^{3} Y_i$$

adds up the earnings for the first 3 companies and

$$\sum_{i=47}^{48} Y_i$$

adds up the earnings for the 47th and 48th companies.

Sometimes, where it is obvious from the context (usually when summing over all companies), the subscript and superscript will be dropped and I will simply write:

$$\sum Y_i.$$

Logarithms

For various reasons (which are explained later on), in some cases the researcher does not work directly with a variable but with a transformed version of this variable. Many such transformations are straightforward. For instance, in comparing different companies financial economists sometimes use the price-to-earnings ratio. This is a transformed version of the stock price and earnings variables where the former is divided by the latter.

One particularly common transformation is the logarithmic one. The logarithm (to the base B) of a number, A, is the power to which B must be raised to give A. The notation for this is: $\log_B(A)$. So, for instance, if $B = 10$ and $A = 100$ then the logarithm is 2 and we write $\log_{10}(100) = 2$. This follows since $10^2 = 100$. In finance, it is common to work with the so-called natural logarithm which has $B = e$ where $e \approx 2.71828$. We will not explain where e comes from or why this rather unusual-looking base is chosen. The natural logarithm operator is denoted by ln; i.e. $\ln(A) = \log_e(A)$.

In this book, you do not really have to understand the material in the previous paragraph. The key thing to note is that the natural logarithmic operator is a common one (for reasons explained later on) and it is denoted by $\ln(A)$. In practice, it can be easily calculated in a spreadsheet such as Excel (or on a calculator).

CHAPTER 2

Basic data handling

This chapter introduces the basics of data handling. It focuses on four important areas:

1. The types of financial data that are commonly used.
2. A brief discussion of the sources from which data can be obtained.[1]
3. An illustration of the types of graphs that are commonly used to present information in a data set.
4. A discussion of simple numerical measures, or descriptive statistics, often presented to summarize key aspects of a data set.

Types of financial data

This section introduces common types of data and defines the terminology associated with their use.

Time series data

Financial researchers are often interested in phenomena such as stock prices, interest rates, exchange rates, etc. This data is collected at specific points in time. In all of these examples, the data are ordered by time and are referred to as **time series** data. The underlying phenomenon which we are measuring (e.g. stock prices, interest rates, etc.) is referred to as a **variable**. Time series data can be observed at many **frequen-**

cies. Commonly used frequencies are: **annual** (i.e. a variable is observed every year), **quarterly** (i.e. four times a year), **monthly, weekly** or **daily**.[2]

In this book, we will use the notation Y_t to indicate an observation on variable Y (e.g. an exchange rate) at time t. A series of data runs from period $t = 1$ to $t = T$. "T" is used to indicate the total number of time periods covered in a data set. To give an example, if we were to use monthly time series data from January 1947 through October 1996 on the UK pound/US dollar exchange – a period of 598 months – then $t = 1$ would indicate January 1947, $t = 598$ would indicate October 1996 and $T = 598$ the total number of months. Hence, Y_1 would be the pound/dollar exchange rate in January 1947, Y_2 this exchange rate in February 1947, etc. Time series data are typically presented in chronological order.

Working with time series data often requires some special tools, which are discussed in Chapters 8–11.

Cross-sectional data

In contrast to the above, some researchers often work with data that is characterized by individual **units**. These units might refer to companies, people or countries. For instance, a researcher investigating theories relating to portfolio allocation might collect data on the return earned on the stocks of many different companies. With such **cross-sectional** data, the ordering of the data typically does not matter (unlike time series data).

In this book, we use the notation Y_i to indicate an observation on variable Y for individual i. Observations in a cross-sectional data set run from unit $i = 1$ to N. By convention, "N" indicates the number of cross-sectional units (e.g. the number of companies surveyed). For instance, a researcher might collect data on the share price of $N = 100$ companies at a certain point in time. In this case, Y_1 will be equal to the share price of the first company, Y_2 the share price of the second company, and so on.

The distinction between qualitative and quantitative data

It is worthwhile stressing an important distinction between types of data. In the preceding example, the researcher collecting data on share prices will have a number corresponding to each company (e.g. the price of a share of company 1 is $25). This is referred to as **quantitative** data.

However, there are many cases where data does not come in the form of a single number. For instance, in corporate finance a researcher may be interested in investigating how companies decide between debt or equity financing of new investments. In this case, the researcher might survey companies and obtain responses of the form "Yes, we financed our investment by taking on debt" or "No, we did not finance our investment by taking on debt (instead we raised money by issuing new equity)". Alternatively, in event-study analysis, interest centers on how events (e.g. a company's earning announcement) affects a company's share price. In some cases, the events a researcher is studying come in the form of a simple Good News/Bad News dichotomy.

Data that comes in categories (e.g. Yes/No or Good News/Bad News) are referred to as **qualitative**. Such data arise often in finance when choices are involved (e.g. the choice to invest or not to invest in a certain stock, to issue new equity or not, etc). Financial researchers will usually convert these qualitative answers into numeric data. For instance, in the debt financing example, we might set Yes = 1 and No = 0. Hence, $Y_1 = 1$ means that the first company financed its investment by taking on debt, $Y_2 = 0$ means that the second company did not. When variables can take on only the values 0 or 1, they are referred to as **dummy** (or **binary**) **variables**. Working with such variables is a topic that will be discussed in detail in Chapter 7.

Panel data

Some data sets will have both a time series and a cross-sectional component. This data is referred to as **panel** data. For instance, research involving portfolio choice might use data on the return earned by many companies' shares for many months. Alternatively, financial researchers studying exchange rate behavior might use data from many countries for many months. Thus, a panel data set on $Y =$ the exchange rate for 12 countries would contain the exchange rate for each country in 1950 ($N = 12$ observations), followed by the exchange rate for the same set of countries in 1951 (another $N = 12$ observations), and so on. Over a period of T years, there would be $T \times N$ observations on Y.[3]

We will use the notation Y_{it} to indicate an observation on variable Y for unit i at time t. In the exchange rate example, Y_{11} will be the exchange rate in country 1, year 1, Y_{12} the exchange rate for country 1 in year 2, etc.

Data transformations: levels, growth rates, returns and excess returns

In this book, we will mainly assume that the data of interest, Y, is directly available. However, in practice, you may be required to take raw data from one source, and then transform it into a different form for your empirical analysis. For instance, you may take raw time series data on the variables $X =$ company earnings, and $W =$ number of shares, and create a new variable: $Y =$ earnings per share. Here the transformation would be $Y = X/W$. The exact nature of the transformation required depends on the problem at hand, so it is hard to offer any general recommendations on data transformation. Some special cases are considered in later chapters. Here it is useful to introduce one common transformation that arises repeatedly in finance when using time series data.

To motivate this transformation, note that in many cases we are not interested in the price of an asset, but in the return that an investor would make from purchase of the asset. This depends on how much the price of the asset will change over time. Suppose, for instance, that we have annual data on the price of a share in a particular company for 1950–1998 (i.e. 49 years of data) denoted by Y_t for $t = 1$ to 49. In many empirical projects, this might be the variable of primary interest. We will refer to such series as the **level** of the share price. However, people are often more interested in the **growth** of the share price. A simple way to measure growth is to take the share price series and calculate a percentage change for each year. The percentage change in the share price between period $t - 1$ and t is calculated according to the formula:

$$\% \text{ change} = \frac{(Y_t - Y_{t-1})}{Y_{t-1}} \times 100.$$

It is worth stressing that a percentage change always has a time scale associated with it (e.g. the percentage change *between period $t - 1$ and t*). For instance, with annual data this formula would produce an annual percentage change, with monthly data the formula would produce a monthly percentage change, etc.

As will be discussed in later chapters, it is sometimes convenient to take the natural logarithm, or $\ln(.)$ of variables. The definition and properties of logarithms can be found in the Appendix to Chapter 1 or virtually any introductory mathematics textbook. Using the properties of logarithms, it can be shown that the percentage change in a variable is approximately $100 \times [\ln(Y_t) - \ln(Y_{t-1})]$. This formula provides an alternative way of calculating a percentage change and is often used in practice.

The percentage change of an asset's price is often referred to as the **growth** of the price or the **change** in the price. It can also be referred to as the **return** if it reflects the return that an investor purchasing the share would earn. However, to interpret the growth of an asset's price as the return an investor would make one has to assume that there are no other income flows coming from holding the asset. For some assets this may be a reasonable assumption. But where it is not reasonable, the formula for a return has to be modified to include all income the investor would receive from holding the asset. For instance, most stocks pay dividends. If we let D_t be the dividend paid between period $t - 1$ and t then the return (which we denote by R_t) made by an investor (measured as a percentage) would be

$$\text{Return} = R_t = \frac{(Y_t - Y_{t-1} + D_t)}{Y_{t-1}} \times 100.$$

Another concept commonly used in finance is that of the **excess return**. This is the difference between an asset's return and that of some benchmark asset which is usually defined as a safe, low-risk asset (e.g. the return on a government bond). The concept of an excess return is an important one, since investors will only take on the risk of purchasing a particular asset if it is expected to earn more than a safe asset. For instance, if the expected return on a (risky) company's stock is 5% this might sound like a good return. But if the investor can earn a 6% return by buying (safe) government bonds, then the expected 5% return on the risky asset becomes much less impressive. It is the excess return of holding a share that is important, not the simple return. If the return on a risk-free asset is denoted by R_{0t}, then the excess return (ER), measured as a percentage, on an asset is defined as:

$$ER_t = R_t - R_{0t}.$$

Time series data will be discussed in more detail in Chapters 8–11. It is sufficient for you to note here that we will occasionally distinguish between the level of a variable and its growth rate, and that it is common to work with the returns an investor would make from holding an asset.

Index numbers

Many variables that financial analysts work with come in the form of **index numbers**. For instance, the common measures of stock price performance reported in the media are indices. The Dow Jones Industrial Average (DJIA) and Standard & Poor's composite share index (S&P500) are stock price indices.

Appendix 2.1, at the end of this chapter, provides a detailed discussion of what these are and how they are calculated. However, if you just want to use an index number in your empirical work, a precise knowledge of how to calculate indices is probably unnecessary. Having a good intuitive understanding of how an index number is interpreted is sufficient. Accordingly, here in the body of the text we provide only an informal intuitive discussion of index numbers.

Suppose you are interested in studying the performance of the stock market as a whole and want a measure of how stock prices change over time. The question arises as to how we measure "prices" in the stock market as a whole. The price of the stock of an individual company (e.g. Microsoft, Ford or Wal-Mart, etc.) can be readily measured, but often interest centers not on individual companies, but on the stock market as a whole. From the point of view of the investor, the relevant price would be the price of a portfolio containing the sorts of shares that a typical investor might buy. The price of this portfolio is observed at regular intervals over time in order to determine how prices are changing in the stock market as a whole. But the price of the portfolio is usually not directly reported. After all, if you are told the price of an individual share (e.g. the price of a share of Microsoft is $2.20), you have been told something informative, but if you are told "the price of a portfolio of representative shares" is $1,400, that statement is not very informative. To interpret this latter number, you would have to know what precisely was in the portfolio and in what quantities. Given the thousands of shares bought and sold in a modern stock market, far too much information would have to be given.

In light of such issues, data often comes in the form of a price **index**. Indices may be calculated in many ways, and it would distract from the main focus of this chapter to talk in detail about how they are constructed (see Appendix 2.1 for more detail). However, the following points are worth noting at the outset. First, indices almost invariably come as time series data. Second, one time period is usually chosen as a base year and the price level in the base year is set to 100.[4] Third, price levels in other years are measured in percentages relative to the base year.

An example will serve to clarify these issues. Suppose a price index for 4 years exists, and the values are: $Y_1 = 100$, $Y_2 = 106$, $Y_3 = 109$ and $Y_4 = 111$. These numbers can be interpreted as follows: The first year has been selected as a base year and, accordingly, $Y_1 = 100$. The figures for other years are all relative to this base year and allow for a simple calculation of how prices have changed since the base year. For instance, $Y_2 = 106$ means that prices have risen from 100 to 106 – a 6% rise since the first year. It can also be seen that prices have risen by 9% from year 1 to year 3 and by 11% from year 1 to year 4. Since the percentage change in stock prices measures the return (exclusive of dividends), the price index allows the person looking at the data to easily see the return earned from buying the basket of shares which go into making up the index. In other words, you can think of a price index as a way of presenting price data that is easy to interpret and understand.

A price index is very good for measuring **changes** in prices over time, but should not be used to talk about the **level** of prices. For instance, it should not be interpreted as an indicator of whether prices are "high" or "low". A simple example illustrates why this is the case. At the time I am writing this, the DJIA is at 10,240 while the S&P500 is at 1,142. This does not mean that the stocks in the DJIA portfolio are worth almost ten times as much as the S&P500 portfolio. In fact, the two portfolios contain shares from many of the same companies. The fact that they are different from one another is due to their having different base years.

In our discussion, we have focussed on stock price indices, and these are indeed by far the most common type of index numbers used in finance. However, it is worth noting that there are many other price indices used in many fields. For example, economists frequently use price indices which measure the prices of goods and services in the economy. The economist faces the same sort of problem that the financial researcher does. The latter has to find ways of combining the information in the stock prices of hundreds of individual companies while the former has to find ways of combining information in the prices of millions of goods in a modern economy. Indices such as the Consumer Price Index (CPI) are the solution and a commonly reported measure of inflation is the change in the CPI. Since inflation plays a role in many financial problems, such economic price indices are also of use to the financial researcher.

Furthermore, other types of indices (e.g. quantity indices) exist and should be interpreted in a similar manner to price indices. That is, they should be used as a basis for measuring how phenomena have changed from a given base year.

This discussion of index numbers is a good place to mention another transformation which is used to deal with the effects of inflation. As an example, consider the interest rate (e.g. the return earned on a savings deposit in a bank or the return on a government bond). In times of high inflation, simply looking at an interest rate can be misleading. If inflation is high (say 10%), then an investor who deposits money in a savings account earning a lower rate of interest (say 5%) will actually lose money on her investment. To be precise, if the investor initially deposits $100 in the savings account, she will have $105 a year from now. But in the meantime the price of the "portfolio of goods" used to construct the CPI will have gone up by 10%. So goods which cost $100 originally will cost $110 a year later. The investor, with only $105 after a year, will actually end up being able to buy fewer goods than she could have originally.

The issues discussed in the previous paragraph lead researchers to want to correct for the effect of inflation. In the case of returns (e.g. the interest rate which measures the return the investor earns on her savings), the way to do this is to subtract the inflation rate from the original return. To introduce some terminology, an interest rate transformed in this way is called a **real interest rate**. The original interest rate is referred to as a **nominal interest rate**. This distinction between real and nominal variables is important in many investment decisions. The key things you should remember is that a real return is a nominal return minus inflation and that real returns have the effects of inflation removed from them.

Obtaining data

All of the data you need in order to understand the basic concepts and to carry out the simple analyses covered in this book can be downloaded from the website associated with this book (**http://www.wiley.com/go/koopafd**). However, in the future you may need to gather your own data for an essay, dissertation or report. Financial data come from many different sources and it is hard to offer general comments on the collection of data. Below are a few key points that you should note about common data sets and where to find them.

It is becoming increasingly common for financial researchers to obtain their data over the Internet, and many relevant World Wide Web (www) sites now exist from which data can be downloaded. You should be forewarned that the web is a rapidly growing and changing place, so that the information and addresses provided here might soon be outdated. Appropriately, this section is provided only to give an indication of what can be obtained over the Internet, and as such is far from complete.

Some of the data sets available on the web are free, but many are not. Most university libraries or computer centers subscribe to various databases which the student can use. You are advised to check with your own university library or computer center to see what data sets you have access to. There are many excellent databases of stock prices and accounting information for all sorts of companies for many years. Unfortunately, these tend to be very expensive and, hence, you should see whether your university has a subscription to a financial database. Two of the more popular ones are DataStream by Thompson Financial (**http://www.datastream.com/**) and Wharton Research Data Services (**http://wrds.wharton.upenn.edu/**). With regards to free data, a more limited choice of financial data is available through popular Internet ports such as Yahoo! (**http://finance.yahoo.com**). The Federal Reserve Bank of St Louis also maintains a free database with a wide variety of data, including some financial time series (**http://research.stlouisfed.org/fred2/**). The Financial Data Finder (**http://www.cob.ohio-state.edu/fin/osudata.htm**), provided by the Fisher College of Business at the Ohio State University is also a useful source. Many academics also make the data sets they have used available on their websites. For instance, Robert Shiller at Yale University has a website which provides links to many different interesting financial data sets (**http://aida.econ.yale.edu/%7Eshiller/index.html**).

An extremely popular website among economists is "Resources for Economists on the Internet" (**http://rfe.wustl.edu/EconFAQ.html**). This site contains all sorts of interesting material on a wide range of economic topics, including links to many sorts of financial data. On this site you can also find links to Journal Data Archives. Many journals encourage their authors to make their data publicly available and, hence, in some cases you can get financial data from published academic papers through Journal Data Archives.

The general advice I want to give here is that spending some time searching the Internet can often be very fruitful.

Working with data: graphical methods

Once you have your data, it is important for you to summarize it. After all, anybody who reads your work will not be interested in the dozens or – more likely – hundreds or more observations contained in the original raw data set. Indeed, you can think of the whole field of financial econometrics as one devoted to the development and dissemination of methods whereby information in data sets is summarized in informative ways. Charts and tables are very useful ways of presenting your data. There are many different types (e.g. bar chart, pie chart, etc.). A useful way to learn about the charts is to experiment with the ChartWizard© in Excel. In this section, we will illustrate a few of the commonly used types of charts.

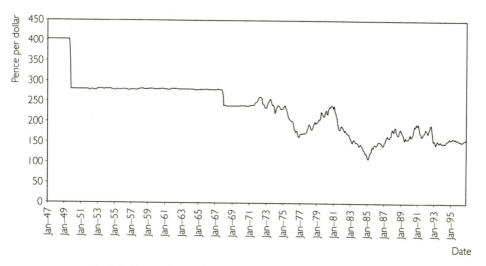

Fig. 2.1 Time series graph of UK pound/US dollar exchange rate.

Since most financial data is either in time series or cross-sectional form, we will briefly introduce simple techniques for graphing both types of data.

Time series graphs

Monthly time series data from January 1947 through October 1996 on the UK pound/US dollar exchange rate is plotted using the "Line Chart" option in Excel's ChartWizard© in Figure 2.1 (this data is located in Excel file EXRUK.XLS). Such charts are commonly referred to as **time series graphs**. The data set contains 598 observations – far too many to be presented as raw numbers for a reader to comprehend. However, a reader can easily capture the main features of the data by looking at the chart. One can see, for instance, the attempt by the UK government to hold the exchange rate fixed until the end of 1971 (apart from large devaluations in September 1949 and November 1967) and the gradual depreciation of the pound as it floated downward through the middle of the 1970s.

Exercise 2.1

(a) File INTERESTRATES.XLS contains data on long-term interest rates and short-term interest rates (measured as a percentage) from 1954Q1 to 1994Q2.[5] Make one time series graph that contains both of these variables.

(b) Transform the long-term interest rate data to growth rates using the fact that percentage changes are approximately $100 \times [\ln(Y_t) - \ln(Y_{t-1})]$. Make a time series graph of the series you have created.

Histograms

With time series data, a chart that shows how a variable evolves over time is often very informative. However, in the case of cross-sectional data, such methods are not appropriate and we must summarize the data in other ways.

A key variable in many studies of international financial development is Gross Domestic Product (GDP) per capita, a measure of income per person. Excel file GDPPC.XLS contains cross-sectional data on real GDP per capita in 1992 for 90 countries.[6]

One convenient way of summarizing this data is through a **histogram**. To construct a histogram, begin by constructing **class intervals** or **bins** that divide the countries into groups based on their GDP per capita. In our data set, GDP per person varies from $408 in Chad to $17,945 in the USA. One possible set of class intervals is 0–2,000, 2,001–4,000, 4,001–6,000, 6,001–8,000, 8,001–10,000, 10,001–12,000, 12,001–14,000, 14,001–16,000 and 16,001 and over (where all figures are in US dollars).

Note that each class interval (with the exception of the 16,001 + category) is $2,000 wide. In other words, the **class width** for each of our bins is 2,000. For each class interval we can count up the number of countries that have GDP per capita in that interval. For instance, there are seven countries in our data set with real GDP per capita between $4,001 and $6,000. The number of countries lying in one class interval is referred to as the **frequency**[7] of that interval. A histogram is a bar chart that plots frequencies against class intervals.[8]

Figure 2.2 is a histogram of our cross-country GDP per capita data set that uses the class intervals specified in the previous paragraph. Note that, if you do not wish to specify class intervals, Excel will do it automatically for you. Excel also creates a **frequency table**, which is located next to the histogram.

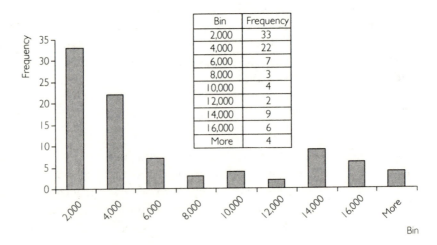

Bin	Frequency
2,000	33
4,000	22
6,000	7
8,000	3
10,000	4
12,000	2
14,000	9
16,000	6
More	4

Fig. 2.2 Histogram.

The frequency table indicates the number of countries belonging to each class interval (or bin). The numbers in the column labeled "Bin" indicate the upper bounds of the class intervals. For instance, we can read that there are 33 countries with GDP per capita less than $2,000; 22 countries with GDP per capita above $2,000 but less than $4,000; and so on. The last row says that there are 4 countries with GDP per capita above $16,000.

This same information is graphed in a simple fashion in the histogram. Graphing allows for a quick visual summary of the cross-country **distribution** of GDP per capita. We can see from the histogram that many countries are very poor, but that there is also a "clump" of countries that are quite rich (e.g. 19 countries have GDP per capita greater than $12,000). There are relatively few countries in between these poor and rich groups (i.e. few countries fall in the bins labeled 8,000, 10,000 and 12,000).

Researchers often refer to this clumping of countries into poor and rich groups as the "twin peaks" phenomenon. In other words, if we imagine that the histogram is a mountain range, we can see a peak at the bin labeled 2,000 and a smaller peak at 14,000. These features of the data can be seen easily from the histogram, but would be difficult to comprehend simply by looking at the raw data.

Exercise 2.2

(a) Recreate the histogram in Figure 2.2.

(b) Create histograms using different class intervals. For instance, begin by letting your software package choose default values and see what you get, then try values of your own.

(c) If you are using Excel, redo questions (a) and (b) with the "Cumulative Percentage" box clicked on. What does this do?

XY-plots

Financial analysts are often interested in the nature of the relationships between two or more variables. For instance: "What is the relationship between capital structure (i.e. the division between debt and equity financing) and firm performance (e.g. profit)?" "What is the relationship between the return on a company's stock and the return on the stock market as a whole?" "What are the effects of financial decisions on the probability that a firm will go bankrupt?" "Are changes in the money supply a reliable indicator of inflation changes?" "Do differences in financial regulation explain why some countries are growing faster than others?"

The techniques described previously are suitable for describing the behavior of only one variable; for instance, the properties of real GDP per capita across countries in Figure 2.2. They are not, however, suitable for examining relationships between pairs of variables.

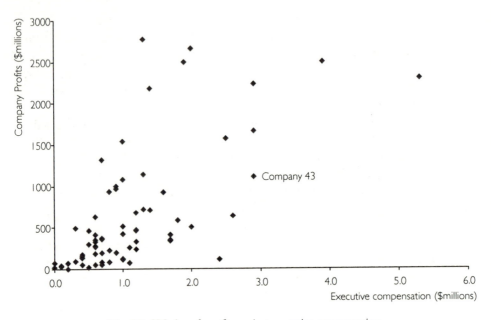

Fig. 2.3 *XY*-plot of profits against executive compensation.

Once we are interested in understanding the nature of the relationships between two or more variables, it becomes harder to use graphs. Future chapters will discuss regression analysis, which is an important tool used by financial researchers working with many variables. However, graphical methods can be used to draw out some simple aspects of the relationship between two variables. **XY-plots** (also called **scatter diagrams**) are particularly useful in this regard.

Figure 2.3 is a graph of data on executive compensation (i.e. the salary paid to the chief executive, expressed in millions of dollars) for 70 companies, along with data on the profits of the companies (i.e. profit expressed in millions of dollars). (This data is available in Excel file EXECUTIVE.XLS.) It is commonly thought that there should be a relationship between these two variables, either because more profitable companies can afford to hire better chief executives (and pay them more) or because executive talent leads to higher profits.

Figure 2.3 is an *XY*-plot of these two variables. Each point on the chart represents a particular company. Reading up the *Y*-axis (i.e. the vertical one) gives us the compensation of the chief executive in that company. Reading across the *X*-axis (i.e. the horizontal one) gives us the profit of the company. It is possible to label each point with its corresponding company name. We have not done so here, since labels for 70 companies would clutter the chart and make it difficult to read. However, one company, Company 43, has been labeled. Note that Company 43 paid its chief executive $2.9 million ($Y = 2.9$) and had profits of $1,113 million ($X = 1,113$).

The *XY*-plot can be used to give a quick visual impression of the relationship between profits and executive compensation. An examination of this chart indicates some support for the idea that a relationship between profits and executive compensation does exist. For instance, if we look at companies with relatively low profits (less than $500 million, say), almost all of them compensate their executives at a relatively low level (less than $1 million). If we look at companies with high profits (e.g. over $1,500 million), almost all of them have high levels of executive compensation (more than $2 million). This indicates that there may be a **positive relationship** between profits and executive compensation (i.e. high values of one variable tend to be associated with high values of the other; and low values, associated with low values). It is also possible to have a **negative relationship**. This might occur, for instance, if we substituted a measure of losses for profits in the *XY*-plot. In this case, high levels of losses might be associated with low levels of executive compensation.

It is worth noting that the positive or negative relationships found in the data are only "tendencies", and, as such, do not hold necessarily for every company. That is, there may be exceptions to the general pattern of profit's association with high rates of compensation. For example, on the *XY*-plot we can observe one company with high profits of roughly $1,300 million, but low executive compensation of only $700,000. Similarly, low profits can also be associated with high rates of compensation, as evidenced by one company with low profits of roughly $150 million, which is paying its chief executive the high amount of almost $2.5 million. As researchers, we are usually interested in drawing out general patterns or tendencies in the data. However, we should always keep in mind that exceptions (in statistical jargon **outliers**) to these patterns typically exist. In some cases, finding out which companies don't fit the general pattern can be as interesting as the pattern itself.

Exercise 2.3

In addition to the variables executive compensation and profit (discussed previously), the file EXECUTIVE.XLS contains data on the percentage change in company sales over the last two years and on the percentage increase in company debt over the same period. Construct and interpret *XY*-plots of these two variables (one at a time) against executive compensation. Does there seem to be a positive relationship between executive compensation and the change in sales? How about between executive compensation and the change in debt?

Working with data: descriptive statistics

Graphs have an immediate visual impact that is useful for livening up an essay or report. However, in many cases it is important to be numerically precise. Later chapters will describe common numerical methods for summarizing the relationship between several variables in greater detail. Here we discuss briefly a few **descriptive statistics** for summarizing the properties of a single variable. By way of motivation, we will return to the concept of distribution introduced in our discussion on histograms.

In our cross-country data set, real GDP per capita varies across the 90 countries. This variability can be seen by looking at the histogram in Figure 2.2, which plots the distribution of GDP per capita across countries. Suppose you wanted to summarize the information contained in the histogram numerically. One thing you could do is to present the numbers in the frequency table in Figure 2.2. However, even this table may provide too many numbers to be easily interpretable. Instead it is common to present two simple numbers called the **mean** and **standard deviation**.

The **mean** is the statistical term for the average. The mathematical formula for the mean is given by:

$$\overline{Y} = \frac{\sum_{i=1}^{N} Y_i}{N}$$

where N is the **sample size** (i.e. number of countries) and Σ is the summation operator (i.e. it adds up real GDP per capita for all countries). In our case, mean GDP per capita is \$5,443.80. Throughout this book, we will place a bar over a variable to indicate its mean (i.e. $\overline{Y}$ is the mean of the variable Y, $\overline{X}$ is the mean of X, etc.).

The concept of the mean is associated with the middle of a distribution. For example, if we look at the previous histogram, \$5,443.80 lies somewhere in the middle of the distribution. The cross-country distribution of real GDP per capita is quite unusual, having the twin peaks property described earlier. It is more common for distributions of economic variables to have a single peak and to be bell-shaped. Figure 2.4 is a histogram that plots just such a bell-shaped distribution. For such distributions, the mean is located precisely in the middle of the distribution, under the single peak.

Of course, the mean or average figure hides a great deal of variability across countries. Other useful summary statistics, which shed light on the cross-country variation in GDP per capita, are the minimum and maximum. For our data set, minimum GDP per capita is \$408 (Chad) and maximum GDP is \$17,945 (USA). By looking at the distance between the maximum and minimum we can see how **dispersed** the distribution is.

The concept of dispersion is quite important in finance and is closely related to the concepts of variability and inequality. For instance, real GDP per capita in 1992 in our data set varies from \$408 to \$17,945. If poorer countries were, in the near future, to grow quickly, and richer countries to stagnate, then the dispersion of real GDP per capita in, say, 2012, might be significantly less. It may be the case that the poorest country at this time will have real GDP per capita of \$10,000 while the richest country will remain at \$17,945. If this were to happen, then the cross-country distri-

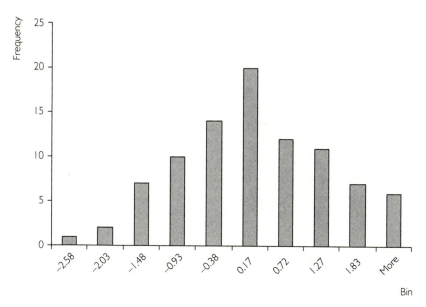

Fig. 2.4 Histogram.

bution of real GDP per capita would be more equal (less dispersed, less variable). Intuitively, the notions of dispersion, variability and inequality are closely related.

The minimum and maximum, however, can be unreliable guidelines to dispersion. For instance, what if, with the exception of Chad, all the poor countries, experienced rapid economic growth between 1992 and 2012, while the richer countries did not grow at all? In this case, cross-country dispersion or inequality would decrease over time. However, since Chad and the USA did not grow, the minimum and maximum would remain at $408 and $17,945, respectively.

A more common measure of dispersion is the **standard deviation**. Its mathematical formula is given by:

$$s = \sqrt{\frac{\sum_{i=1}^{N}(Y_i - \overline{Y})^2}{N-1}}$$

although in practice you will probably never have to calculate it by hand.[9] You can calculate it easily in Excel using either the Tools/Descriptive Statistics or the Functions facility. Confusingly, statisticians refer to the square of the standard deviation as the **variance** (s^2) and it is common to see either terminology used. So it is important to remember this close relationship between the standard deviation and the variance.

These measures have little direct intuition. In our cross-country GDP data set, the standard deviation is $5,369.496 and it is difficult to get a direct feel for what this number means in an **absolute** sense. However, the standard deviation can be interpreted in a **comparative** sense. That is, if you compare the standard deviations of two different distributions, the one with the smaller standard deviation will always exhibit less dispersion. In our example, if the poorer countries were to suddenly experience economic growth and the richer countries to stagnate, the standard deviation would decrease over time. As another example, consider the returns of two stocks observed for many months. In some months the stocks earn high returns, in other months they earn low returns. This variability in stock returns is measured by the variance. If one stock has a higher variance than the other stock, then we can say it exhibits more variability. As the variability in stock returns relates to the risk involved in holding the stock, the variance is very important in portfolio management.

Exercise 2.4

Construct and interpret descriptive statistics for all the variables in EXECUTIVE.XLS.

Expected values and variances

In the previous section we talked about means and variances. If this were a statistics textbook, we would actually have called them **sample means** and **sample variances**. The word "sample" is added to emphasize that they are calculated using an actual "sample" of data. For instance, in our cross-country GDP data set we took the data we had and calculated (using Excel) exact numbers for $\bar{Y}$ and s. We found these to be \$5,443.80 and \$5,369.496, respectively. These are the sample mean and standard deviation calculated using the data set at hand.

As another example, suppose we have collected data on the return to holding stock in a company for the past 100 months. We can use this data to calculate the mean and variance. However, these numbers are calculated based on the historical performance of the company. In finance, we are often interested in predicting future stock returns. By definition we do not know exactly what these will be, so we cannot calculate sample means and variances as we did above. But a potential investor would be interested in some similar measures. That is, this investor would be interested in the typical return which she might expect. She might also be interested in the risk involved in purchasing the stock. The concept of a typical expected value sounds similar to the ideas we discussed relating to the mean. The concept of riskiness sounds similar to the idea of a variance we discussed above. In short, we need concepts like the sample mean and variance, but for cases when we do not actually have data to calculate them. The relevant concepts are the **population mean** and **population variance**.

If this were a statistics book, we would now get into a long discussion of the distinction between population and sample concepts involving probability theory and many equations. However, for the student who is interested in doing financial data analysis, it is enough to provide some intuition and definitions.

A conventional statistics textbook might begin motivating population and sample concepts through an example. Consider, for instance, the height of every individual in the USA. In the population as a whole there is some average height (the population mean height) and some variance of heights (the population variance). This population mean and variance will be unknown, unless someone actually went out and measured the height of every person in the USA.

However, a researcher might have data on the actual heights of 100 people (e.g. a medical researcher might measure the height of each of 100 patients). Using the data for 100 people, the researcher could calculate $\overline{Y}$ and s^2. These are the sample mean and variance. These will be actual numbers. The medical researcher could then use these numbers as estimates (or approximations) for what is going on in the country as a whole (i.e. sample means and variances can be used as estimates for population means and variances). However, despite these relationships it is important to stress that sample and population concepts are different with the former being actual numbers calculated using the data at hand and the latter being unobserved.

Perhaps the previous two paragraphs are enough to intuitively motivate the distinction between sample and population means and variances. To see why financial analysts need to know this distinction (and to introduce some notation), let us use our example of a potential investor interested in the potential return she might make from buying a stock. Let Y denote next month's return on this stock. From the investor's point of view, Y is unknown. The typical return she might expect is measured by the population mean and is referred to as the **expected value**. We use the notation $E(Y)$ to denote the expected return. Its name accurately reflects the intuition for this statistical concept. The "expected value" sheds light on what we expect will occur.

However, the return on a stock is rarely exactly what is expected [i.e. rarely will you find Y to turn out to be exactly $E(Y)$]. Stock markets are highly unpredictable, sometimes the return on stocks could be higher than expected, sometimes it could be lower than expected. In other words, there is always risk associated with purchasing a stock. A potential investor will be interested in a measure of this risk. Variance is a common way of measuring this risk. We use the notation $\text{var}(Y)$ for this.

To summarize, in the previous section on descriptive statistics we motivated the use of the sample mean and variance, $\overline{Y}$ and s^2, to give the researcher an idea of the average value and dispersion, respectively, in a data set. In this section, we have motivated their population counterparts, $E(Y)$ and $\text{var}(Y)$, as having similar intuition but being relevant for summarizing information about an uncertain outcome (e.g. the return on a stock next month). This is probably enough intuition about the mean and variance operator for you to master the concepts and techniques used in this book. However, for the reader interested in how $E(Y)$ and $\text{var}(Y)$ are calculated, we provide the following example.

Suppose you are an investor trying to decide whether to buy a stock based on its return next month. You do not know what this return will be. You are quite confident (say, 70% sure) that the markets will be stable, in which case you will earn a 1% return. But you also know there is a 10% chance the stock market will crash, in which case the stock return will be −10%. There is also a 20% probability that good news will boost the stock markets and you will get a 5% return on your stock.

Let us denote this information using symbols as there being three possible outcomes (good, normal, bad) as 1, 2, 3. So, for instance, $Y_1 = 0.05$ will denote the 5% return if good times occur. We will use the symbol "P" for probability and the same subscripting convention. Thus, $P_3 = 0.10$ will denote the 10% probability of a stock market crash. We can now define the expected return as a weighted average of all the possible outcomes:

$$E(Y) = P_1 Y_1 + P_2 Y_2 + P_3 Y_3 = 0.20 \times 0.05 + 0.70 \times 0.01 + 0.10 \times (-0.10) = 0.007$$

In words, the expected return on the stock next month is 0.7% (i.e. a bit less than 1%).

In our example, we have assumed that there are only three possible outcomes next month. In general, if there are K possible outcomes,[10] the formula for the expected value is:

$$E(Y) = \sum_{i=1}^{K} P_i Y_i.$$

The formula for var(Y) is similar to that for s^2 presented in the previous section. It also has a similar lack of intuition and, hence, we shall not discuss it in detail. For the case where we have K possible outcomes, the variance of Y is defined as:

$$\text{var}(Y) = \sum_{i=1}^{K} P_i [Y_i - E(Y)]^2.$$

The key thing to remember is that var(Y) is a measure of the dispersion of the possible outcomes which could occur and, thus, is closely related to the concept of risk.

Chapter summary

1. Financial data come in many forms. Common types are time series, cross-sectional and panel data.
2. Financial data can be obtained from many sources. The Internet is becoming an increasingly valuable repository for many data sets.
3. Simple graphical techniques, including histograms and XY-plots, are useful ways of summarizing the information in a data set.
4. Many numerical summaries can be used. The most important are the mean, a measure of the location of a distribution, and the standard deviation, a measure of how spread out or dispersed a distribution is.
5. If Y is a variable which could have many outcomes, then the expected value, $E(Y)$, is a measure of the typical or expected outcome (e.g. the expected return on a stock next month) and the variance, var(Y), is a measure of the dispersion of possible outcomes (e.g. relating to the riskiness in holding a stock next month).

Appendix 2.1: Index numbers

To illustrate the basic ideas in constructing a stock price index, we use the data shown in Table 2.1.1 on the stock price of three fictitious companies: Megaco, Monstroco and Minico.

Calculating a Megaco price index

We begin by calculating a price index for a single company, Megaco, before proceeding to the calculation of a stock price index. As described in the text, calculating a price index involves first selecting a base year. For our Megaco price index, let us choose the year 2000 as the base year (although it should be stressed that any year can be chosen). By definition, the value of the Megaco price index is 100 in this base year. How did we transform the price of Megaco in the year 2000 to obtain the price index value of 100? It can be seen that this transformation involved taking the price of Megaco in 2000 and dividing by the price of Megaco in 2000 (i.e. dividing the price by itself) and multiplying by 100. To maintain comparability, this same transformation must be applied to the price of Megaco in every year. The result is a stock price index for Megaco (with the year 2000 as the base year). This is illustrated in Table 2.1.2.

From the Megaco stock price index, it can be seen that between 2000 and 2003 the price of stock in Megaco increased by 4.4% and in 1999 the price of Megaco's stock was 97.8%, as high as in 2000.

Table 2.1.1   Stock prices of companies in different years.

	Megaco	Monstroco	Minico
1999	0.89	0.44	1.58
2000	0.91	0.43	1.66
2001	0.91	0.46	1.90
2002	0.94	0.50	2.10
2003	0.95	0.51	2.25

Table 2.1.2   Calculating a Megaco stock price index.

	Price of Megaco	Transformation	Price index
1999	0.89	×100 ÷ 0.91	97.8
2000	0.91	×100 ÷ 0.91	100
2001	0.91	×100 ÷ 0.91	100
2002	0.94	×100 ÷ 0.91	103.3
2003	0.95	×100 ÷ 0.91	104.4

Calculating a stock price index

When calculating the Megaco stock price index (a single company), all we had to look at was the stock price of Megaco. However, if we want to calculate a stock price index (involving several companies), then we have to combine the prices of all stocks together somehow. One thing you could do is simply average the prices of all stock prices together in each year (and then construct a price index in the same manner as for the Megaco stock price index). However, this strategy is usually inappropriate since it implicitly weights all companies equally to one another. Let us suppose, as their names indicate, that Megaco and Monstroco are huge companies with a large amount of stock outstanding, traded on many stock exchanges. In contrast, we suppose Minico to be a tiny company with only a small amount of stock outstanding, traded only rarely on a local stock exchange. A simple average just would add up the stock prices of these three companies and divide by three. In our example (and many real world applications), this equal weighting is unreasonable.[11] An examination of Table 2.1.1 reveals that the stock prices of Megaco and Monstroco are going up only slightly over time (and, in some years, they are not changing or even dropping). However, the price of Minico's stock is going up rapidly over time. Megaco and Monstroco are common stocks purchased frequently by many people, whereas Minico is a small obscure company purchased by a tiny minority of people. In light of this, it is unreasonable to weight all three companies equally when calculating a stock price index. A stock price index which was based on a simple average would reveal stock prices were growing at a fairly rapid rate (i.e. combining the slow growth of Megaco and Monstroco's stocks with the very fast growth of Minico would yield a stock price index which indicates moderately fast growth). However, if the financial analyst were to use such a price index to report "stock prices are increasing at a fairly rapid rate", the vast majority of people would find this report inconsistent with their own experience. That is, the vast majority of people only have shares of Megaco and Monstroco in their portfolios and their prices are growing only slowly over time.

The line of reasoning in the previous paragraph suggests that a stock price index which weights all companies equally will not often be a sensible one. It also suggests how one might construct a sensible stock price index: use a weighted average of the prices of all stocks to construct an index where the weights are chosen so as to reflect the importance of each company. In our stock price index, we would want to attach more weight to Megaco and Monstroco (the big companies) and little weight to the tiny Minico.

There are many different ways of choosing such weights. But most share the idea that stocks should be weighted by the size or importance of the underlying company. The S&P500 weights companies by their market capitalization (i.e. the price per share times the total number of shares outstanding).[12] Sometimes, such indices are referred to as "value-weighted". For empirical work, it is usually acceptable to understand this intuition and a knowledge of the precise calculations performed in calculating a value-weighted stock price index is not necessary. However, for the interested reader, the remainder of Appendix 2.1 describes these calculations in the context of our simple example.

A value-weighted stock price index can be written in terms of a mathematical formula. Let P denote the price of a stock, Q denote the market capitalization and subscripts denote the company and year with Megaco being company 1, Monstroco company 2 and Minico company 3. Thus, for instance, $P_{1,2000}$, is the stock price of Megaco in the year 2000, $Q_{3,2002}$ is the market capitalization of Minico in 2002, etc. See the Appendix 1.1 if you are having trouble understanding this subscripting notation or the summation operator used below.

With this notational convention established, a value-weighted price index (PI) in year t (for $t = 1999, 2000, 2001, 2002$ and 2003) can be written as:

$$PI_t = \frac{\sum_{i=1}^{3} P_{it} Q_{it}}{\sum_{i=1}^{3} P_{i,2000} Q_{it}} \times 100.$$

Note that the numerator of this formula takes the price of each stock and multiplies it by the current market capitalization. This ensures that Megaco and Monstroco receive much more weight in the index than Minico. We will not explain the denominator. For the more mathematically inclined, the denominator ensures that the weights in the weighted average sum to one (which is necessary to ensure that it is a proper weighted average) and that 2000 is the base year.

Table 2.1.3 presents the market capitalization (in millions of dollars) for our three companies. Table 2.1.4 shows the calculation of the value-weighted stock price index using the stock price data of Table 2.1.1 and the market capitalization data of Table 2.1.3.

The values from the last column can be interpreted as with any price index. So, for instance, we can say that stock prices rose by 10.4% between 2000 and 2003.

Table 2.1.3 Market capitalization (millions of dollars).

	Megaco	Monstroco	Minico
1999	100	78	1
2000	100	82	1
2001	98	86	3
2002	94	87	4
2003	96	88	5

Table 2.1.4 Calculating the value-weighted stock price index.

	Numerator = $\Sigma_{j=1}^{3} P_{it} Q_{it}$	Denominator = $\Sigma_{j=1}^{3} P_{i,2000} Q_{it}$	Price index
1999	124.90	126.20	99.0
2000	127.92	127.92	100
2001	134.44	131.14	102.5
2002	140.26	129.59	108.2
2003	147.33	133.50	110.4

Appendix 2.2: Advanced descriptive statistics

The mean and standard deviation are the most common descriptive statistics but many others exist. The mean is the simplest **measure of location** of a distribution. The word "location" is meant to convey the idea of the center of the distribution. The mean is the average. Other common measures of location are the **mode** and **median**.

To distinguish between the mean, mode and median, consider a simple example. Seven people report their respective incomes in £ per annum as: £18,000, £15,000, £9,000, £15,000, £16,000, £17,000 and £20,000. The mean, or average, income of these seven people is £15,714.

The **mode** is the most common value. In the present example, two people have reported incomes of £15,000. No other income value is reported more than once. Hence, £15,000 is the modal income for these seven people.

The **median** is the middle value. That is, it is the value that splits the distribution into two equal halves. In our example, it is the income value at which half the people have higher incomes and half the people have lower incomes. Here the median is £16,000. Note that three people have incomes less than the median and three have incomes higher than it.

The mode and median can also be motivated through consideration of Figures 2.2 and 2.4, which plot two different histograms or distributions. A problem with the mode is that there may not be a most common value. For instance, in the GDP per capita data set (GDPPC.XLS), no two countries have precisely the same values. So there is no value that occurs more than once. For cases like this, the mode is the highest point of the histogram. A minor practical problem with defining the mode in this way is that it can be sensitive to the choice of class intervals (and this is why Excel gives a slightly different answer for the mode for GDPPC.XLS than the one given here). In Figure 2.2, the histogram is highest over the class interval labeled 2,000. Remember, Excel's choice of labeling means that the class interval runs from 0 to 2,000. Hence, we could say that "the class interval 0 to 2,000 is the modal (or most likely) value". Alternatively, it is common to report the middle value of the relevant class interval as the mode. In this case, we could say, "the mode is $1,000". The mode is probably the least commonly used of the three measures of location introduced here.

To understand the median, imagine that all the area of the histogram is shaded. The median is the point on the X-axis which divides this shaded area precisely in half. For Figure 2.4 the highest point (i.e. the mode) is also the middle point that divides the distribution in half (i.e. the median). It turns out it is also the mean. However, in Figure 2.2 the mean ($5,443.80), median ($3,071.50) and mode ($1,000) are quite different.

Other useful summary statistics are based on the notion of a **percentile**. Consider our GDP per capita data set. For any chosen country, say Belgium, you can ask "how many countries are poorer than Belgium?" or, more precisely, "what proportion of countries are poorer than Belgium?". When we ask such questions we are, in effect, asking what percentile Belgium is at. Formally, the Xth percentile is the data value (e.g. a GDP per capita figure) such that $X\%$ of the observations (e.g. countries) have lower data values. In the cross-country GDP data set, the 37th percentile is $2,092. This is the GDP per capita figure for Peru. 37% of the countries in our data set are poorer than Peru.

Several percentiles relate to concepts we have discussed before. The 50th percentile is the median. The minimum and maximum are the 0th and 100th percentile. The percentile divides the data range up into hundredths, while other related concepts use other basic units. **Quartiles** divide the data range up into quarters. Hence, the first quartile is equivalent to the 25th percentile, the second quartile, the 50th percentile (i.e. the median) and the third quartile, the 75th percentile. **Deciles** divide the data up into tenths. In other words, the first decile is equivalent to the 10th percentile, the second decile, the 20th percentile, etc.

After the standard deviation, the most common measure of dispersion is the **inter-quartile range**. As its name suggests, it measures the difference between the third and first quartiles. For the cross-country data set, 75% of countries have GDP per capita less than $9,802 and 25% have GDP per capita less than $1,162. In other words, $1,162 is the first quartile and $9,802 is the third quartile. The inter-quartile range is $9,802-$1,162 = $8,640.

Endnotes

1. As emphasized in Chapter 1, this is not a book about collecting data. Nevertheless, it is useful to offer a few brief pointers about how to look for data sets.
2. Some researchers even work with data observed more frequently than this. For instance, in a stock market one can record the price of a stock every time it is traded. Since, for some companies' shares, the time between trades is measured in seconds (or even less) such data is recorded at a very high frequency. Such data sets are useful for investigating market micro-structure. We will not discuss such data sets nor models of market micro-

structure in this book. *The Econometrics of Financial Markets* by Campbell, Lo and MacKinlay has a chapter on this topic.

3. Another type of data occurs if, say, a researcher carries out a survey of *a different set* of companies each year. This is not the same as panel data and is referred to as repeated cross-sectional data.

4. Some indices set the base year value to 1.00, 10 or 1000 instead of 100.

5. 1954Q1 means the first quarter (i.e. January, February and March) of 1954.

6. Real GDP per capita in every country has been converted into US dollars using purchasing power parity exchange rates. This allows us to make direct comparisons across countries.

7. Note that the use of the word "frequency" here as meaning "the number of observations that lie in a class interval" is somewhat different from the use of the word "frequency" in time series analysis (see the discussion of time series data above).

8. Excel creates the histogram using the Histogram command (in Tools/Data Analysis). It simply plots the bins on the horizontal axis and the frequency (or number of observations in a class) on the vertical axis. Note that most statistics books plot class intervals against frequencies *divided by class width*. This latter strategy corrects for the fact that class widths may vary across class intervals. In other words, Excel does not calculate the histogram correctly. Provided the class intervals are the same width (or nearly so) this error is not of great practical importance.

9. In some textbooks, a slightly different formula for calculating the standard deviation is given where the $N-1$ in the denominator is replaced by N.

10. The case where there is a continuity of possible outcomes has similar intuition to the case with K outcomes, but is mathematically more complicated. Since we are only interested in providing intuition, we will not discuss this case.

11. An exception to this is the DJIA which does equally weight the stock prices of all companies included in making the index. Note, however, that the DJIA is based only on a set of large companies, so the problem of different-sized companies receiving equal weight in a simple average is lessened.

12. This statement holds for the most commonly reported S&P500 Index, although we note that Standard & Poor's produces many stock price indices, including an S&P500 Equal Weight Index.

CHAPTER 3

Correlation

Often financial analysts are interested in investigating the nature of the relationship between different variables, such as the amount of debt that companies hold and their market capitalization or their risk and return. Correlation is an important way of numerically quantifying the relationship between two variables. A related concept, introduced in future chapters, is regression, which is essentially an extension of correlation to cases of three or more variables. As you will quickly find as you read through this chapter and those that follow, it is no exaggeration to say that correlation and regression are the most important unifying concepts of this book.

In this chapter, we will first describe the theory behind correlation, and then work through a few examples designed to think intuitively about the concept in different ways.

Understanding correlation

Let X and Y be two variables (e.g. market capitalization and debt, respectively) and let us also suppose that we have data on $i = 1, \ldots, N$ different units (e.g. companies). The **correlation** between X and Y is denoted by the small letter, r, and its precise mathematical formula is given in Appendix 3.1. Of course, in practice, you will never actually have to use this formula directly. Any spreadsheet or statistics software package will do it for you. In Excel, you can use the Tools/Data Analysis or Function Wizard[©] to calculate them. It is usually clear from the context to which variables r refers. However, in some cases we will use subscripts to indicate that r_{XY} is the correlation between variables X and Y, r_{XZ} the correlation between variables X and Z, etc.

Once you have calculated the correlation between two variables you will obtain a number (e.g. $r = 0.55$). It is important that you know how to interpret this number. In this section, we will try to develop some intuition about correlation. First, however, let us briefly list some of the numerical properties of correlation.

Properties of correlation

1. r always lies between -1 and 1. That is, $-1 \leq r \leq 1$.
2. Positive values of r indicate a positive correlation between X and Y. Negative values indicate a negative correlation. $r = 0$ indicates that X and Y are uncorrelated.
3. Larger positive values of r indicate stronger positive correlation. $r = 1$ indicates perfect positive correlation. Larger negative values[1] of r indicate stronger negative correlation. $r = -1$ indicates perfect negative correlation.
4. The correlation between Y and X is the same as the correlation between X and Y.
5. The correlation between any variable and itself (e.g. the correlation between Y and Y) is 1.

Understanding correlation through verbal reasoning

Statisticians use the word "correlation" in much the same way as the layperson does. The following continuation of the executive compensation/profit example from Chapter 2 will serve to illustrate verbal ways of conceptualizing the concept of correlation.

Example: The correlation between executive compensation and profit

Let us suppose that we are interested in investigating the relationship between executive compensation and profit. Remember that Excel file EXECUTIVE.XLS contains data on these variables (and others) for a cross-section of 70 companies. Using Excel, we find that the correlation between executive compensation (Y) and profit (X) is 0.66. Being greater than zero, this number allows us to make statements of the following form:

1. There is a positive relationship (or positive association) between executive compensation and profit.

2. Companies with high profits tend to have high levels of executive compensation. Companies with low profits tend to have low levels of executive compensation. Note that we use the word "tend" here. A positive correlation does not mean that **every** company with high profits necessarily has a high level of executive compensation but, rather, that this is the **general tendency**. It is possible that a few individual companies do not follow this pattern (see the discussion of outliers in Chapter 2).
3. Compensation levels vary across companies as do profits (for this reason we call them "variables"). Some companies pay their executives well, others pay them relatively poorly. This high/low cross-company variance in compensation tends to "match up" with the high/low variance in profits.

All that the preceding statements require is for r to be positive.[2] It is somewhat more difficult to get an intuitive feel for the exact number of the correlation (e.g. how is a correlation of 0.66 different from 0.26?). The XY-plots discussed below offer some help, but here we will briefly note an important point to which we shall return when we discuss regression:

4. The degree to which executive compensation varies across companies can be measured numerically using the formula for the standard deviation (and variance) discussed in Chapter 2. As mentioned in point 3 above, the fact that compensation and profits are positively correlated means that their patterns of cross-company variability tend to match up. The correlation squared (r^2) measures the proportion of the cross-company variability in compensation that matches up with, or is explained by, the variance in profits. In other words, correlation is a numerical measure of the degree to which patterns in X and Y correspond. In our compensation/profits example, since $0.66^2 = 0.44$, we can say that 44% of the cross-company variance in compensation can be explained by the cross-company variance in profits.

Exercise 3.1

(a) Using the data in EXECUTIVE.XLS, calculate and interpret the mean, standard deviation, minimum and maximum of executive compensation and profits.
(b) Verify that the correlation between these two variables is 0.66.

Example: The determinants of market capitalization

Investors and financial researchers are interested in understanding how the stock market values a firm's equity (i.e. its shares). In a fundamental sense, the value of a firm's shares (i.e. its market capitalization) should reflect investors' expectations of the firm's future profitability. However, data on expected future profitability is non-existent. Instead, empirical financial studies must use measures such as current income, sales, assets and debt of the firm as variables we can observe now but may influence the future prospects of the firm.

Excel file EQUITY.XLS contains data on $N = 309$ US firms in 1996. Data on the following variables is provided. All variables are measured in millions of US dollars.

- MARKETCAP = the total value of all shares. This is calculated as the price per share times the number of shares outstanding.
- DEBT = the amount of long-term debt held by the firm.
- SALES = total sales of the firm.
- INCOME = net income of the firm.
- ASSETS = book value of the assets of the firm (i.e. what an accountant would judge the firm's assets to be worth).

We will use this data set in subsequent chapters, but here we focus on $Y =$ MARKETCAP and $X =$ SALES. If we calculate the correlation between these two variables, we find $r_{XY} = 0.41$.

The following statements can be made about market capitalization using this data set:

1. Companies with large sales tend to be worth more (as measured by market capitalization) than those with small sales.
2. There is a positive relationship between sales and market capitalization.
3. The variance in sales accounts for 17% (i.e. $0.41^2 = 0.17$) of the variability in market capitalization.

Example: House prices in Windsor, Canada

Many financial theories involve pricing of a good or an asset. Here we give an example of pricing a particularly important asset: a house. For most people, the house they own is the biggest asset they have. Thus, housing is a big component in most people's portfolios. Given the importance of housing, many researchers in finance and real estate economics have sought to understand how houses are priced.

The Excel file HPRICE.XLS contains data relating to $N = 546$ houses sold in Windsor, Canada in the summer of 1987. It contains the selling price (in Canadian dollars) along with many characteristics for each house. We will use this data set extensively in future chapters, but for now let us focus on just a few variables. In particular, let us assume that $Y =$ the sales price of the house and $X =$ the size of its lot in square feet, lot size being the area occupied by the house itself plus its garden or yard. The correlation between these two variables is $r_{XY} = 0.54$.

The following statements can be made about house prices in Windsor:

1. Houses with large lots tend to be worth more than those with small lots.
2. There is a positive relationship between lot size and sales price.
3. The variance in lot size accounts for 29% (i.e. $0.54^2 = 0.29$) of the variability in house prices.

Now let us add a third variable, $Z =$ number of bedrooms. Calculating the correlation between house prices and number of bedrooms, we obtain $r_{YZ} = 0.37$. This result says, as we would expect, that houses with more bedrooms tend to be worth more than houses with fewer bedrooms.

Similarly, we can calculate the correlation between number of bedrooms and lot size. This correlation turns out to be $r_{XZ} = 0.15$, and indicates that houses with larger lots also tend to have more bedrooms. However, this correlation is very small and quite unexpectedly, perhaps, suggests that the link between lot size and number of bedrooms is quite weak. In other words, you may have expected that houses on larger lots, being bigger, would have more bedrooms than houses on smaller lots. But the correlation indicates that there is only a weak tendency for this to occur.

The above example allows us to motivate briefly an issue of importance, namely, that of **causality**. Researchers are often interested in finding out whether one variable "causes" another. We will not provide a formal definition of causality here but instead will use the word in its everyday meaning. In this example, it is sensible to use the positive correlation between house price and lot size to reflect a causal relationship. That is, lot size is a variable that directly influences (or causes) house prices. However, house prices do not influence (or cause) lot size. In other words, the direction of causality flows from lot size to house prices, not the other way around. In our sales/market capitalization example a similar story can be told. Companies with high sales (indicating financial health) are valued more highly by the market. It is the high sales which cause the markets to value them highly, not the high market valuation which boosts sales.

Another way of thinking about these issues is to ask yourself what would happen if a homeowner were to purchase some adjacent land, and thereby increase the lot size of her house. This action would tend to increase the value of the house (i.e. an increase in lot size would cause the price of the house to increase). However, if you reflect on the opposite question: "will increasing the price of the house cause lot size to increase?" you will see that the opposite causality does not hold (i.e. house price increases do not cause lot size increases). For instance, if house prices in Windsor were suddenly to rise for some reason (e.g. due to a boom in the economy) this would not mean that houses in Windsor suddenly got bigger lots. Similarly, financial analysts, noting an increase in a firm's sales, may be tempted to purchase the stock (driving up its price and, hence, its market capitalization). But if the market capitalization of a firm increases, that will not cause its sales to increase.

The discussion in the previous paragraph could be repeated with "lot size" replaced by "number of bedrooms". That is, it is reasonable to assume that the positive correlation between Y = house prices and Z = number of bedrooms is due to Z's influencing (or causing) Y, rather than the opposite. Note, however, that it is difficult to interpret the positive (but weak) correlation between X = lot size and Y = number of bedrooms as reflecting causality. That is, there is a tendency for houses with many bedrooms to occupy large lots, but this tendency does not imply that the former causes the latter.

One of the most important things in empirical work is knowing how to interpret your results. The house example illustrates this difficulty well. It is not enough just to report a number for a correlation (e.g. $r_{XY} = 0.54$). Interpretation is important too. Interpretation requires a good intuitive knowledge of what a correlation is in addition to a lot of common sense about the financial phenomenon under study. Given the importance of interpretation in empirical work, the following section will present several examples to show why variables are correlated and how common sense can guide us in interpreting them.

Exercise 3.2

(a) Using the data in HPRICE.XLS, calculate and interpret the mean, standard deviation, minimum and maximum of Y = house price (labeled "sale price" in HPRICE.XLS), X = lot size and Z = number of bedrooms (labeled "#bedroom").

(b) Verify that the correlation between X and Y is the same as given in the example. Repeat for X and Z then for Y and Z.

(c) Now add a new variable, W = number of bathrooms (labeled "#bath"). Calculate the mean of W.

(d) Calculate and interpret the correlation between W and Y. Discuss to what extent it can be said that W causes Y.

(e) Repeat part (d) for W and X and then for W and Z.

Understanding why variables are correlated

In our executive compensation/profits example, we discovered that executive compensation and profits are indeed correlated positively, indicating a positive relationship between the two. But what exact form does this relationship take? As discussed above, we often like to think in terms of causality or influence, and it may indeed be the case that correlation and causality are closely related. For instance, the finding that profits and compensation are correlated could mean that the former directly causes the latter. Similarly, the finding of a positive correlation between sales and market capitalization could be interpreted as meaning that more profit does directly influence market capitalization. However, as the following examples demonstrate, the interpretation that correlation implies causality is not always necessarily an accurate one.

Example: Correlation does not necessarily imply causality

It is widely accepted that cigarette smoking causes lung cancer. Let us assume that we have collected data from many people on (a) the number of cigarettes each person smokes per week (X) and (b) on whether they have ever had or now have lung cancer (Y). Since smoking causes cancer we would undoubtedly find $r_{XY} > 0$; that is, that people who smoked tend to have higher rates of lung cancer than non-smokers. Here the positive correlation between X and Y indicates direct causality.

Now suppose that we also have data on the same people, measuring the amount of alcohol they drink in a typical week. Let us call this variable Z. In practice, it is the case that heavy drinkers also tend to smoke and, hence, $r_{XZ} > 0$. This correlation does not mean that cigarette smoking also causes people to drink. Rather it probably reflects some underlying social attitudes. It may reflect the fact, in other words, that people who smoke do not worry about their nutrition, or that their social lives revolve around the pub, where drinking and smoking often go hand in hand. In either case, the positive correlation between smoking and drinking probably reflects some underlying cause (e.g. social attitude), which in turn causes both. Thus, a correlation between two variables does not necessarily mean that one causes the other. It may be the case that an underlying third variable is responsible.

Now consider the correlation between lung cancer and heavy drinking. Since people who smoke tend to get lung cancer more, and people who smoke also tend to drink more, it is not unreasonable to expect that lung cancer rates will be higher among heavy drinkers (i.e. $r_{YZ} > 0$). Note that this positive correlation does not imply that alcohol consumption causes lung cancer. Rather, it is cigarette smoking that causes cancer, but smoking and drinking are related to some underlying social attitude. This example serves to indicate the kind of complicated patterns of causality which occur in practice, and how care must be taken when trying to relate the concepts of correlation and causality.

In our house price example, however, it is likely that the positive correlations we observed reflect direct causality. For instance, having a larger lot is considered by most people to be a good thing in and of itself, so that increasing the lot size should directly increase the value of a house. There is no other intervening variable here, and hence we say that the causality is direct.[3]

The general message that should be taken from these examples is that *correlations can be very suggestive, but cannot on their own establish causality*. In the smoking/cancer example above, the finding of a positive correlation between smoking and lung cancer, in conjunction with medical evidence on the manner in which substances in cigarettes trigger changes in the human body, have convinced most people that smoking causes cancer. In the house price example, common sense tells us that the variable, number of bedrooms, directly influences house prices. In finance, the concept of correlation can be used in conjunction with common sense or a convincing financial theory to establish causality.

Exercise 3.3

People with university education tend to hold higher paying jobs than those with fewer educational qualifications. This could be due to the fact that a university education provides important skills that employers value highly. Alternatively, it could be the case that smart people tend to go to university and that employers want to hire these smart people (i.e. a university degree is of no interest in and of itself to employers).

Suppose you have data on Y = income, X = number of years of schooling and Z = the results of an intelligence test[4] of many people, and that you have calculated r_{XY}, r_{XZ} and r_{YZ}. In practice, what signs would you expect these correlations to have? Assuming the correlations do have the signs you expect, can you tell which of the two stories in the paragraph above is correct?

Understanding correlation through XY-plots

Intuition about the meaning of correlations can also be obtained from the *XY*-plots described in Chapter 2. Recall that in this chapter we discussed positive and negative relationships based on whether the *XY*-plots exhibited a general upward or down-

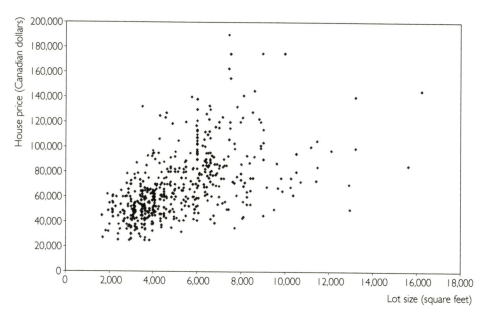

Fig. 3.1 *XY*-plot of house price versus lot size.

ward slope.[5] If two variables are correlated, then an *XY*-plot of one against the other will also exhibit such patterns. For instance, the *XY*-plot of executive compensation density against profit exhibits an upward sloping pattern (see Figure 2.3). This plot implies that these two variables should be positively correlated, and we find that this is indeed the case from the correlation, $r = 0.66$. The important point here is that positive correlation is associated with upward sloping patterns in the *XY*-plot and negative correlation is associated with downward sloping patterns. All the intuition we developed about *XY*-plots in the previous chapter can now be used to develop intuition about correlation.

Figure 3.1 uses the Windsor house price data set (HPRICE.XLS) to produce an *XY*-plot of $X =$ lot size against $Y =$ house price. Recall that the correlation between these two variables was calculated as $r_{XY} = 0.54$, which is a positive number. This positive (upward sloping) relationship between lot size and house price can clearly be seen in Figure 3.1. That is, houses with small lots (i.e. small *X*-axis values) also tend to have small prices (i.e. small *Y*-axis values). Conversely, houses with large lots tend to have high prices.

The previous discussion relates mainly to the sign of the correlation. However, *XY*-plots can also be used to develop intuition about how to interpret the magnitude of a correlation, as the following examples illustrate.

Figure 3.2 is an *XY*-plot of two perfectly correlated variables (i.e. $r = 1$). Note that they do not correspond to any actual financial data, but were simulated on the computer. All the points lie exactly on a straight line.

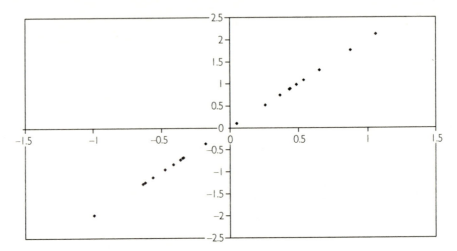

Fig. 3.2 *XY*-plot of two perfectly correlated variables (*r* = 1).

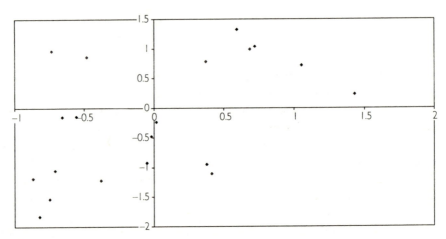

Fig. 3.3 *XY*-plot of two positively correlated variables (*r* = 0.51).

Figure 3.3 is an *XY*-plot of two variables which are positively correlated (*r* = 0.51), but not perfectly correlated. Note that the *XY*-plot still exhibits an upward sloping pattern, but that the points are much more widely scattered.

Figure 3.4 is an *XY*-plot of two completely uncorrelated variables (*r* = 0). Note that the points seem to be randomly scattered over the entire plot.

Plots for negative correlation exhibit downward sloping patterns, but otherwise the same sorts of patterns noted above hold for them. For instance, Figure 3.5 is an *XY*-plot of two variables that are negatively correlated (*r* = −0.58).

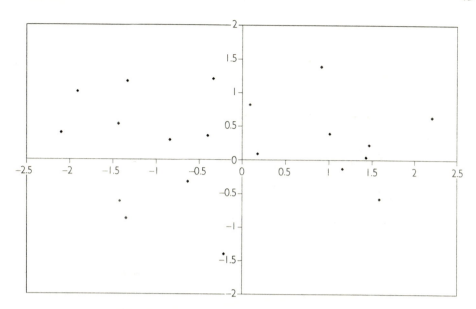

Fig. 3.4 *XY*-plot of two uncorrelated variables ($r = 0$).

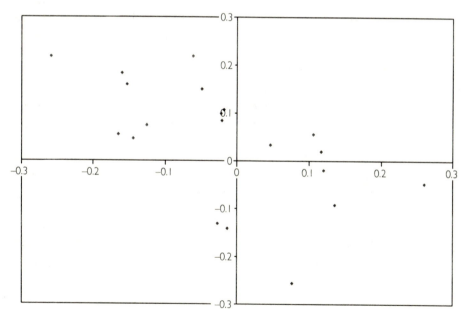

Fig. 3.5 *XY*-plot of two negatively correlated variables ($r = -0.58$).

These figures illustrate one way of thinking about correlation: correlation indicates how well a straight line can be fit through an XY-plot. Variables that are strongly correlated fit on or close to a straight line. Variables that are weakly correlated are more scattered in an XY-plot.

Exercise 3.4

The file EX34.XLS contains four variables: Y, X_1, X_2 and X_3.

(a) Calculate the correlation between Y and X_1. Repeat for Y and X_2 and for Y and X_3.

(b) Create an XY-plot involving Y and X_1. Repeat for Y and X_2 and for Y and X_3.

(c) Interpret your results for (a) and (b).

Correlation between several variables

Correlation is a property that relates two variables together. Frequently, however, researchers must work with several variables. For instance, market capitalization might depend on the firm's assets, income, debts and many other characteristics of the firm. As we shall see in subsequent chapters, regression is the most appropriate tool for use if the analysis contains more than two variables. Yet it is also not unusual for empirical researchers, when working with several variables, to calculate the correlation between each pair. This calculation is laborious when the number of variables is large. For instance, if we have three variables, X, Y and Z, then there are three possible correlations (i.e. r_{XY}, r_{XZ} and r_{YZ}). However, if we add a fourth variable, W, the number increases to six (i.e. r_{XY}, r_{XZ}, r_{XW}, r_{YZ}, r_{YW} and r_{ZW}). In general, for M different variables there will be $M \times (M - 1)/2$ possible correlations. A convenient way of ordering all these correlations is to construct a matrix or table, as illustrated by the following example.

CORMAT.XLS contains data on three variables labeled X, Y and Z. X is in the first column, Y the second and Z the third. Using Excel, we can create the following correlation matrix (Table 3.1) for these variables.

Table 3.1   The correlation matrix for X, Y, and Z.

	Column 1	Column 2	Column 3
Column 1	1		
Column 2	0.318237	1	
Column 3	−0.13097	0.096996	1

The number 0.318237 is the correlation between the variable in the first column (X), and that in the second column (Y). Similarly, -0.13097 is the correlation between X and Z, and 0.096996, the correlation between Y and Z. Note that the 1s in the correlation matrix indicate that any variable is perfectly correlated with itself.

Exercise 3.5

(a) Using the data in EXECUTIVE.XLS, calculate and interpret a correlation matrix involving executive compensation, profit, change in sales and change in debt.

(b) Repeat part (a) using the following variables in the data set HPRICE.XLS: house price, lot size, number of bedrooms, number of bathrooms and number of stories. How many individual correlations have you calculated?

Covariances and population correlations

In the previous chapter, we discussed means and variances and distinguished between sample and population variants. So, for instance, the sample mean was denoted by $\overline{Y}$ and was the average calculated using the data at hand. The population mean was denoted by $E(Y)$ and called the expected value. It was a more theoretical concept. We motivated it with an example where Y was next month's return on a stock. This is not known exactly, but the financial analyst is often able to predict what he would expect the return to be. This is $E(Y)$. However, there is uncertainty associated with the analyst's prediction and this is measured through the (population) variance, denoted var(Y).

The same sample/population distinction holds with correlations. We will use the notation ρ to denote the population correlation (remember r is our notation for the sample correlation). To motivate why such a concept might be useful, consider a portfolio consisting of the shares of two companies. The expected return of the portfolio depends on the expected returns of the two individual stocks. What is the risk of this portfolio? In the preceding chapter we related the risk of an individual stock to its variance. But with a portfolio of stocks the correlation between their returns is also important. The financial analyst is, thus, interested in ρ when evaluating the riskiness of a portfolio.

To illustrate the previous point, suppose an investor is interested in investing over the summer months in the shares of two companies: an umbrella manufacturer and an ice cream maker. Sales of these two companies are susceptible to the weather. If it is a hot, sunny summer, then ice cream makers do well (and owners of their stock make large returns). But if the summer is rainy, sales are very poor for the ice cream makers (and owners of their stock make small or negative returns). Hence, it seems like shares in the ice cream company are very risky. Shares in the umbrella manufacturer are also very risky – but for exactly the opposite reasons. Sunny summers are bad for umbrella sales, whereas rainy summers ensure good sales.

However, the overall portfolio is much less risky than the individual stocks. Whenever one of the stocks does poorly, the other does well. In a rainy summer, the investor will earn a good return on the part of her portfolio in umbrella stocks but a bad return on the part in ice cream stocks. In a sunny summer, the opposite will occur. Hence, the investor's portfolio will be quite safe – earning an adequate return regardless of the weather.

In statistical language, the previous example shows how the correlation between the returns on the shares in the two companies is a crucial factor in assessing the riskiness of a portfolio. In our example, this correlation was negative (i.e. whenever one stock made a good return, the other made a bad return). In practice, of course, the correlations between the returns in shares of two different companies may be positive or negative.

The previous discussion is meant to motivate why correlation is an important concept for the financial analyst. To develop a formula for exactly what the population correlation is requires us to take a slight detour and introduce the concept of a **covariance**. Remember that, in Chapter 2, we introduced the formula for the variance. We considered a case where Y was an unknown variable (e.g. the return of a stock in a future month) and supposed there were K possible outcomes (e.g. return of 1%, return of 2%, etc.). The probability of each outcome occurring was denoted by P_i for $i = 1, \ldots, K$. The variance of Y is defined as:

$$\mathrm{var}(Y) = \sum_{i=1}^{K} P_i [Y_i - E(Y)]^2.$$

Covariance is a closely related concept, except that two variables, Y and X are involved. The formula for covariance is:

$$\mathrm{cov}(X, Y) = \sum_{i=1}^{K} P_i [Y_i - E(Y)][X_i - E(X)].$$

The population correlation is the covariance normalized so as to have the same properties as the sample correlation (see the list "Properties of correlation" near the beginning of this chapter and replace r by ρ). It has the following formula:

$$\rho = \frac{\mathrm{cov}(X, Y)}{\sqrt{\mathrm{var}(X)\,\mathrm{var}(Y)}}.$$

Knowledge of this exact formula is rarely required in this textbook. However, it is crucial to have some intuition about correlation and how it depends on the variances and covariances of two variables.

As with means and variances, it is common for sample concepts to be used as estimates of population concepts. So, to return to our ice cream/umbrella example, the portfolio manager would be interested in knowing ρ: the population correlation between the stock returns in the two companies. The portfolio manager might collect data from the last 20 summers on stock returns for the two companies and use this data to calculate r: the sample correlation. The sample correlation could then be used as an estimate of ρ.

Chapter summary

1. Correlation is a common way of measuring the relationship between two variables. It is a number that can be calculated using Excel or any spreadsheet or econometric software package.
2. Correlation can be interpreted in a common sense way as a numerical measure of a relationship or association between two variables.
3. Correlation can also be interpreted graphically by means of XY-plots. That is, the sign of the correlation relates to the slope of a best fitting line through an XY-plot. The magnitude of the correlation relates to how scattered the data points are around the best fitting line.
4. Correlations can arise for many reasons. However, correlation does not necessarily imply causality between two variables.
5. The population correlation, ρ, is a useful concept when talking about many issues in finance (e.g. portfolio management).

Appendix 3.1: Mathematical details

The **correlation** between X and Y is referred to by the small letter r and is calculated as:

$$r = \frac{\sum_{i=1}^{N}(Y_i - \overline{Y})(X_i - \overline{X})}{\sqrt{\sum_{i=1}^{N}(Y_i - \overline{Y})^2}\sqrt{\sum_{i=1}^{N}(X_i - \overline{X})^2}},$$

where $\overline{X}$ and $\overline{Y}$ are the means of X and Y (see Chapter 2). More intuitively, note that if we were to divide the numerator and denominator of the previous expression by $N - 1$, then the denominator would contain the product of the standard deviations of X and Y, and the numerator, the covariance between X and Y.

Endnotes

1. By "larger negative values" we mean more negative. For instance, −0.9 is a larger negative value than −0.2.
2. If *r* were negative, the opposite of these statements would hold. For instance, *high* values of *X* would be associated with *low* values of *Y*, etc.
3. An alternative explanation is that good neighborhoods tend to have houses with large lots. People are willing to pay extra to live in a good neighborhood. Thus, it is possible that houses with large lots tend also to have higher sales prices, not because people want large lots, but because they want to live in good neighborhoods. In other words, "lot size" may be acting as a proxy for the "good neighborhood" effect. We will discuss such issues in more detail in later chapters on regression. You should merely note here that the interpretation of correlations can be quite complicated and a given correlation pattern may be consistent with several alternative stories.
4. It is a controversial issue among psychologists and educators as to whether intelligence tests really are meaningful measures of intelligence. For the purposes of answering this question, avoid this controversy and assume that they are indeed an accurate reflection of intelligence.
5. We will formalize the meaning of "upward" or "downward" sloping patterns in the *XY*-plots when we come to regression. To aid in interpretation, think of drawing a straight line through the points in the *XY*-plot that best captures the pattern in the data (i.e. is the best fitting line). The upward or downward slope discussed here refers to the slope of this line.

CHAPTER 4

An introduction to simple regression

Regression is an important tool financial researchers use to understand the relationship among two or more variables. Even when, as done in later chapters, we move beyond regression and use slightly more complicated methods, the intuition provided by regression is of great use. This motivates why we devote this chapter (and the next three) to regression. It is important for the reader to develop the basic tools of regression before proceeding on to more sophisticated methods.

In finance, most empirical work involves time series data. However, as we shall see in the second half of this book, working with time series data requires some specialized tools. Hence, with some exceptions,[1] for the next few chapters you will not see too many examples involving financial time series data. The examples in this chapter will mostly involve cross-sectional data. The reader interested in more traditional applications involving financial time series can be reassured that they will reappear starting in Chapter 8. However, before we get to time series methods, a good understanding of basic regression is required.

Regression is particularly useful for the common case where there are many variables and the interactions between them are complex. All of the examples considered in Chapter 3 really should have involved many variables. For instance, market capitalization likely depends on many characteristics of the firm, such as sales, assets, income, etc. Executive compensation likely does not depend solely on firm profits, but also on other firm characteristics. The price of a house, as well, depends on many characteristics (e.g. number of bedrooms, number of bathrooms, location of house, size of lot, etc.). Many variables must be included in a model seeking to explain why some houses are more expensive than others.

These examples are not unusual. Many problems in finance are of a similar level of complexity. Unfortunately, the basic tool you have encountered so far – simple correlation analysis – cannot handle such complexity. For these more complex cases – that is, those involving more than two variables – regression is the tool to use.

Regression as a best fitting line

As a way of understanding regression, let us begin with just two variables (Y and X). We refer to this case as simple regression. Multiple regression, involving many variables, will be discussed in Chapter 6. Beginning with simple regression makes sense since graphical intuition can be developed in a straightforward manner and the relationship between regression and correlation can be illustrated quite easily.

Let us return to the XY-plots used previously (e.g. Figure 2.3 which plots profits against executive compensation for many companies or Figure 3.1 which plots lot size against house price). We have discussed in Chapters 2 and 3 how an examination of these XY-plots can reveal a great deal about the relationship between X and Y. In particular, a straight line drawn through the points on the XY-plot provides a convenient summary of the relationship between X and Y. In regression analysis, we formally analyze this relationship.

To start with, we assume that a linear relationship exists between Y and X. As an example, you might consider Y to be the market capitalization variable and X to be the sales variable from data set EQUITY.XLS. Remember that this data set contained the market capitalization of 309 American firms with several characteristics for each firm. It is sensible to assume that the sales of the firm affects its market capitalization.

We can express the linear relationship between Y and X mathematically as:[2]

$$Y = \alpha + \beta X,$$

where α is the intercept of the line and β is the slope. This equation is referred to as the **regression line**. If in actuality we knew what α and β were, then we would know what the relationship between Y and X was. In practice, of course, we do not have this information. Furthermore, even if our **regression model**, which posits a linear relationship between Y and X, were true, in the real world we would never find that our data points lie precisely on a straight line. Factors such as measurement error mean that individual data points might lie close to but not exactly on a straight line.

For instance, suppose the price of a house (Y) depends on the lot size (X) in the following manner: $Y = 34{,}000 + 7X$ (i.e. $\alpha = 34{,}000$ and $\beta = 7$). If X were 5,000 square feet, this model says the price of the house should be $Y = 34{,}000 + 7 \times 5{,}000 = \$69{,}000$. But, of course, not every house with a lot size of 5,000 square feet will have a sales price of precisely \$69,000. No doubt in this case, the regression model is missing some important variables (e.g. number of bedrooms) that may affect the price of a house. Furthermore, the price of some houses might be higher than they should be (e.g. if they were bought by irrationally exuberant buyers). Alternatively, some houses may sell for less than their true worth (e.g. if the sellers have to relocate to a different city and must sell their houses quickly). For all these reasons, even if $Y = 34{,}000 + 7X$ is an accurate description of a straight line relationship between Y and X, it will not be the case that every data point lies exactly on the line.

Our house price example illustrates a truth about regression modeling: **the linear regression model will always be only an approximation of the true relationship**. The truth may differ in many ways from the approximation implicit in the linear regression model. In many financial applications, the most probable source of error is due to missing variables, usually because we cannot observe them. In our previous example, house prices reflect many variables for which we can easily collect data (e.g. number of bedrooms, number of bathrooms, etc.). But they will also depend on many other factors for which it is difficult if not impossible to collect data (e.g. the number of loud parties held by neighbors, the degree to which the owners have kept the property well-maintained, the quality of the interior decoration of the house, etc.). The omission of these variables from the regression model will mean that the model makes an error.

We call all such errors e. The regression model can now be written as:

$$Y = \alpha + \beta X + e.$$

In the regression model, Y is referred to as the **dependent** variable, X the **explanatory** variable, and α and β, **coefficients**. It is common to implicitly assume that the explanatory variable "causes" Y, and the coefficient β measures the influence of X on Y. In light of the comments made in the previous chapter about how correlation does not necessarily imply causality, you may want to question the assumption that the explanatory variable causes the dependent variable. There are two responses that can be made to this statement.

First, note that we talk about the regression **model**. A model specifies how different variables interact. For instance, models of salary determination posit that executive compensation should depend on firm profitability. Such models have the causality "built-in" and the purpose of a regression involving Y = executive compensation and X = profit is to measure the magnitude of the effect of profit on compensation only (i.e. the causality assumption may be reasonable and we do not mind assuming it). Secondly, we can treat the regression purely as a technique for generalizing correlation and interpret the numbers that the regression model produces purely as reflecting the association between variables. (In other words, we can drop the causality assumption if we wish.[3])

In light of the error, e, and the fact that we do not know what α and β are, the first problem in regression analysis is how we can figure approximately, or **estimate**, what α and β are. It is standard practice to refer to the estimates of α and β as $\hat{\alpha}$ and $\hat{\beta}$ (i.e. $\hat{\alpha}$ and $\hat{\beta}$ are actual numbers that the computer calculates, for instance, $\hat{\alpha} = 34{,}136$ and $\hat{\beta} = 6.599$, which are estimates of the unknown true values

$\alpha = 34{,}000$ and $\beta = 7$). One can interpret the estimates as being obtained from a line drawn through the points on an XY-plot which fits best. Hence, we must define what we mean by "best fitting line".

Before we do this, it is useful to make a distinction between **errors** and **residuals**. The error is defined as the distance between a particular data point and the true regression line. Mathematically, we can rearrange the regression model to write $e_i = Y_i - \alpha - \beta X_i$. This is the **error** for the ith observation. However, if we replace α and β by their estimates $\hat{\alpha}$ and $\hat{\beta}$, we get a straight line which is generally a little different from the true regression line. The deviations from this estimated regression line are called **residuals**. We will use the notation "u" when we refer to residuals. That is, the residuals are given by $u_i = Y_i - \hat{\alpha} - \hat{\beta} X_i$. If you find the distinction between errors and residuals confusing, you can probably ignore it in the rest of this book and assume errors and residuals are the same thing. However, if you plan on further study of financial econometrics, this distinction becomes crucial.

If we return to some basic geometry, note that we can draw one (and only one) straight line connecting any two distinct points. Thus, in the case of two points, there is no doubt about what the best fitting line through an XY-plot is. However, typically we have many points – for instance, our executive compensation/profit example has 70 different companies and the XY-plots 70 points – and there is ambiguity about what is the "best fitting line". Figure 4.1 plots three data points (A, B and C) on an XY graph. Clearly, there is no straight line that passes through all three points. The line I have drawn does not pass through any of them; each point, in other words, is a little bit off the line. To put it another way: the line drawn implies residuals that are labeled u_1, u_2 and u_3. The residuals are the vertical difference between a data point and the line. A good fitting line will have small residuals.

The usual way of measuring the size of the residuals is by means of the sum of squared residuals (**SSR**), which is given by:

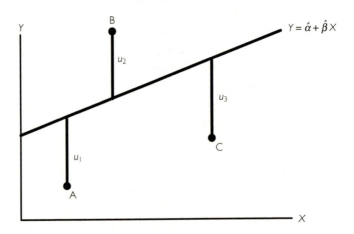

Fig. 4.1 Best fitting line for three data points.

$$\text{SSR} = \sum_{i=1}^{N} u_i^2,$$

for $i = 1, \ldots, N$ data points. We want to find the best fitting line which minimizes the sum of squared residuals. For this reason, estimates found in this way are called **least squares** estimates (or ordinary least squares – **OLS** – to distinguish them from more complicated estimators which we will not discuss in this book).

In practice, software packages such as Excel can automatically find values for $\hat{\alpha}$ and $\hat{\beta}$ which will minimize the sum of squared residuals. The exact formulae for $\hat{\alpha}$ and $\hat{\beta}$ can be derived using simple calculus, but we will not derive them here (see Appendix 4.1 for more details).

Example: The regression of executive compensation on profits

Consider again the data set EXECUTIVE.XLS, which contains data on profits and executive compensation for 70 companies. It makes sense to assume that profitability influences executive pay rather than the other way around.[4] Thus we choose executive compensation as the dependent variable (i.e. $Y =$ executive compensation) and profits as the explanatory variable (i.e. $X =$ profits). Using Excel (Tools/Data Analysis/Regression) we obtain $\hat{\alpha} = 0.60$ and $\hat{\beta} = 0.000842$. To provide some more jargon, note that when we estimate a regression model it is common to say that "we run a regression of Y on X".

Note also that it is actually very easy to calculate these numbers in most statistical software packages. Appropriately, we will turn instead to the more important issue: how do we interpret these numbers.

Interpreting OLS estimates

In the example of the relationship between executive compensation and profits, we obtained OLS estimates for the intercept and slope of the regression line. The question now arises: how should we interpret these estimates? The intercept in the regression model, α, usually has little financial interpretation so we will not discuss it here. However, β is typically quite important. This coefficient is the slope of the best fitting straight line through the XY-plot. In the executive compensation/profits example, $\hat{\beta}$ was positive. Remembering the discussion on how to interpret correlations in the previous chapter, we note that since $\hat{\beta}$ is positive X and Y are positively correlated. However, we can go further in interpreting $\hat{\beta}$ if we differentiate the regression model and obtain:

$$\frac{dY}{dX} = \beta.$$

Even if you do not know calculus, the verbal intuition of the previous expression is not hard to provide. Derivatives measure how much Y changes when X is changed by a small (marginal) amount. Hence, β can be interpreted as the **marginal effect** of X on Y and is a measure of how much X influences Y. To be more precise, we can interpret β as a measure of how much Y tends to change when X is changed by one unit.[5] The definition of "unit" in the previous sentence depends on the particular data set being studied and is best illustrated through examples. Before doing this, it should be stressed that regressions measure tendencies in the data (note the use of the word "tends" in the explanation of β above). It is not necessarily the case that every observation (e.g. company or house) fits the general pattern established by the other observations. In Chapter 2 we called such unusual observations outliers and argued that, in some cases, examining outliers could be quite informative. In the case of regression, outliers are those with residuals that stand out as being unusually large. Hence, examining the residuals from a regression is a common practice. (In Excel you can examine the residuals by clicking on the box labeled "Residuals" in the regression menu.)

Example: Regression of executive compensation on profits (continued from page 53)

In the executive compensation/profits example we obtained $\hat{\beta} = 0.000842$. This is a measure of how much executive compensation tends to change when profit changes by a small amount. Since profit and compensation are measured in millions of dollars, this figure implies that if profit goes up by $1 million (i.e. a change of one unit in the explanatory variable), then executive compensation will tend to increase by 0.000842 million dollars (or $842).

Exercise 4.1

The Excel data set EXECUTIVE.XLS contains data on Y = executive compensation, X = profits, W = percentage change in sales and Z = percentage change in debt.

(a) Run a regression of Y on X and interpret the results.

(b) Run a regression of Y on W and one of Y on Z and interpret the results.

(c) Create a new variable, V, by dividing X by 100. What are the units in terms of which V is measured?

(d) Run a regression of Y on V. Compare your results to those for (a). How do you interpret your coefficient estimate of β? How does $\hat{\alpha}$ differ between a) and d)?

(e) Experiment with scaling dependent and explanatory variables (i.e. by dividing them by a constant) and see what effect this has on your coefficient estimates.

Fitted values and R^2: measuring the fit of a regression model

In the preceding discussion we learned how to calculate and interpret regression coefficients, $\hat{\alpha}$ and $\hat{\beta}$. Furthermore, we explained that regression finds the "best fitting" line in the sense that it minimizes the SSR. However, it is possible that the "best" fit is not a very good fit at all. Appropriately, it is desirable to have some measure of fit (or a measure of how good the best fitting line is). The most common measure of fit is referred to as the R^2. It relates closely to the correlation between Y and X. In fact, for the simple regression model, it is the correlation squared. This provides the formal statistical link between regression and correlation. However, the previous discussion should make the informal links between correlation and regression clear. Both are interested in quantifying the degree of association between different variables and both can be interpreted in terms of fitting lines through XY-plots.

To derive and explain R^2, we will begin with some background material. We start by clarifying the notion of a **fitted value**. Remember that regression fits a straight line through an XY-plot, but does not pass precisely through each point on the plot (i.e. an error is made). In the case of our executive compensation/profits example, this meant that individual companies did not lie on the regression line. The fitted value for observation i is the value that lies on the regression line corresponding to the X_i value for that particular observation (e.g. house, company). In other words, if you draw a straight vertical line through a particular point in the XY-plot, the intersection of this vertical line and the regression line is the fitted value corresponding to the point you chose.

Alternatively, we can think of the idea of a fitted value in terms of the formula for the regression model:

$$Y_i = \alpha + \beta X_i + e_i.$$

Remember that adding i subscripts (e.g. Y_i) indicates that we are referring to a particular observation (e.g. the ith company or the house). If we ignore the error, we can say that the model's prediction of Y_i should be equal to $\alpha + \beta X_i$. If we replace α and β by the OLS estimates $\hat{\alpha}$ and $\hat{\beta}$, we obtain a so-called "fitted" or "predicted" value for Y_i:

$$\hat{Y}_i = \hat{\alpha} + \hat{\beta} X_i.$$

Note that we are using the value of the explanatory variable and the OLS estimates to predict the dependent variable. By looking at actual (Y_i) versus fitted ($\hat{Y}_i$) values we can gain a rough impression of the "goodness of fit" of the regression model. Many software packages allow you to print out the actual and fitted values for each observation. An examination of these values not only gives you a rough measure of how well the regression model fits, they allow you to examine individual observations to determine which ones are close to the regression line and which are not. Since the regression line captures general patterns or tendencies in your data set, you can see which observations conform to the general pattern and which do not.

Exercise 4.2

Using the data in EXECUTIVE.XLS (see Exercise 4.1), run a regression of Y on X and graphically and numerically compare actual and fitted values. In Excel this can be done by running the regression with the box clicked on labeled "Line Fit Plot" in the Regression menu (i.e. look at the columns labeled "Residual Output" and the accompanying display chart).

We have defined the residual made in fitting our best fitting line previously. Another way to express this residual is in terms of the difference between the actual and fitted values of Y. That is:

$$u_i = Y_i - \hat{Y}_i.$$

Software packages such as Excel can also plot or list the residuals from a regression model. These can be examined in turn to give a rough impression of the goodness of fit of the regression model. We emphasize that unusually big residuals are outliers and sometimes these outliers are of interest.

Exercise 4.3

(a) Using the data in EXECUTIVE.XLS (see Exercise 4.1) run a regression of Y on X and graphically and numerically compare residuals. In Excel this can be done with the boxes labeled "Residuals" and "Residual Plots" in the regression menu clicked on. How would you interpret the residuals? Are there any outliers?

(b) Repeat question (a) for the other variables, W and Z in this data set.

To illustrate the kind of information with which residual analysis can provide us, take a look at your computer output from Exercise 4.3 (a). In the Residual Output, observation 39 has a fitted value of 2.93 and a residual of −1.63. By adding these two figures together (or by looking at the original data), you can see that the actual compensation paid to the chief executive by this company is 1.3. What do all these numbers imply? Note that the regression model is predicting a much higher value (2.93) for compensation than actually occurred (1.3) in this company. This means that this company is getting a much cheaper chief executive than the regression model implies.

The ideas of a residual and a fitted value are important in developing an informal understanding of how well a regression model fits. However, we still lack a formal numerical measure of fit. At this stage, we can now derive and motivate such a measure: R^2.

Recall that variance is the measure of dispersion or variability of the data. Here we define a closely related concept, the total sum of squares or TSS:

$$TSS = \sum (Y_i - \bar{Y})^2,$$

Note that the formula for the variance of Y is $TSS/(N-1)$ (see Chapter 2). Loosely speaking, the $N-1$ term will cancel out in our final formula for R^2 and, hence, we ignore it. So think of TSS as being a measure of the variability of Y. The regression model seeks to explain the variability in Y through the explanatory variable X. It can be shown that the total variability in Y can be broken into two parts as:

$$TSS = RSS + SSR,$$

where RSS is the regression sum of squares, a measure of the explanation provided by the regression model.[6] RSS is given by:

$$RSS = \sum (\hat{Y}_i - \bar{Y})^2.$$

Remembering that SSR is the sum of squared residuals and that a good fitting regression model will make the SSR very small, we can combine the equations above to yield a measure of fit:

$$R^2 = 1 - \frac{SSR}{TSS}$$

or, equivalently,

$$R^2 = \frac{RSS}{TSS}.$$

Intuitively, the R^2 measures the proportion of the total variance of Y that can be explained by X. Note that TSS, RSS and SSR are all sums of squared numbers and, hence, are all non-negative. This implies $TSS \geq RSS$ and $TSS \geq SSR$. Using these facts, it can be seen that $0 \leq R^2 \leq 1$.

Further intuition about this measure of fit can be obtained by noting that small values of SSR indicate that the regression model is fitting well. A regression line which fits all the data points perfectly in the XY-plot will have no errors and hence $SSR = 0$ and $R^2 = 1$. Looking at the formula above, you can see that values of R^2 near 1 imply a good fit and that $R^2 = 1$ implies a perfect fit. In sum, high values of R^2 imply a good fit and low values a bad fit.

An alternative source of intuition is provided by the RSS. RSS measures how much of the variation in Y the explanatory variables explain. If RSS is near TSS, then the explanatory variables account for almost all of the variability and the fit will be a good one. Looking at the previous formula you can see that the R^2 is near one in this case.

Another property of R^2 can be used to link regression and correlation. It turns out that the R^2 from the regression of Y on X is exactly equal to the square of the correlation between Y and X. Regression is really just an extension of correlation. Yet, regression also provides you with an explicit expression for the marginal effect (β), which is often important for policy analysis.

Exercise 4.4

(a) Using the data in EXECUTIVE.XLS (see exercise 4.1) run a regression of Y on X using Excel. What is the R^2?

(b) Calculate the correlation between Y and X.

(c) Discuss the relationship between your answers in (a) and (b).

(d) Redo (a) for various regressions involving the variables W, X, Y and Z in the data set. Comment on the fit of each of these regressions.

Example: The capital asset pricing model

This book is about the analysis of financial data, not about financial theory (e.g. the theory of investor behavior).[7] However, it is instructive occasionally to give a flavor of some of the theory that financial analysts use to motivate their empirical work. In this example, we briefly describe a simple variant of the capital asset pricing model (CAPM). This is a very popular model and it, or extensions of it, are widely used by financial analysts. We show how it yields a simple regression which can be estimated using OLS. Of the concepts used in this example, we have discussed the return and excess return of an asset in Chapter 2, the expected value and variance operators in Chapter 2 and the covariance in Chapter 3. Please review this material now if you cannot remember what they are.

An important issue when deciding on an investment portfolio is the trade-off between risk and expected return. After all, some assets the investor could purchase are very safe (e.g. government bonds or cash), while others are moderately safe (e.g. purchasing the shares of an established blue-chip company) and others are much more risky (e.g. purchasing the shares of a newly established dot.com). As discussed in Chapter 2, variance can be related to risk (e.g. variance can be interpreted as measuring the variability of the return on an asset). There is a large theoretical literature on **mean-variance efficient portfolios** that trade off risk and return in an optimal manner. The CAPM is an implication of this theory. To explain the CAPM, we need to define the returns on three types of assets. We will let R be the return on the asset under study (e.g. the return on holding a share in a particular company, call it Company A), R_f be the **risk free rate of interest** (e.g. the return on a very safe investment such as a government bond) and R_m be the return on the **market portfolio**. The market portfolio is formally defined as a portfolio containing the shares of every possible company with portfolio weights proportional to each company's market capitalization. In empirical work, the market portfolio is usually proxied using a stock market index such as the S&P500, NYSE or FTSE.

We will not derive the CAPM, but merely state some of its main implications and provide some intuitive motivation for it. When deciding on a portfolio, the investor does not know for certain the return of the stocks that are available for purchase; hence we have to talk in terms of expected returns. It is assumed that the return on the risk free asset is known (e.g. when the investor buys government bonds she knows how much their return will be in the future). The CAPM implies:

$$E(R) = R_f + \beta[E(R_m) - R_f].$$

Thus, the expected return on the share of Company A is equal to the risk free rate plus β times the expected excess return on the market portfolio (remember that an excess return is a return minus the return on a safe asset). On a broad level, this makes sense. Investors could have bought the safe asset or the market portfolio. Investors' decisions on whether to buy shares in Company A will thus depend on the returns on the other available options. And investors' decisions determine the price of shares in Company A. Thus, its expected return can reasonably be expected to depend on R_f and $E(R_m)$.

The precise relationship depends on β, which is commonly referred to as the **CAPM beta** or **investor's beta** which is given by:

$$\beta = \frac{\text{cov}(R, R_m)}{\text{var}(R_m)}.$$

The CAPM β thus depends on the covariance between the return on Company A's shares and the return on the market portfolio. Thus, it is closely related to the correlation between these two variables (see the section on Covariances and Population Correlations in Chapter 3). This is sensible since it relates to the old adage that one should not put all one's eggs in one basket. That is, it is wise for an investor to diversify their portfolio since this will reduce risk.

To understand the CAPM better, consider what happens when Company A's shares are just as volatile as the stock market as a whole and movements in the one perfectly match the other. Every time the stock market rises, Company A's shares rise by the same amount. Every time the stock market falls, Company A's shares fall by the same amount. In this case, it can be confirmed that $\beta = 1$ and the CAPM equation implies that both expected returns have to be the same as one another. Intuitively, if shares in Company A and the stock market as a whole are exactly as risky as one another then their expected returns must be the same. If the stock market index had a higher expected return, then no investor would ever buy the (equally risky, but with lower expected return) shares of Company A.

In contrast, consider what would happen if returns to Company A's stock were negatively correlated with the stock market as a whole. Then, it can be seen that β is negative. Note that the expected excess return on the market portfolio is positive (since if $E(R_m) < R_f$ then no one would ever invest in the stock market – they would prefer the safe higher return of the risk free asset). Using these facts in the CAPM equation, it can be seen that they imply $E(R) < R_f$ and the expected excess return to Company's A shares is actually negative! How can this be? In this case, Company A's shares would be very attractive to investors. After all, if their returns are negatively correlated with the stock market as a whole, then whenever there is a stock market crash, the shares in Company A would actually rise. In fact, in a sense they are even safer than a risk free asset such as cash. In a stock market crash, cash would still hold its value, but shares in Company A would actually increase in value. So to an investor who hates risk, they would be an ideal purchase. Such investors would be willing to buy shares in Company A even if their expected return was lower than the risk free rate.

The stories in the two previous paragraphs are intended to motivate the CAPM equation and its importance for investment decisions. Of course, in practice, the CAPM β can take a wide range of values. It is common to find $\beta > 1$. In this case the expected excess return to holding Company A's shares is higher than the expected excess return on the market portfolio. This indicates Company A's shares are riskier than the stock market as a whole and investors require a higher expected return in order to compensate them for bearing this risk.

Given its importance for investment decisions, financial analysts often try to estimate what the CAPM β is for individual company's shares. This can be done using regression methods. Of course, one cannot obtain data on the expected excess return of a share or a market portfolio. However, if we replace expected returns with the actual returns of a stock from the past we can run a regression based on the CAPM equation. That is, we set Y = excess returns on Company A's shares (measured as the actual return minus the return on a risk free asset such as a government bond) and X = excess returns on the market portfolio (measured as the actual return on a major stock market index minus the return on a risk free asset such as a government bond) and run a simple regression.

The file CAPM.XLS contains monthly data on Y = the excess returns on Company A's stock for the last 10 years as well as data on X = excess returns on a stock market index for the same time period. If we run the regression of Y on X we obtain $\hat{\alpha} = 0.43$ and $\hat{\beta} = 1.77$. Thus, our estimate of the CAPM β for Company A is 1.77.

Nonlinearity in regression

So far, we have used the linear regression model and fit a straight line through XY-plots. However, this may not always be appropriate. Consider the XY-plot in Figure 4.2. It looks like the relationship between Y and X is not linear. If we were to fit a straight line through the data, it might give a misleading representation of the relationship between Y and X. In fact, we have artificially generated this data by assuming the relationship between Y and X is of the form:

$$Y_i = 6X_i^2,$$

such that the true relationship is quadratic. A cursory glance at the XY-plots can often indicate whether fitting a straight line is appropriate or not.

What should you do if a quadratic relationship rather than a linear relationship exists? The answer is surprisingly simple: rather than regressing Y on X, regress Y on X^2 instead.

Of course, the relationship revealed by the XY-plot may be found to be neither linear nor quadratic. It may appear that Y is related to $\ln(X)$ or $1/X$ or X^3 or any other transformation of X. However, the same general strategy holds: transform the X variable as appropriate and then run a regression of Y on the transformed variable. You can even transform Y if it seems appropriate.

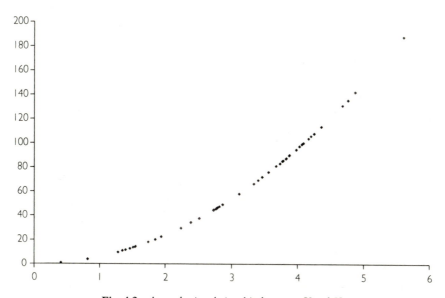

Fig. 4.2 A quadratic relationship between X and Y.

A very common transformation, of both the dependent and explanatory variables, is the logarithmic transformation (see Appendix 1.1 for a discussion of logarithms). Even if you are not familiar with logarithms, they are easy to work with in any spreadsheet or econometric software package, including Excel.[8] Often financial researchers work with natural logarithms, for which the symbol is ln. In this book, we will always use natural logarithms and simply refer to them as "logs" for short. It is common to say that: "we took the log of variable X" or that "we worked with log X". The mathematical notation is $\ln(X)$. One thing to note about logs is that they are only defined for positive numbers. So if your data contains zeros or negative numbers, you cannot take logs (i.e. the software will display an error message).

Why is it common to use $\ln(Y)$ as the dependent variable and $\ln(X)$ as the explanatory variable? First, the expressions will often allow us to interpret results quite easily. Second, data transformed in this way often does appear to satisfy the linearity assumption of the regression model.

To fully understand the first point, we need some background in calculus, which is beyond the scope of this book. Fortunately, the intuition can be stated verbally. In the following regression:

$$\ln(Y) = \alpha + \beta \ln(X) + e,$$

β can be interpreted as an **elasticity**. Recall that, in the basic regression without logs, we said that "Y tends to change by β **units** for a one **unit** change in X". In the regression containing both logged dependent and explanatory variables, we can now say that "Y tends to change by β **percent** for a one **percent** change in X". That is, instead of having to worry about units of measurement, regression results using logged variables are always interpreted as elasticities. Logs are convenient for other reasons too. For instance, as discussed in Chapter 2, when we have time series data, the percentage change in a variable is approximately $100 \times [\ln(Y_t) - \ln(Y_{t-1})]$. This transformation will turn out to be useful in later chapters in this book.

The second justification for the log transformation is purely practical: With many data sets, if you take the logs of dependent and explanatory variables and make an XY-plot the resulting relationship will look linear. This is illustrated in Figures 4.3 and 4.4. Figure 4.3 is an XY-plot of two data series, Y and X, neither of which has been transformed in any way. Figure 4.4 is an XY-plot of $\ln(X)$ and $\ln(Y)$. Note that the points in the first figure do not seem to lie along a straight line. Rather the relationship is one of a steep-sloped pattern for small values of X, that gradually flattens out as X increases. This is a typical pattern for data which should be logged. Figure 4.4 shows that, once the data is logged, the XY-plot indicates a linear pattern. An OLS regression will fit a straight line with a high degree of accuracy in Figure 4.4. However, fitting an accurate straight line through Figure 4.3 is a very difficult (and probably not the best) thing to do.

On what basis should you log your data (or for that matter take any other transformation)? There is no simple rule that can be given. Examining XY-plots of the

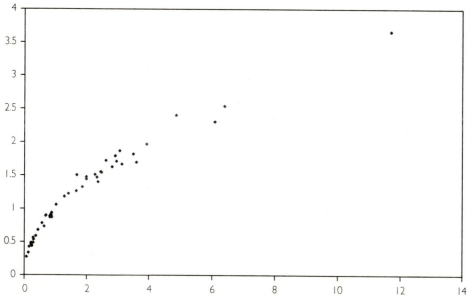

Fig. 4.3 X and Y need to be logged.

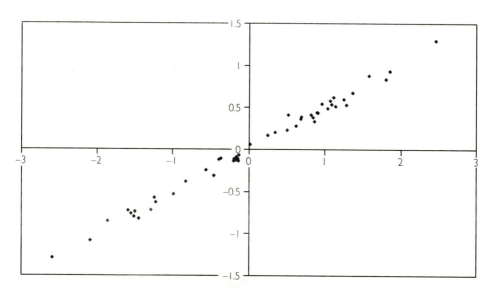

Fig. 4.4 $\ln(X)$ versus $\ln(Y)$.

data transformed in various ways is often instructive. For instance, begin by looking at a plot of X against Y. This may look roughly linear. If so, just go ahead and run a regression of Y on X. If the plot does not look linear, it may exhibit some other pattern that you recognize (e.g. the quadratic form of Figure 4.2 or the logarithmic form of Figure 4.3). If so, create an XY-plot of suitable transformed variables (e.g. $\ln(Y)$ against $\ln(X)$) and see if it looks linear. Such a strategy will likely work well in a simple regression containing only one explanatory variable. In Chapter 6, we will move on to cases with several explanatory variables. In these cases, the examination of XY-plots may be quite complicated since there are so many possible XY-plots that could be constructed.

Exercise 4.5

Using the data in EXECUTIVE.XLS examine different XY-plots involving the variables X, Y, W and Z (see Exercise 4.1 for a definition of these variables). Does there seem to be a nonlinear relationship between any pair of variables?

Exercise 4.6

Data set EX46.XLS contains two variables, labeled Y and X.

(a) Make an XY-plot of these two variables. Does the relationship between Y and X appear to be linear?
(b) Calculate the square root of variable X. Note the Excel function for square root is SQRT.
(c) Make an XY-plot of the square root of X against Y. Does this relationship appear to be linear?

Chapter summary

1. Simple regression quantifies the effect of an explanatory variable, X, on a dependent variable, Y. Hence, it measures the relationship between two variables.
2. The relationship between Y and X is assumed to take the form, $Y = \alpha + \beta X$, where α is the intercept and β the slope of a straight line. This is called the regression line.
3. The regression line is the best fitting line through an XY graph.

4. No line will ever fit perfectly through all the points in an XY graph. The distance between each point and the line is called a residual.
5. The ordinary least squares, OLS, estimator is the one which minimizes the sum of squared residuals.
6. OLS provides estimates of α and β which are labeled $\hat{\alpha}$ and $\hat{\beta}$.
7. Regression coefficients should be interpreted as marginal effects (i.e. as measures of the effect on Y of a small change in X).
8. R^2 is a measure of how well the regression line fits through the XY graph.
9. OLS estimates and the R^2 are calculated in computer software packages such as Excel.
10. Regression lines do not have to be linear. To carry out nonlinear regression, merely replace Y and/or X in the regression model by a suitable nonlinear transformation (e.g. $\ln(Y)$ or X^2).

Appendix 4.1: Mathematical details

The OLS estimator defines the best fitting line through the points on an XY-plot. Mathematically, we are interested in choosing $\hat{\alpha}$ and $\hat{\beta}$ so as to minimize the sum of squared residuals. The SSR can be written as:

$$SSR = \sum_{i=1}^{N}\left(Y_i - \hat{\alpha} - \hat{\beta}X_i\right)^2.$$

Optional exercise

Take first and second derivatives with respect to $\hat{\alpha}$ and $\hat{\beta}$ of the above expression for SSR. Use these to find values of $\hat{\alpha}$ and $\hat{\beta}$ that minimize SSR. Verify that the solution you have found does indeed minimize (rather than maximize) SSR.

If you have done the previous exercise correctly, you should have obtained the following:

$$\hat{\beta} = \frac{\sum_{i=1}^{N}(Y_i - \overline{Y})(X_i - \overline{X})}{\sum_{i=1}^{N}(X_i - \overline{X})^2}$$

and

$$\hat{\alpha} = \overline{Y} - \hat{\beta}\overline{X},$$

where $\overline{Y}$ and $\overline{X}$ are the means of Y and X (see Chapter 2). These are the OLS estimators for α and β. Note that there are several equivalent ways of writing the formula for $\hat{\beta}$. If you consult other textbooks you will find alternative expressions for the OLS estimator.

These equations can be used to demonstrate the consequences of taking **deviations from means**. By way of explanation, note that we have assumed above that the dependent and explanatory variables, X and Y, are based on the raw data. However, in some cases researchers do not work with just X and Y, but rather with X and Y minus their respective means:

$$y_i = Y_i - \overline{Y}$$

and

$$x_i = X_i - \overline{X}.$$

Consider using OLS to estimate the regression:

$$y = a + bx + e,$$

where we have used the symbols a and b to distinguish them from the coefficients α and β in the regression involving Y and X.

It turns out that the relationship between OLS estimates from the original regression and the one where deviations from means have been taken is a simple one. The OLS estimate of b is always exactly the same as $\hat{\beta}$ and the OLS estimate of a is always zero. In other words, taking deviations from means simplifies the regression model by getting rid of the intercept (i.e. there is no point in including an intercept since its coefficient is always zero). This simplification does not have any affect on the slope coefficient in the regression model. It is unchanged by taking deviations from means and still has the same interpretation as a marginal effect.

It is not too hard to prove the statements in the previous paragraph and, if you are mathematically inclined, you might be interested in doing so. As a hint, note that the means of y and x are zero.

In Chapter 6, we will consider the case where there are several explanatory variables. In this case, if you take deviations from means of the dependent and all of the explanatory variables, you obtain the same result. That is, the intercept disappears from the regression, but all other coefficient estimates are unaffected.

Endnotes

1. The regression methods outlined in the next few chapters can be used with time series variables if they are stationary. At this stage, you will not know what the term "stationary" means, but you can be assured that the examples in this chapter and the next involving time series data involve stationary data. The concept of stationarity will be explained in Chapter 9.

2. Note that, at many places, we will omit multiplication signs for simplicity. For instance, instead of saying $Y = \alpha + \beta \times X$ we will just say $Y = \alpha + \beta X$.

3. Some statistics books draw a dividing line between correlation and regression. They argue that correlation should be interpreted only as a measure of the *association* between two variables, not the *causality*. In contrast, regression should be based on causality in the manner of such statements as: "Financial theory tells us that X causes Y". Of course, this division simplifies the interpretation of empirical results. After all, it is conceptually easier to think of your dependent variable – isolated on one side of the regression equation – as being "caused" by the explanatory variables on the other. However, it can be argued that this division is in actuality an artificial one. As we saw in Chapter 3, there are many cases for which correlation does indeed reflect causality. Furthermore, in future chapters we will encounter some cases in which the regressions are based on causality, some in which they are not, and others about which we are unsure. The general message here is that you need to exercise care when interpreting regression results as reflecting causality. The same holds for correlation results. Common sense and financial theory will help you in your interpretation of either.

4. Some may disagree with this assumption. If the management skills of the chief executive are the key factor in firm profitability, and compensation directly reflects management skills, then one can argue that the executive compensation should be the explanatory variable. But, for reasons of exposition, let us accept that the assumption made in the text is reasonable.

5. If you cannot see this construct your own numerical example. That is, choose any values for α, β and X, then use the equation $Y = \alpha + \beta X$ to calculate Y (call this "original Y"). Now increase X by one, leaving α and β unchanged and calculate a new Y. No matter what values you originally chose for α, β and X, you will find new Y minus original Y is precisely β. In other words, β is a measure of the effect on Y of increasing X by one unit.

6. Excel prints out TSS, RSS and SSR in a table labeled ANOVA. The column labeled "SS" contains these three sums of squares. At this stage, you probably do not know what ANOVA means, but we will discuss it briefly in Chapter 7 (Regression with Dummy Variables).

7. Any finance textbook will describe the theoretical derivations in this example in detail. See, for instance, *Quantitative Financial Economics* by Keith Cuthbertson, published by John Wiley & Sons, Ltd.

8. You can calculate the natural logarithm of any number in Excel by using the formula bar. For instance, if you want to calculate the log of the number in cell D4 move to the formula bar and type "= ln(D4)" then press enter.

CHAPTER 5

Statistical aspects
of regression

Statistics is a field of study based on mathematics and probability theory. However, since this book assumes you have little knowledge of these topics, a complete understanding of statistical issues in the regression model will have to await further study.[1] What we will do instead in this chapter is to: (1) discuss what statistical methods in the regression model are designed to do; (2) show how to carry out a regression analysis using these statistical methods and interpret the results obtained; and (3) provide some graphical intuition in order to gain a little insight into where statistical results come from and why these results are interpreted in the manner that they are.

We will begin by stressing a distinction which arose in the previous chapter between the regression coefficients, α and β, and the OLS estimates of the regression coefficients, $\hat{\alpha}$ and $\hat{\beta}$. Remember that we began Chapter 4 with a regression model of the form:

$$Y_i = \alpha + \beta X_i + e_i,$$

for $i = 1, \ldots, N$ observations. As noted previously, α and β measure the relationship between Y and X. We pointed out that we do not know what this relationship is, i.e., what precisely α and β are. We derived so-called ordinary least squares or OLS estimates which we then labeled $\hat{\alpha}$ and $\hat{\beta}$. We emphasized that α and β are the unknown true coefficients while $\hat{\alpha}$ and $\hat{\beta}$ are merely estimates (and almost certainly not precisely the same as α and β).

These considerations lead us to ask whether we can gauge how accurate these estimates are. Fortunately we can, using statistical techniques. In particular, these techniques enable us to provide **confidence intervals** for, and to enable us to carry out, **hypothesis tests** on, our regression coefficients.

To provide some jargon, we say that OLS provides **point estimates** for β (e.g. $\hat{\beta} = 0.000842$ is the point estimate of β in the regression of executive compensation on profits in the previous chapter). You can think of a point estimate as your best guess at what β is. Confidence intervals provide **interval estimates**, allowing us to make statements that reflect the uncertainty we may have about the true value of β (e.g. "We are confident that β is greater than 0.0006 and less than 0.0010"). We can obtain different confidence intervals corresponding to different levels of confidence. For instance, in the case of a 95% confidence interval we can say that "we are 95% confident that β lies in the interval"; in the case of a 90% confidence interval we can say that "we are 90% confident that β lies in the interval"; and so on. The degree of confidence we have in a chosen interval (e.g. 95%) is referred to as the **confidence level**.

The other major activity of the empirical researcher is **hypothesis testing**. An example of a hypothesis that a researcher may want to test is $\beta = 0$. If the latter hypothesis is true, then this means that the explanatory variable has no explanatory power. Hypothesis testing procedures allow us to carry out such tests.

Both confidence interval and hypothesis testing procedures will be explained further in the rest of this chapter. For expository purposes, we will focus on β, since it is usually more important than α in economic problems. However, all the procedures we will discuss for β apply equally well for α.

Which factors affect the accuracy of the estimate $\hat{\beta}$?

We have artificially created four different data sets for X and Y from regression models with $\alpha = 0$ and $\beta = 1$. XY-plots for these four different data sets are presented in Figures 5.1, 5.2, 5.3 and 5.4. All of these data sets have the same true coefficient values of $\alpha = 0$ and $\beta = 1$, and we hope to obtain $\hat{\alpha}$ and $\hat{\beta}$ values that are roughly equal to 0 and 1, respectively, when we estimate the model from any of these four data sets. However, if you imagine trying to fit a straight line (as does OLS) through these XY-plots, you would not expect all four of these lines to be equally accurate.

How confident would you feel about the accuracy of the straight line that you have just fitted? It is intuitively straightforward to see that the line fitted for Figure 5.3 would be the most accurate. That is, the straight-line relationship between X and Y "leaps out" in Figure 5.3. Even if a ruler were used and you were to draw a best-fitting line by hand through this XY-plot you would find that the intercept (α) was very close to zero and the slope (β) close to 1. In contrast, you would probably be much less confident about the accuracy of a best-fitting straight line that you drew for Figures 5.1, 5.2 and 5.4.

These figures illustrate three main factors that affect the accuracy of OLS estimates and the uncertainty that surrounds our knowledge of what the true value of β really is:

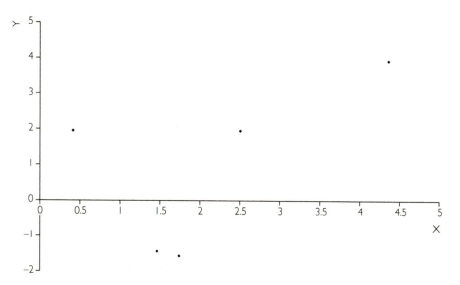

Fig. 5.1 Very small sample size.

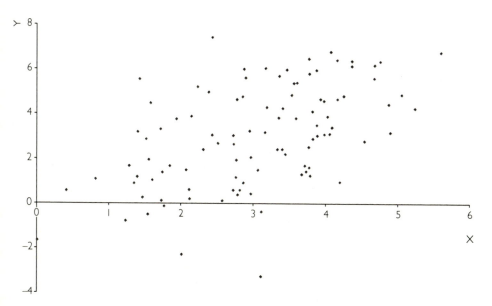

Fig. 5.2 Large sample size, large error variance.

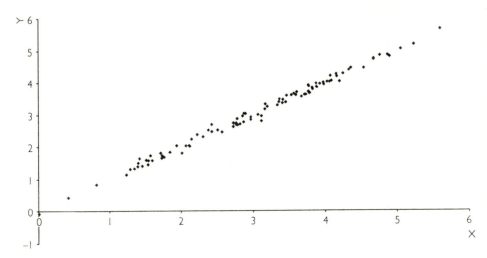

Fig. 5.3 Large sample size, small error variance.

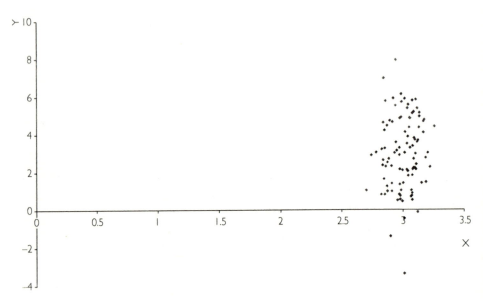

Fig. 5.4 Limited range of X values.

1. Having more data points improves accuracy of estimation. This can be seen by comparing Figure 5.1 ($N = 5$) and Figure 5.3 ($N = 100$).
2. Having smaller errors improves accuracy of estimation. Equivalently, if the SSR is small or the variance of the errors is small, the accuracy of the estimation will be improved. This can be seen by comparing Figure 5.2 (large variance of errors) with Figure 5.3 (small variance of errors).[2]

3. Having a larger spread of values (i.e. a larger variance) of the explanatory variable (X) improves accuracy of estimation. This can be seen by comparing Figure 5.3 (values of the explanatory variable spread all the way from 0 to 6) to Figure 5.4 (values of the explanatory variable all clustered around 3).

The influence of these three factors is intuitively reasonable. With regards to the first two factors, it is plausible that having either more data or smaller errors should increase accuracy of estimation. The third factor is perhaps less intuitive, but a simple example should help you to understand it.

Suppose you are interested in investigating the influence of business education levels (X = years of business education) on the income people receive (Y = income). To understand the nature of this relationship, you will want to go out and interview all types of people (e.g. people with no qualifications, people with an undergraduate degree in business, people with an MBA, people with PhDs in finance, etc.). In other words, you will want to interview a broad spectrum of the population in order to capture as many of these different education levels as possible. In statistical jargon, this means that you will want X to have a high variance. If you do not follow this strategy – for example, were you to interview only those people possessing PhDs in finance – you would get a very unreliable picture of the effect of education on income. In this case, you would not know whether the relationship between education and income was positive. For instance, without collecting data on people who had an MBA you would not know for sure that they are making less income than the PhDs.

Thus, we can summarize by saying that having a large spread of values (i.e. a larger variance) for the explanatory variable, X, is a desirable property in an analysis, whereas having a large spread of values (i.e. a larger variance) for the error, e, is not.

Calculating a confidence interval for β

The above three factors are reflected in a commonly used interval estimate for β: the confidence interval. This interval reflects the uncertainty surrounding the accuracy of the estimate $\hat{\beta}$. If the confidence interval is small, it indicates accuracy. Conversely, a large confidence interval indicates great uncertainty over β's true value. In many cases researchers choose to present the confidence interval in addition to (or even in place of) the OLS point estimate.

The mathematical formula for the confidence interval for β is:[3]

$$\left[\hat{\beta} - t_b s_b, \, \hat{\beta} + t_b s_b\right].$$

An equivalent way of expressing the equation above is to say that there is a high level of confidence that the true value of β obeys the following inequality:

$$\hat{\beta} - t_b s_b \leq \beta \leq \hat{\beta} + t_b s_b.$$

The equations above use three numbers that must be calculated: $\hat{\beta}$, t_b and s_b. The first of these, $\hat{\beta}$, we have already discussed in detail; the latter two you may not have seen before. The confidence interval can be calculated automatically in computer packages such as Excel. Thus, you can calculate confidence intervals without knowing either the above formula or the precise definitions of t_b and s_b. At the most basic level, you can just think of $\hat{\beta}$, t_b and s_b as three numbers calculated by the computer. However, it is worthwhile to have at least some intuition about where the confidence interval comes from as this will aid in your understanding of results.

Below, we discuss each of the three numbers required to calculate a confidence interval, relating them to the issues raised in our discussion of Figures 5.1 through 5.4 on the factors affecting the accuracy of estimation of $\hat{\beta}$.

First, $\hat{\beta}$ is always included in the confidence interval (in fact, it will be right in the middle of it).

Second, s_b is the standard deviation of $\hat{\beta}$. Somewhat confusingly, s_b is often referred to as the **standard error** as opposed to the standard deviation. In Chapter 2, we introduced the standard deviation as a measure of dispersion (i.e. spread, or variability) of a variable. For instance, Figure 2.2 plots a histogram for the variable GDP per capita using the cross-country data set GDPPC.XLS. In Chapter 2, we argued that the standard deviation of GDP per capita was a measure of how much GDP per capita varied across countries. Although it may seem a little odd, we can treat $\hat{\beta}$ as a variable in the same way as GDP per capita is a variable. In other words, we can calculate its standard deviation and use it as a measure of our uncertainty about the accuracy of the estimate.

Large values of s_b will imply large uncertainty. In this case, $\hat{\beta}$ may be a very inaccurate estimate of β. In contrast, small values of s_b will imply small uncertainty. If the latter, then $\hat{\beta}$ will be an accurate estimate of β.

In other chapters, we have put mathematical formulae in appendices. However, to properly draw out the connections between the formula for the confidence interval and the graphical intuition provided in Figures 5.1–5.4, a small amount of mathematics is required. We present (but do not derive) the following formula for the standard deviation of $\hat{\beta}$:

$$s_b = \sqrt{\frac{\text{SSR}}{(N-2)\sum(X_i - \overline{X})^2}}.$$

This expression, which measures the variability or uncertainty in $\hat{\beta}$, reflects all of the issues raised in the context of our discussion of Figures 5.1, 5.2, 5.3 and 5.4.

Looking at the formula for the confidence interval, we can see that the larger s_b is, the wider the confidence interval is. If we combine this consideration with a careful analysis of the components of the formula for s_b, we can say that:

1. s_b and, hence, the width of the confidence interval, varies **directly** with SSR (i.e. more variable errors/residuals imply wider confidence intervals and, thus, less accurate estimation).

2. s_b and, hence, the width of the confidence interval, vary **inversely** with N (i.e. more data points imply narrower confidence intervals and, thus, more accurate estimation).

3. s_b and, hence, the width of the confidence interval, vary **inversely** with $\Sigma(X_i - \overline{X})^2$ (i.e. more variability in X implies more accurate estimation).

Note that, as described in Chapter 2, $\Sigma(X_i - \overline{X})^2$ is a key component of the standard deviation of X. In particular, large values of this expression are associated with large standard deviations of X.

We stress that these three factors (i.e. N, SSR and the standard deviation of X), which affect the width of the confidence interval, are the same as those discussed above as affecting the accuracy of the OLS estimate $\hat{\beta}$ in Figures 5.1 through 5.4.

The third number in the formula for the confidence interval is t_b. It is hard to provide much intuition about this number without some knowledge of statistics. For those with some knowledge of statistics, note that t_b is a value taken from statistical tables for the Student-t distribution. Appendix 5.1 provides some additional discussion about t_b. Some informal intuition for what it means, however, can be obtained from the following example.

Example: Election polls

You may have encountered "point estimates" and something akin to a confidence interval in political polls, which are regularly taken in the weeks and months before an election. These are usually carried out by staffers telephoning a few hundred potential voters and asking them which party they intend to support on election day. Suppose Party A is running in the election. The newspaper reports that 43% of those surveyed will support Party A. This is the newspaper's point estimate of what voters will do on election day. Of course, in reality the actual result on election day will rarely, if ever, be exactly that indicated by the pre-election poll. This discrepancy illustrates a point we stressed earlier in this chapter in the context of the regression model: a point estimate (e.g. $\hat{\beta}$) will rarely, if ever, be identical to the true value (e.g. β).

Newspapers typically recognize that their surveys will not be precisely accurate and often add statements to their coverage such as: "This result is accurate to within +/− 2 percentage points." Although they do not explicitly say it, they are getting this result from a confidence interval (usually a 95% confidence interval).[4] An equivalent statement would be: "We are 95% confident that Party A will receive between 41% and 45% of the vote on election day".

This example provides some additional intuition about what confidence intervals are. If you understand this example, you can also see that different confidence levels imply different confidence intervals. As a trivial example, consider the 100% confidence level. We can be certain that Party A is going to receive between 0% and 100% of the vote on election day. A 100% confidence interval for Party A's percentage of the vote would thus be [0, 100].

Now consider the other extreme: how confident can we be that Party A is going to receive almost precisely 43% of the vote? Probably not very confident for, as noted, in reality we rarely find that opinion polls and election day results will match identically. For this reason, a confidence interval right around 43% (e.g. [42.9, 43.1]) will have a very low confidence level (perhaps 10%).

Note that the more confident you wish to be about your interval, the wider it becomes. For instance, 99% confidence intervals will always be wider than 95% confidence intervals. It turns out that the confidence level determines the number t_b. If the level of confidence is high (e.g. 99%) t_b will be large, while if the level of confidence is low (e.g. 50%) it will be small.

To return to the general statistical theory of regression, we should stress (without explanation beyond that given in the previous example) the following:

1. t_b decreases with N (i.e. the more data points you have the smaller the confidence interval will be).
2. t_b increases with the level of confidence you choose.

Researchers usually present 95% confidence intervals, although other intervals are possible (e.g. 99% or 90% confidence intervals are sometimes presented). A useful (but formally incorrect) intuition for 95% confidence intervals is conveyed by the following statement: "There is a 95% probability that the true value of β lies in the 95% confidence interval". A correct (but somewhat awkward) interpretation of this statement is: "If you repeatedly used (in different data sets) the above formula for calculating confidence intervals, 95% of the confidence intervals constructed would contain the true value for β". Similar statements can be made for 99% or 90% confidence intervals, simply by replacing "95%" with the desired confidence level. Thus, the interpretation of confidence intervals is relatively straightforward (and will be further illustrated in subsequent examples in this chapter).

The preceding material is intended to provide some intuition and motivation for the statistical theory underlying confidence intervals. Even if you do not fully understand this material, confidence intervals can be calculated quite easily in most standard computer software packages. For example, when you run a regression in Excel it automatically calculates the confidence interval and labels the bounds of the 95% confidence interval as "lower 95%" and "upper 95%". Excel also enables you to change the level of confidence, e.g. from 99% to 90%.

Example: Confidence intervals for the data sets in Figures 5.1–5.4

Figures 5.1 through 5.4 contained four different data sets, all of which have $\alpha = 0$ and $\beta = 1$. Remember that the data set used in Figure 5.3 has some very desirable properties, i.e. large sample size, spread-out values for the explanatory variables, and small errors. These properties are missing to varying degrees in the other three data sets. Table 5.1 contains OLS point estimates, $\hat{\beta}$, and 90%, 95% and 99% confidence intervals for these four data sets.

Table 5.1   OLS estimates and confidence intervals.

Data Set	$\hat{\beta}$	90% Confidence interval	95% Confidence interval	99% Confidence interval
Figure 5.1	0.91	[−0.92, 2.75]	[−1.57, 3.39]	[−3.64, 5.47]
Figure 5.2	1.04	[0.75, 1.32]	[0.70, 1.38]	[0.59, 1.49]
Figure 5.3	1.00	[0.99, 1.01]	[0.99, 1.02]	[0.98, 1.03]
Figure 5.4	1.52	[−1.33, 4.36]	[−1.88, 4.91]	[−2.98, 6.02]

The following points are worth emphasizing:

1. Reading across any row, we can see that as the confidence level gets higher the confidence interval gets wider. The widest interval is the 99% confidence interval for the data set in Figure 5.4. In this case, if you want to be 99% confident, you have to say β could be anywhere between −2.98 and 6.02!
2. The data set in Figure 5.3 – the one with the most desirable properties of all the data sets – yields an OLS estimate of 1.00 which is equal to the true value to two decimal places (more precisely, $\hat{\beta} = 1.002577$ for this data set).
3. The data set in Figure 5.3 yields confidence intervals which are much narrower than those for Figures 5.1, 5.2 and 5.4. This makes sense since we would expect the OLS estimate using the data set in Figure 5.3 to be more accurate than the other data sets.
4. The data sets in Figures 5.1, 5.2 and 5.4 yield a variety of results. Figure 5.2 contains a data set of the sort usually found in a well-designed empirical project (rarely does one get a data set as good as Figure 5.3). This data set has mostly desirable properties, but the errors are moderately large, reflecting the measurement error and imperfections in the underlying economic theory which so often occur in practice. For this representative data set, $\beta = 1.04$ which is not too far off the true value of $\beta = 1$. With respect to this data set, we can make statements of the form: "The value of β lies in the interval [0.70, 1.38] with a 95% confidence level" or "We are 99% confident that β lies between 0.59 and 1.49".

Exercise 5.1

The data sets used to calculate Figures 5.1, 5.2, 5.3 and 5.4 are in FIG51.XLS, FIG52.XLS, FIG53.XLS and FIG54.XLS.

(a) Calculate the OLS estimates $\hat{\alpha}$ and $\hat{\beta}$ for these four data sets. How close are they to 0 and 1 (the values we used to artificially simulate the data)?

(b) Calculate confidence intervals for α for the four data sets. Examine how the width of the confidence interval relates to N and the variability of the errors.

(c) Calculate 99% and 90% confidence intervals for the data sets. How do these differ from the 95% confidence intervals in (b)?

Example: The regression of executive compensation on profits

Let us go back to our executive compensation (Y) and profit (X) data set (EXECUTIVE.XLS). We saw in the last chapter that $\hat{\beta} = 0.000842$. In other words, the marginal effect of profit on executive pay was 0.000842. A 95% confidence interval for this effect is [0.00061, 0.001075], indicating (with a great deal of certitude) that the marginal effect of profit on executive pay is greater than 0.00061 and less than 0.001075.

Example: The regression of lot size on house price

In Chapter 3 we investigated the effect of X = lot size on Y = the sales price of a house, using data on 546 houses sold in Windsor, Canada (see data set HPRICE.XLS). Running a regression of Y on X we obtain the following estimated relationship:

$$Y = 34{,}136 + 6.59X,$$

or, equivalently, $\hat{\alpha} = 34{,}136$ and $\hat{\beta} = 6.59$. We can say that the OLS estimate of the marginal effect of X on Y is 6.59. Our best guess would be that increasing lot size by an extra square foot of lot is associated with a $6.59 increase in house price.

The 95% confidence interval for β is [5.72, 7.47]. Although the effect of lot size on house price is estimated at $6.59, we are not certain that this figure is exactly correct. However, we are extremely confident (i.e. 95% confident) that the effect of lot size on house is at least $5.72 and at most $7.47. This interval would be enough for a potential buyer or seller to have a good idea of the value of lot size.

Example: The capital asset pricing model

In Chapter 4, we introduced the CAPM, a theory that implied that the excess return on the stock of a particular company should depend on the excess return on the market portfolio. This motivated a regression using monthly data on Y = the excess returns on Company A's stock for the last 10 years on X = excess returns on a stock market index for the same time period. When we ran a regression of Y on X we obtain $\hat{\alpha} = 0.43$ and $\hat{\beta} = 1.77$. Thus, our estimate of the CAPM β for Company A was 1.77. The 95% confidence interval corresponding to our estimate is [1.37, 2.17]. Thus, we can conclude that, with high confidence, the CAPM β is at least 1.37 and at most 2.17.

Exercise 5.2

The file EQUITY.XLS contains data on Y = market capitalization and X = debt (both measured in millions of dollars) for $N = 309$ companies in the USA.

(a) Run a regression of Y on X and obtain 95% confidence intervals for α and β.
(b) Write a sentence explaining verbally what the 95% confidence interval for β means in terms of the possible range of values that the effect of the explanatory variable on the dependent variable may take.

Exercise 5.3

The file EQUITY.XLS also contains data on other potential explanatory variables: sales, income and assets (all measured in millions of dollars). Repeat Exercise 5.2 using these explanatory variables one at a time.

Testing whether $\beta = 0$

Hypothesis testing is another exercise commonly carried out by the empirical researcher. As with confidence intervals, we will not go into the statistical theory that underlies hypothesis testing. Instead we will focus on the practical details of how to carry out hypothesis tests and interpret the results. Classical hypothesis testing involves specifying a hypothesis to test. This is referred to as the **null hypothesis**, and is labeled as H_0. It is compared to an **alternative hypothesis**, labeled H_1. A common hypothesis test is whether $\beta = 0$. Formally, we say that this is a test of H_0: $\beta = 0$ against H_1: $\beta \neq 0$.

Note that, if $\beta = 0$ then X does not appear in the regression model; that is, the explanatory variable fails to provide any explanatory power whatsoever for the dependent variable. If you think of the kinds of questions of interest to researchers (e.g. "Does a certain characteristic influence the price of an asset or good?", "Will a certain advertising strategy increase sales?", "Does the debt burden of a firm influence its market capitalization?", etc.) you will see that many are of the form "Does the explanatory variable have an effect on the dependent variable?" or "Does $\beta = 0$ in the regression of Y on X?". The purpose of the hypothesis test of $\beta = 0$ is to answer this question.

The first point worth stressing is that hypothesis testing and confidence intervals are closely related. In fact, one way of testing whether $\beta = 0$ is to look at the confidence interval for β and see whether it contains zero. If it does not then we can, to introduce some statistical jargon, "reject the hypothesis that $\beta = 0$" or conclude "X has significant explanatory power for Y" or "β is significantly different from zero" or "β is statistically significant". If the confidence interval does include zero then we change the word "reject" to "accept" and "has significant explanatory power" to "does not have significant explanatory power", and so on. This confidence interval approach to hypothesis testing is exactly equivalent to the formal approach to hypothesis testing discussed below.

Just as confidence intervals came with various levels of confidences (e.g. 95% is the usual choice), hypothesis tests come with various **levels of significance**. If you use the confidence interval approach to hypothesis testing, then the level of significance is 100% minus the confidence level. That is, if a 95% confidence interval does not include zero, then you may say "I reject the hypothesis that $\beta = 0$ at the 5% level of significance" (i.e. $100\% - 95\% = 5\%$). If you had used a 90% confidence interval (and found it did not contain zero) then you would say: "I reject the hypothesis that $\beta = 0$ at the 10% level of significance".

The alternative way of carrying out hypothesis testing is to calculate a **test statistic**. In the case of testing whether $\beta = 0$, the test statistic is known as a t-statistic (or t-ratio or t-stat). It is calculated as:

$$t = \frac{\hat{\beta}}{s_b}.$$

"Large" values (in an absolute value sense) of t indicate that $\beta \neq 0$, while "small" values indicate that $\beta = 0$. Mathematical intuition for the preceding sentence is given as: if $\hat{\beta}$ is large relative to its standard deviation, s_b, then we can conclude that β is significantly different from zero. The question arises as to what we mean by "large" and "small". In a formal statistical sense, the test statistic is large or small relative to a "critical value" taken from statistical tables of the "Student-t distribution". A discussion of how to do this is given in Appendix 5.1. Fortunately, we do not have to trouble ourselves with statistical tables since most common computer software packages such as Excel print out something called a **P-value** automatically. The P-value provides a direct measure of whether the t is "large" or "small". A useful (but formally incorrect) intuition would be to interpret the P-value as measuring the probability that $\beta = 0$. If the P-value is small, $\beta = 0$ is unlikely to be true. Accordingly,

1. If the P-value is less than 5% (usually written as 0.05 by the computer) then t is "large" and we conclude that $\beta \neq 0$.
2. If the P-value is greater than 5% then t is "small" and we conclude that $\beta = 0$.

The preceding test used the 5% level of significance. However, if we were to replace the figure 5% in the above expressions with 1% (i.e. reject $\beta = 0$ if the P-value is less than 1%) our hypothesis test would be carried out at the 1% level of significance.

As an aside, it is worth noting that we are focussing on the test of $\beta = 0$ partly because it is an important one, but also because it is the test that is usually printed out by computer packages. You can use it without fully understanding the underlying statistics. However, in order to test other hypotheses (e.g. H_0: $\beta = 1$ or hypotheses involving many coefficients in the multiple regression case in the next chapter) you would need more statistical knowledge than is covered here (see Appendix 5.1 for more details). The general structure of a hypothesis test is always of the form outlined above. That is, (i) specify the hypothesis being tested, (ii) calculate a test statistic and (iii) compare the test statistic to a critical value. The first of these three steps is typically easy, but the second and third can be much harder. In particular, to obtain the test statistic for more complicated hypothesis tests will typically require some extra calculations beyond merely running the regression. Obtaining the critical value will involve the use of statistical tables. Hence, if you wish to do more complicated hypothesis tests you will have to resort to a basic statistics or econometrics textbook (see endnote 1 of this chapter for some suggestions).

As a practical summary, note that regression techniques provide the following information about β:

1. $\hat{\beta}$, the OLS point estimate, or best guess, of what β is.
2. The 95% confidence interval, which gives an interval where we are 95% confident β will lie.
3. The standard deviation (or standard error) of $\hat{\beta}$, s_b, which is a measure of how accurate $\hat{\beta}$ is. s_b is also a key component in the mathematical formula for the confidence interval and the test statistic for testing $\beta = 0$.
4. The test statistic, t, for testing $\beta = 0$.
5. The P-value for testing $\beta = 0$.

These five components, ($\hat{\beta}$, confidence interval, s_b, t and the P-value) are usually printed out in a row in computer packages like Excel. In practice, the most important are $\hat{\beta}$, the confidence interval, and the P-value. You can usually interpret your empirical findings without explicit reference to t and s_b. The following examples will serve to illustrate how regression results are presented and can be interpreted.

Example: The regression of executive compensation on profits (continued from page 78)

If we regress Y = executive compensation on X = profit using Excel, the following output will be produced (other software packages will provide output of a similar form):

Table 5.2   The regression of executive compensation on profits.

	Coefficient	Standard error	t-stat	P-value	Lower 95%	Upper 95%
Intercept	0.599965	0.112318	5.341646	1.15E − 06	0.375837	0.824093
X-variable	0.000842	0.000117	7.227937	5.5E − 10	0.00061	0.001075

The row labeled "Intercept" contains results for α, and the row labeled "X-variable", results for β. We will focus discussion on this latter row. The column labeled "Coefficient" presents the OLS estimate and, as we have seen before, $\hat{\beta} = 0.000842$, indicating that an increase in profit of 1 million dollars is associated with an increase in executive pay of \$842. The columns labeled "Lower 95%" and "Upper 95%" give the lower and upper bounds of the 95% confidence interval. For this data set, and as discussed previously, the 95% confidence interval for β is [0.00061, 0.001075]. Thus, we are 95% confident that the marginal effect of profit on executive pay is between \$610 and \$1,075.

The columns labeled "Standard error" and "t-Stat" indicate that $s_b = 0.000117$ and $t = 7.227937$. These numbers are not essential to carrying out a hypothesis test of $\beta = 0$ when the P-value is given. For most purposes we can ignore these two columns.[5]

The hypothesis test of $\beta = 0$ can be done in two equivalent ways. First, we can find a 95% confidence interval for β of [0.00061, 0.001075]. Since this interval does not contain 0, we can reject the hypothesis that $\beta = 0$ at the 5% level of significance. In other words, there is strong evidence for the hypothesis that $\beta \neq 0$ and that profit has significant power in explaining executive pay. Second, we can look at the P-value which is 5.5×10^{-10},[6] and much less than 0.05. This means that we can reject the hypothesis that profit has no effect on executive pay at the 5% level of significance. In other words, we have strong evidence that profit does indeed affect executive pay.

Example: The capital asset pricing model
(continued from page 79)

With the CAPM, the hypothesis that $\beta = 0$ is rarely tested. It implies that the excess return on the stock of a particular company is completely unrelated to the market portfolio (something which rarely occurs in practice). However, if you look back at our discussion of the CAPM in Chapter 4 you will note that the original CAPM equation did not contain an intercept. Thus, the CAPM implies that there should be no intercept in the regression of Y = the excess returns on Company A's stock on X = excess returns on a stock market index. This motivates an interest in testing the hypothesis that $\alpha = 0$. The hypothesis test of $\alpha = 0$ can be done in exactly the same manner as testing $\beta = 0$. That is, you can look at the P-value corresponding to the intercept and check whether it is less than 0.05. With our data set (CAPM.XLS) we find that the P-value is 0.052. Thus, it is (very slightly) larger than 0.05 and we can (very marginally) accept the hypothesis that $\alpha = 0$ at the 5% level of significance.

Exercise 5.4

Using the table above (or running a regression yourself using data set EXECUTIVE.XLS) test the hypothesis that $\alpha = 0$.

Exercise 5.5

The Excel data set EXECUTIVE.XLS contains data on Y = executive compensation, X = profits, W = change in sales and Z = change in debt.

(a) Run a regression of Y on W and interpret your results. Can you reject the hypothesis that changes in sales has an effect on executive compensation?
(b) Run a regression of Y on Z and interpret your results. Can you reject the hypothesis that changes in debt have an effect on executive compensation?

Exercise 5.6

Use data sets FIG51.XLS, FIG52.XLS, FIG53.XLS and FIG54.XLS.

(a) Test whether $\beta = 0$ using the confidence interval approach for each of the four data sets.

(b) Test whether $\beta = 0$ using the P-value approach and the four data sets. Use the 5% level of significance.

(c) Redo (a) and (b) for α.

(d) Redo parts (a), (b) and (c) using the 1% level of significance.

(e) Are your results sensible in light of the discussion in this chapter of the factors affecting the accuracy of OLS estimates?

Example: The regression of lot size on house price (continued from page 78)

Previously, we found a 95% confidence interval in the regression of $Y =$ house price on $X =$ lot size to be [5.27, 7.47]. Since this interval does not contain zero, we can reject the hypothesis that $\beta = 0$ at the 5% level of significance. Lot size does indeed seem to have a statistically significant effect on house prices.

Alternatively, the P-value is 6.77×10^{-42}, which is much less than 0.05. As before, we can reject the hypothesis that $\beta = 0$ at the 5% level of significance. Note also that, since, 6.77×10^{-42} is less than 0.01 we can also reject the hypothesis that $\beta = 0$ at the 1% level of significance. This is strong evidence indeed that lot size affects house prices.

Exercise 5.7

The file ADVERT.XLS contains data on the sales and advertising expenditures of 84 companies. Set up and run a regression using this data and discuss your results verbally as you would in a report. Include a discussion of the marginal effect of advertising on sales and a discussion of whether this marginal effect is statistically significant.

Hypothesis testing involving R^2: the F-statistic

Most computer packages which include regression, such as Excel, also print out results for the test of the hypothesis $H_0: R^2 = 0$. The definition and interpretation of R^2 was given in the previous chapter. Recall that R^2 is a measure of how well the regression line fits the data or, equivalently, of the proportion of the variability in Y

that can be explained by X. If $R^2 = 0$ then X does not have any explanatory power for Y. The test of the hypothesis $R^2 = 0$ can therefore be interpreted as a test of whether the regression explains anything at all. For the case of simple regression, this test is equivalent to a test of $\beta = 0$.

In the next chapter, we will discuss the case of multiple regression (where there are many explanatory variables), in which case this test will be different. To preview our discussion of the next chapter, note that the test of $R^2 = 0$ will be used as a test of whether all of the explanatory variables jointly have any explanatory power for the dependent variable. In contrast, the t-statistic test of $\beta = 0$ will be used to investigate whether a single individual explanatory variable has explanatory power.

The strategy and intuition involved in testing $R^2 = 0$ proceed along the same lines as above. That is, the computer software calculates a test statistic which you must then compare to a critical value. Alternatively, a P-value can be calculated which directly gives a measure of the plausibility of the null hypothesis $R^2 = 0$ against the alternative hypothesis, $R^2 \neq 0$. Most statistical software packages will automatically calculate the P-value and, if so, you don't need to know the precise form of the test statistic or how to use statistical tables to obtain a critical value. For completeness, though, we present the test statistic, the F-statistic,[7] which is calculated as:

$$F = \frac{(N-2)R^2}{(1-R^2)}.$$

This expression is calculated automatically by Excel and is labeled simply as "F". As before, "large" values of the test statistic indicate $R^2 \neq 0$ while "small" values indicate $R^2 = 0$. As for the test of $\beta = 0$, we use the P-value to decide what is "large" and what is "small" (i.e. whether R^2 is significantly different from zero or not). Note, however, that Excel refers to the P-value for this test as "Significance F". The test is performed according to the following strategy:

1. If Significance F is less than 5% (i.e. 0.05), we conclude $R^2 \neq 0$.
2. If Significance F is greater than 5% (i.e. 0.05), we conclude $R^2 = 0$.

The previous strategy provides a statistical test with a 5% level of significance. To carry out a test at the 1% level of significance, merely replace 5% (0.05) by 1% (0.01) in the preceding sentences. Other levels of significance (e.g. 10%) can be calculated in an analogous manner.

Other computer packages might use a slightly different notation than Excel does. For instance, MicroFit labels the F-statistic "F-stat." and puts the P-value in brackets next to F.

**Example: The regression of executive compensation on profits
             (continued from page 82)**

In the case of the executive pay/profit data set, $F = 52.24308$. Is this "large"?
If you said yes you are right, since Significance $F = 5.5 \times 10^{-10}$, which is less
than 0.05. We can conclude in light of this finding that executive compensation
does have explanatory power for Y. Formally, we can say that "R^2 is significantly
different from zero at the 5% level", or that "X has statistically significant
explanatory power for Y" or that "The regression is significant". Note that Significance F is equal to the P-value in the test of $\beta = 0$, stressing the equivalence
of these two tests in the case of simple regression.

Exercise 5.8

Use data sets FIG51.XLS, FIG52.XLS, FIG53.XLS and FIG54.XLS.
   Test whether $R^2 = 0$ for each of the four data sets. Compare your results with
those of Exercise 5.6.

Chapter summary

1. The accuracy of OLS estimates depends on the number of data points, the
   variability of the explanatory variable and the variability of the errors.
2. The confidence interval provides an interval estimate of β (i.e. an interval
   in which you can be confident β lies). It is calculated in most computer software packages.
3. The width of the confidence interval depends on the same factors as affect
   the accuracy of OLS estimates. In addition, the width of the confidence
   interval depends on the confidence level (i.e. the degree of confidence you
   want to have in your interval estimate).
4. A hypothesis test of whether $\beta = 0$ can be used to find out whether the
   explanatory variable belongs in the regression. The P-value, which is calculated automatically in most spreadsheet or statistical computer packages, is
   a measure of how plausible the hypothesis is.
5. If the P-value for the hypothesis test of whether $\beta = 0$ is less than 0.05 then
   you can reject the hypothesis at the 5% level of significance. Hence, you
   can conclude that X does belong in the regression.

6. If the P-value for the hypothesis test of whether $\beta = 0$ is greater than 0.05 then you cannot reject the hypothesis at the 5% level of significance. Hence, you cannot conclude that X belongs in the regression.

7. A hypothesis test of whether $R^2 = 0$ can be used to investigate whether the regression helps explain the dependent variable. A P-value for this test is calculated automatically in most spreadsheet and statistical computer packages and can be used in a similar manner to that outlined in points 5 and 6.

Appendix 5.1: Using statistical tables for testing whether $\beta = 0$

The P-value is all that you will need to know in order to test the hypothesis that $\beta = 0$. Most computer software packages (e.g. Excel, MicroFit, Stata or SHAZAM) will automatically provide P-values. However, if you do not have such a computer package or are reading a paper which presents the t-statistic, not the P-value, then it is useful to know how to carry out hypothesis testing using statistical tables. Virtually any statistics or econometrics textbook will describe the method in detail and will also provide the necessary statistical table for you to do so. Here we offer only a brief discussion along with a rough rule of thumb which is applicable to the case when the sample size, N, is large.

Remember that hypothesis testing involves the comparison of a test statistic to a number called a critical value. If the test statistic is larger (in absolute value) than the critical value, the hypothesis is rejected. Here, the test statistic is the t-stat given in the body of the chapter. This must be compared to a critical value taken from the Student-t statistical table. It turns out that this critical value is precisely what we have called t_b in our discussion of confidence intervals. If N is large and you are using the 5% level of significance, then $t_b = 1.96$. This suggests the following rule of thumb:

If the t-statistic is greater than 1.96 in absolute value (i.e. $|t| > 1.96$), then reject the hypothesis that $\beta = 0$ at the 5% level of significance. If the t-statistic is less than 1.96 in absolute value, then accept the hypothesis that $\beta = 0$ at the 5% level of significance.

If the hypothesis that $\beta = 0$ is rejected, then we say that "X is significant" or that "X provides statistically significant explanatory power for Y".

This rule of thumb is likely to be quite accurate if the sample size is large. Formally, the critical value equals 1.96 if sample size is infinity. However, even moderately large sample sizes will yield similar critical values. For instance, if $N = 120$, the critical value is 1.98. If $N = 40$, it is 2.02. Even the quite small sample size of $N = 20$ yields a critical value of 2.09 which is not that different from 1.96. However, you should be careful when using this rule of thumb if N is very small or the t-statistic is very close to 2.00. If you look back at the examples included in the body of this chapter you can see that the strategy outlined here works quite well. That is, both the P-value and confidence interval approaches lead to the same conclusion as the approximate strategy described in this appendix.

The previous discussion related to the 5% level of significance. The large sample critical value for the 10% level of significance is 1.65. For the 1% level of significance, it is 2.58.

By far the most common hypothesis to test for is H_0: $\beta = 0$. Using the techniques outlined in this appendix we can generalize this hypothesis slightly to that of: H_0: $\beta = c$, where c is some number that may not be zero (e.g. $c = 1$). In this case, the test statistic changes slightly, but the critical value is exactly the same as for the test of $\beta = 0$. In particular, the test statistic becomes:

$$t = \frac{\hat{\beta} - c}{s_b}.$$

This will not be produced automatically by a computer package, but it can be calculated quite easily in a spreadsheet or on a calculator. That is, $\hat{\beta}$ and s_b are calculated by the computer, and you have to provide c, depending on the hypothesis that you are interested in testing. These three numbers can be combined using the equation above to give you a value for your test statistic. If this value is greater than 1.96 in absolute value, you will conclude that $\beta \neq c$ at the 5% level of significance. The caveats about using this rule of thumb if your sample size is very small apply here.

Endnotes

1. As mentioned previously, a good basic statistics book is *Introductory Statistics for Business and Economics* by Thomas Wonnacott and Ronald Wonnacott (Fourth edition, John Wiley & Sons, Ltd, 1990). A good introductory econometrics textbook is that by Carter Hill, William Griffiths and George Judge, *Undergraduate Econometrics* (Second edition, John Wiley & Sons, Ltd, 2000).
2. If you are having trouble grasping this point, draw a straight line with intercept = 0 and slope = 1 through Figures 5.2 and 5.3 and then look at some of the resulting residuals (constructed as in Figure 4.1). You should see that most of the residuals in Figure 5.2 will be much bigger (in absolute value) than those in Figure 5.3. This will result in a larger SSR (see the formula in Chapter 4) and, since residuals and errors are very similar things, a bigger variance of the errors (see the formula for the standard deviation of a variable in the descriptive statistics section of Chapter 2 and remember that the variance is just the standard deviation squared).
3. The notation that "β lies between a and b" or "β is greater than or equal to a and less than or equal to b" is expressed mathematically as "β lies in the interval $[a, b]$". We will use this mathematical notation occasionally in this book.

4. The choice of a 95% confidence interval is by far the most common one, and whenever a confidence interval is not specified you can assume it is 95%.
5. In the examples in this book we never use s_b and rarely use t. For future reference, the only places we use t are in the Dickey-Fuller and Engle-Granger tests which will be discussed in Chapters 9 and 10, respectively.
6. Note that $5.5E - 10$ is the way most computer packages write 5.5×10^{-10} which can also be written as 0.00000000055.
7. Formally, the F-statistic is only one in an entire class of test statistics that take their critical values from the so-called "F-distribution". Appendix 11.1 offers some additional discussion of this topic.

CHAPTER 6

Multiple regression

The discussion of simple regression in Chapter 5 involved two variables: the dependent variable, Y, and the explanatory variable, X. As we discussed at the beginning of Chapter 4, many analyses in business and finance involve many variables. Multiple regression extends simple regression to the case where there are many explanatory variables. Fortunately, most of the intuition and statistical techniques of multiple regression are very similar to those of simple regression.

The key elements of Chapters 4 and 5 were:

1. The development of graphical intuition for regression techniques as the fitting of a straight line through an XY-plot.
2. The introduction of the regression coefficient as measuring a marginal effect.
3. The description of the OLS estimate as a best fitting line (in terms of minimizing the sum of squared residuals) through an XY-plot.
4. The introduction of R^2 as a measure of fit of a regression model.
5. The introduction of statistical techniques such as confidence intervals and hypothesis tests.

With some exceptions (highlighted below) these five elements do not differ for the multiple regression model. You should look back on Chapters 4 and 5 if you are having difficulty remembering the underlying intuition or statistical aspects of regression. This chapter covers these five elements for the multiple regression case very briefly, summarizing similarities with and differences from the simple regression model. Much of the chapter will involve the discussion of examples that illustrate how to interpret multiple regression results.

Example: Explaining house prices

Much research in finance and marketing focusses on the pricing of goods. One common approach involves building a model in which the price of a good depends on the characteristics of that good. Data set HPRICE.XLS contains data on an application of this so-called hedonic pricing approach to the housing market. We worked with part of this data set in previous chapters. Recall that it contains data on $N = 546$ houses sold in Windsor, Canada. Our dependent variable, Y, was the sales price of the house in Canadian dollars, and lot size was our explanatory variable.

Of course, the price of a house is affected by more than just lot size. Any serious attempt to explain the determinants of house prices must include more explanatory variables than lot size. In this chapter, we focus on the following four explanatory variables:

- X_1 = the lot size of the property (in square feet)
- X_2 = the number of bedrooms
- X_3 = the number of bathrooms
- X_4 = the number of storeys (excluding the basement).

The data set HPRICE.XLS also contains other explanatory variables that we will use in later chapters and in exercises.

Exercise 6.1

(a) Create XY-plots using the four explanatory variables in the house pricing example one at a time (i.e. plot Y and X_1, then plot Y and X_2, etc.).
(b) Perform simple regressions using the explanatory variables one at a time (i.e. regress Y on X_1, then regress Y on X_2, etc.).
(c) Comment on the relationships you find in (a) and (b).

Example: The capital asset pricing model
(continued from page 83)

In contrast to the house price example, the CAPM implies that there should not be a large number of explanatory variables in the regression. Remember that this theory that implied that the excess return on the stock of a particular company should depend on the excess return on the market portfolio – and only on the excess return of market portfolio through the CAPM β. That is, the only thing relevant for the investor should be the expected return and riskiness of the stock (as measured by the CAPM β). CAPM suggests that any other explanatory variables, such as the size of the company, its capital structure, etc. should not matter. In Chapters 4 and 5, we discussed a regression of $Y =$ the excess returns on Company A's stock on $X =$ excess returns on a stock market index using the data in CAPM.XLS. This file also contains data on the sales and debt of Company A (measured in thousands of dollars). Theory tells us that these need not be significant explanatory variables. However, a simple theory such as CAPM may not be sophisticated enough to capture the true behavior of investors. Hence, many researchers have investigated whether other variables (such as sales, debt, etc.) do have explanatory power. In some cases researchers have found that such explanatory variables are important, casting doubt on the simple version of the CAPM and provoking development of extensions of the CAPM model. In short, even though CAPM theory tells us that a simple regression should be adequate, the search to test the adequacy of this theory has lead some researchers to be interested in multiple regression.

Regression as a best fitting line

As we saw in Chapter 4, the simple regression model can be thought of as a technique aimed at fitting a line through an XY-plot. Since multiple regression implies the existence of more than two variables (e.g. X_1, X_2, X_3, X_4 and Y), we cannot draw an XY-plot in a two-dimensional graph, in which one variable is plotted on the vertical axis and the other on the horizontal axis. Nevertheless, the same line-fitting intuition holds (although this could only be illustrated if we could somehow create high-dimensional graphs). For instance, if we had three explanatory variables, we could show how multiple regression involves fitting a surface through a four-dimensional graph, in which Y is plotted on one axis, X_1 on the second, X_2 on the third, and X_3 on the fourth. The graph would be very messy and actually impossible to create (i.e. what does a four-dimensional graph look like?).

Ordinary least squares estimation of the multiple regression model

The multiple regression model with k explanatory variables is written as:[1]

$$Y = \alpha + \beta_1 X_1 + \beta_2 X_2 + \ldots + \beta_k X_k + e.$$

Instead of estimating just α and β, we now have α and $\beta_1, \beta_2, \ldots, \beta_k$. However, the strategy for finding estimates for all these coefficients is exactly the same as for the simple regression model. That is, we define the sum of squared residuals:

$$SSR = \sum\left(Y_i - \widehat{\alpha} - \widehat{\beta}_1 X_{1i} - \ldots - \widehat{\beta}_k X_{ki}\right)^2,$$

where X_{1i} is the ith observation on the first explanatory variable (for $i = 1, \ldots, N$ observations, e.g. lot size of house i for houses $i = 1, \ldots, 546$). The other explanatory variables are defined in an analogous way. The OLS estimates (which can be interpreted as providing the best fitting line) are found by choosing the values of $\widehat{\alpha}$ and $\widehat{\beta}_1, \widehat{\beta}_2, \ldots \widehat{\beta}_k$ that minimize the SSR. Conceptually, this is a straightforward mathematical problem.[2] The resulting formulae are complicated and are not listed here.[3] Note that computer software packages like Excel will calculate these OLS estimates $(\widehat{\alpha}, \widehat{\beta}_1, \ldots, \widehat{\beta}_k)$ automatically.

Statistical aspects of multiple regression

As noted, the statistical aspects of multiple regression are essentially identical to the simple regression case (see Chapter 5). In particular, the R^2 is still a measure of fit and is calculated in the same way. Note, however, that it should be interpreted as a measure of the explanatory power of all the explanatory variables together rather than as just the one explanatory variable in the simple regression model. Similarly, the F-statistic for testing if $R^2 = 0$, has a slightly different formula ($N - 2$ is replaced by $N - k - 1$) but is essentially the same and you still look at "Significance F" in the Excel output. If we find that $R^2 \neq 0$, then we can say that "The explanatory variables in the regression, taken together, help explain the dependent variable", whereas if we find $R^2 = 0$, we can say that "The explanatory variables are not significant and do not provide any explanatory power for the dependent variable".

The general formulae for calculating confidence intervals for the regression coefficients and for testing whether they are equal to zero are the same as in the previous chapter. However, the actual numbers that comprise the formulae (e.g. s_b) are calculated in a slightly more complicated way. Nevertheless, the practical intuition remains unchanged. In other words, a 95% confidence interval will provide an interval estimate such that you can say that "I am 95% confident that my coefficient lies in the 95% confidence interval". In Excel, the "Lower 95%" and "Upper 95%" columns are still the lower and upper bounds of the 95% confidence interval. If the number in the "P-value" column is less than 0.05, we can conclude that the relevant explanatory variable is significant at the 5% level. It is worth stressing that there is now a P-value and a confidence interval associated with each of the coefficients, $\beta_1, \ldots, \beta_k$ rather than just the one β in the simple regression model. However, from the point of view of a researcher wishing to interpret computer output for use in a report, the statistical aspects of multiple regression are essentially the same as for simple regression.[4]

Interpreting OLS estimates

It is in the interpretation of OLS estimates that some subtle (and important) distinctions exist between the simple and multiple regression case. This section will provide a few ways of thinking about or interpreting coefficients in the multiple regression model. Before we begin, it is important to be clear about the notation we will use.

When we speak of a property that holds generally for any of the coefficients we will denote the coefficient by β_j (i.e. the coefficient on the jth explanatory variable where j could be any number between 1 and k). When we wish to talk about a specific coefficient we will give an exact number for j (e.g. β_1 has $j = 1$ and is the coefficient on the first explanatory variable).

In the simple regression case we saw how β could be interpreted as a marginal effect (i.e. as a measure of the effect that a change in X has on Y or as a measure of the influence of X on Y). In multiple regression, β_j still can be interpreted as a marginal effect, but in a slightly different way. In particular, β_j is the marginal effect of X_j on Y, **holding all other explanatory variables constant**. The Latin phrase for this concept is *ceteris paribus*, which is commonly used. The *ceteris paribus* qualification is of critical importance to the correct interpretation of regression results. For this reason, we will spend some time illustrating precisely what we mean by it, by way of consideration of our house price example.

Example: Explaining house prices (continued from page 92)

Table 6.1 below contains results from the regression of Y = sale price on X_1 = lot size, X_2 = number of bedrooms, X_3 = number of bathrooms and X_4 = number of storeys. The table is organized in the form of an Excel output, but other regression packages provide output organized in a similar way.

The first column lists the explanatory variables. In this example there are four of them (plus the intercept). Each row contains the same information as in the table for the simple regression model (i.e. the OLS estimate of the relevant coefficient followed by its standard deviation, t-statistic, P-value for testing whether $\beta_j = 0$ and the lower and upper bounds of the 95% confidence interval for the coefficient). As stressed above, each of these statistical results is now available for each coefficient and they will all be different (e.g. the P-value for testing $\beta_1 = 0$ will be different from the P-value for testing $\beta_3 = 0$).

Table 6.1 Regression of house price on lot size, number of bedrooms, number of bathrooms and number of storeys.*

	Coefficient	Standard error	*t*-stat	P-value	Lower 95%	Upper 95%
Intercept	−4009.5500	3603.109	−1.1128	0.266287	−11087.3	3068.248
$X1$	5.4291737	0.369250	14.70325	2.05E − 41	4.703835	6.154513
$X2$	2824.61379	1214.808	2.325153	0.020433	438.2961	5210.931
$X3$	17105.1745	1734.434	9.862107	3.29E − 21	13698.12	20512.22
$X4$	7634.897	1007.974	7.574494	1.57E − 13	5654.874	9614.92

*Note that in this table, as elsewhere, we write numbers as Excel produces them. That is, we include as many decimal places as possible and use the "E" notation for exponents. In a report you probably would want to use only a few decimal places and replace, say, 1.57E − 13 with 1.57×10^{-13}. Furthermore, $R^2 = 0.54$ and the P-value for testing $R^2 = 0$ (which is labeled "Significance F" by Excel) is 1.18E − 88.

Using the information in Table 6.1, we can write the fitted regression equation as:

$$\hat{Y} = -4009.55 + 5.43X_1 + 2824.61X_2 + 17105.17X_3 + 7634.90X_4.$$

As an example, consider the coefficient for the first explanatory variable, lot size. It can be seen that $\hat{\beta}_1 = 5.43$. Below are some (very similar) ways of verbally stating what this value means.

1. "An extra square foot of lot size will tend to add another \$5.43 on to the price of a house, *ceteris paribus*".
2. "If we consider houses with the same number of bedrooms, bathrooms and storeys, an extra square foot of lot size will tend to add another \$5.43 onto the price of the house".
3. "If we compare houses with the same number of bedrooms, bathrooms and storeys, those with larger lots tend to be worth more. In particular, an extra square foot of lot size is associated with an increased price of \$5.43".

It is worth expanding on the motivation for the latter two expressions. We cannot simply say that "houses with bigger lots are worth more" since this is not the case (e.g. some nice houses on small lots will be worth more than poor houses on large lots). However, we can say that "if we consider houses that vary in lot size, **but are comparable in other respects**, those with larger lots tend to be worth more". The two expressions above explicitly incorporate the qualification "but are comparable in other respects". We did not have to include this qualification in Chapter 4.

Alternatively, let us consider $\hat{\beta}_2$ (the coefficient on the number of bedrooms), which is 2842.61. This might be expressed as:

1. "Houses with an extra bedroom tend to be worth $2,842.61 more than those without the extra bedroom, *ceteris paribus*".
2. "If we consider comparable houses (e.g. those with 5,000 square foot lots, two bathrooms and two storeys), those with three bedrooms tend to be worth $2,842.61 more than those with two bedrooms".

There are many different ways to express the interpretation of these coefficients. However, the general point we wish to make is as follows: In the case of simple regression we can say that "β measures the influence of X on Y"; in the multiple regression we say that "β_j measures the influence of X_j on Y **all other explanatory variables being equal**". The expressions above are just different ways of verbally saying "all other explanatory variables being equal".

The coefficients on the other explanatory variables can be interpreted in analogous ways. For instance, $\hat{\beta}_3 = 17105.174$. In words, we might say that "Houses with an extra bathroom tend to be worth $17,105.17 more, *ceteris paribus*". Since $\beta_4 = 7634.897$, we might say "If we compare houses that are similar in all other respects, those with an extra storey tend to be worth $7,634.90 more".

Remember that in a discussion of the statistical properties of the regression coefficients, the confidence interval and the P-value are the most important numbers. These can be interpreted in the same way as for the simple regression. For instance, since the P-values for all of the explanatory variables (except the intercept) are less than 0.05 we can say that "The coefficients β_1, β_2, β_3 and β_4 are statistically significant at the 5% level", or equivalently, that "We can reject the four separate hypotheses that any of the coefficients is zero at the 5% level of significance".

By way of another example, let us consider the 95% confidence interval for β_2, which is [438.2761, 5210.931]. This information might be presented verbally as: "Although our point estimate indicates that the marginal effect of number of bedrooms on house prices is $2,842.61, this estimate is imprecise. The 95% confidence interval indicates that we can only be confident that this marginal effect lies somewhere between $438.28 and $5,210.93". Alternatively, the confidence interval for β_4 is [5654.874, 9614.92] and we can say: "We are 95% confident that the marginal effect of the number of storeys on house price lies between $5,654.87 and $9,614.92".

The hypothesis test of whether $R^2 = 0$ yields a P-value of much less than 5%, indicating that X_1, X_2, X_3 and X_4 have statistically significant explanatory power for the dependent variable. In fact, variations in lot size and the number of bedrooms, bathrooms and storeys account for 54% of the variability in house prices.

**Example: The capital asset pricing model
(continued from page 93)**

The data set CAPM.XLS contains the following variables:

- Y = the excess return on shares in Company A (a percentage)
- X_1 = the excess return on a stock index (a percentage)
- X_2 = the sales of Company A (thousands of dollars)
- X_3 = the debt of Company A (thousands of dollars).

The theory underlying the CAPM implies that the explanatory variables sales and debt should not be significant. And, indeed, if we use the 5% level of significance we do find that these two explanatory variables are not significant. However, since the P-value for testing whether $\beta_3 = 0$ is less than 0.10, the debt variable is significant at the 10% level. This illustrates how the choice of significance level can have an important effect on the outcome of a hypothesis test.

Remember that the coefficient on X_1 is of crucial importance since it provides us with an estimate of the CAPM beta. The OLS estimate of the CAPM beta is 1.747, which is very similar to the value we found in the previous chapter (1.77) using a simple regression.

Table 6.2   Regression results for the CAPM example.

	Coefficient	Standard error	t-stat	P-value	Lower 95%	Upper 95%
Intercept	2.530	1.335	1.895	0.061	−0.115	5.175
X1	1.747	0.202	8.631	3.73E − 14	1.346	2.148
X2	−0.0003	0.001	−0.323	0.748	−0.002	0.002
X3	−0.022	0.012	−1.867	0.064	−0.045	0.001

Furthermore, $R^2 = 0.41$ and the P-value for testing $R^2 = 0$ (which is labeled "Significance" by Excel) is 2.83E − 13.

Pitfalls of using simple regression in a multiple regression context

To emphasize the difference between simple and multiple regression, we will return to the house price example and run a simple regression of Y = sales price on X_2 = number of bedrooms. Table 6.3 contains the results from this regression. Since $\hat{\beta} = 13,269.98$ in this simple regression, we are able to make statements of the kind:

"The marginal effect of number of bedrooms on house prices is $13,269.98", or "Houses with an extra bedroom tend to cost $13,269.98 more." You should contrast this statement with the ones we made above using the multiple regression. For the simple regression we have left out the *ceteris paribus* conditions that are implicit in the part of the sentence: "If we consider comparable houses (e.g. those with 5,000 square foot lots, two bathrooms and two storeys) . . .".

Table 6.3   Regression of sale price on number of bedrooms.

	Coefficient	Standard error	*t*-stat	P-value	Lower 95%	Upper 95%
Intercept	28773.4327	4413.753	6.519	1.6E – 10	20103.34	37443.53
X2	13269.9801	1444.598	9.186	8.5E – 19	10432.30	16107.66

Table 6.4   Correlation matrix of variable in house price example.

	Sale price	Lot size	#bedrooms	#bath	#storeys
Sale price	1				
Lot size	0.535795	1			
#bedrooms	0.366447	0.151851	1		
#bath	0.516719	0.193833	0.373768	1	
#storeys	0.421190	0.083674	0.407973	0.324065	1

Note also that the coefficient on number of bedrooms in the simple regression is much higher than for the multiple regression. Why is this the case? To answer this question, first imagine that a friend in Windsor wanted to build an extra bedroom in her house and asked you how much that extra bedroom would add to the value of the house. How would you answer?

The simple regression here contains data only on house price and number of bedrooms. You can think of it as observing all the houses in the sample and concluding that those with more bedrooms tend to be more expensive (e.g. those with three bedrooms tend to be worth $13,269.98 more than those with two bedrooms).

However, this does not necessarily mean that adding an extra bedroom to the house will raise its price by $13,269.98. The reason is that there are many factors other than the number of bedrooms that potentially influence house prices. Furthermore, these factors may be highly correlated (i.e. in practice, big houses tend to have more bedrooms, more bathrooms, more storeys and larger lot size). To investigate the possibility, let us first examine the correlation matrix (see Chapter 3) of all the variables in this example (Table 6.4).

Since all the elements of the correlation matrix are positive, it follows that each pair of variables is positively correlated with each other (e.g. the correlation between the number of bathrooms and the number of bedrooms is 0.37, indicating that houses with more bathrooms also tend to have more bedrooms). In cases like this, simple regression cannot disentangle the influences of the individual variables on house prices. So when the simple regression method examines all the houses and notes that those with more bedrooms cost more, this does not necessarily mean that bedrooms are adding value to the house. Buyers may really be valuing bathrooms or lot size over bedrooms. In other words, houses with more bathrooms may be worth more. Yet, houses with more bathrooms also have more bedrooms. The simple regression model simply looks at house price and number of bedrooms and sees that those with more bedrooms tend to be worth more. What it does not realize is that it is really the number of bathrooms that people value. Thus, if you advise your friend that an extra bedroom is worth $13,269.98, you may be seriously misleading her. In essence, in the simple regression model, we leave out important explanatory variables such as lot size, the number of bathrooms and the number of storeys. The regression combines the contribution of all these factors together and allocates it to the only explanatory variable it can: bedrooms. Hence $\hat{\beta}$ is very big.[5]

In contrast, multiple regression allows us to disentangle the individual contributions of the four explanatory variables assumed to affect house prices. The figure of $\hat{\beta}_2 = \$2,842.61$ comes closer to being a genuine measure of the effect of adding an extra bedroom, although even this multiple regression is likely to be omitting some important explanatory variables. By presenting this figure to your friend, you can be confident that you are not making the error above. That is, you can be sure that it is more likely to be the bedroom that is adding the value – and that you are not confounding the contributions of the various explanatory variables.

Omitted variables bias

The problems discussed in the previous section relate to a statistical issue called **omitted variables bias**. We will not develop the statistical theory necessary to formally explain what this means. Informally, however, we can say that if we omit explanatory variables that should be present in the regression and if these omitted variables are correlated with those that are included, then the coefficients on the included variables will be wrong. In the previous example, the simple regression of $Y =$ sales price on $X =$ number of bedrooms, omitted many variables that were important for explaining house prices (e.g. lot size, number of bathrooms, etc.). These omitted variables were also correlated with number of bedrooms. Hence the coefficient estimate $\hat{\beta} = 13,269.98$ is unreliable due to omitted variables bias.

In contrast, in the CAPM example the simple regression (see Chapter 5) and multiple regression provided very similar estimates of the CAPM β. In this case, the extra explanatory variables in the multiple regression (sales and debt) did not have significant explanatory power. Hence, the simple regression did not suffer from omitted variables bias.

The intuition behind why the omission of variables causes bias is provided in the previous section. For instance, lot size is an important explanatory variable for house prices, and thus "wants to" enter into the regression. If we omit it from the regression, it will try to enter in the only way it can – through its positive correlation with the explanatory variable: number of bedrooms. In other words, the coefficient on number of bedrooms will confound the effect of bedrooms and lot size on house prices.

One practical consequence of omitted variables bias is that you should always try to include all those explanatory variables that could affect the dependent variable. Unfortunately, in practice, this is rarely possible. House prices, for instance, depend on many other explanatory variables than those found in the data set HPRICE.XLS (e.g. the state of repair of the house, how pleasant the neighbors are, closet and storage space, whether the house has hardwood floors, the quality of the garden, etc.). In practice, there are too many variables on which to collect data, and many will be subjective (e.g. how do you measure "pleasantness of the neighbors"?). You will virtually always have omitted variables and there is little that can be done about it – other than to hope that the omitted variables do not have much explanatory power and that they are not correlated with the explanatory variables included in the analysis.

The previous paragraphs provide a justification for working with as many explanatory variables as possible. However, there is a counter argument to be made for using as *few* explanatory variables as possible. It can be shown that the inclusion of irrelevant variables decreases the accuracy of the estimation of all the coefficients (even the ones that are not irrelevant). This decrease in accuracy will be reflected in overly large confidence intervals and P-values.

How should we trade off the benefits of including many variables (i.e. reducing the risk of omitted variables bias) with the costs of possibly including irrelevant variables (i.e. reducing the accuracy of estimation)? A common practice is to begin with as many explanatory variables as possible,[6] then discard those that are not statistically significant (and then re-run the regression with the new set of explanatory variables). Statistical significance of an individual explanatory variable can, of course, be assessed using the P-values produced by computer packages like Excel. Once you have discarded the insignificant explanatory variables, you can run a new regression involving fewer explanatory variables, in which the risk of including irrelevant variables is greatly reduced.

Exercise 6.2

Use data set HPRICE.XLS and let Y = house price be the dependent variable and consider the following potential explanatory variables:

- X_1 = the lot size of the property (in square feet)
- X_2 = the number of bedrooms

- X_3 = the number of bathrooms
- X_4 = the number of storeys (excluding the basement).

(a) Regress Y on X_1, X_2, X_3 and X_4 (i.e. recreate the example above) and discuss your results.

(b) Regress Y on various subsets of X_1, X_2, X_3 and X_4 and discuss your results.

(c) Comparing your results for (a) and (b), examine the effect of omitting explanatory variables.

Multicollinearity

Multicollinearity is a statistical issue that relates to the previous discussion. It is a problem that arises if some or all of the explanatory variables are highly correlated with one another. If it is present, the regression model has difficulty telling which explanatory variable(s) is influencing the dependent variables. A multicollinearity problem reveals itself through low t-statistics and therefore high P-values. In these cases, you may conclude that coefficients are insignificant and hence should be dropped from the regression. In an extreme case, it is possible for you to find all the coefficients are insignificant using t-statistics, while the R^2 is quite large and significant. Intuitively, this means that the explanatory variables together provide a great deal of explanatory power, but that multicollinearity makes it impossible for the regression to decide which particular explanatory variable(s) is providing the explanation. (This is not important when doing prediction.)

There is not too much that can be done to correct this problem other than to drop out some of the highly correlated variables from the regression. However, there are many cases when you would not want to do so. For instance, in our house price example, if number of bedrooms and number of bathrooms had been found to be highly correlated, multicollinearity would be a problem. But you may hesitate to throw out one of these variables since common sense indicates that both of them significantly influence housing prices. The following example illustrates a case where a multicollinearity problem exists and how to correct for it by omitting an explanatory variable.

Example: The effect of interest rates on the exchange rate

Suppose you want to examine the effect of interest rate policy on the exchange rate. One way would be to select an exchange rate (e.g. the £/$ rate) as the dependent variable and run a regression of it on the interest rate. But there are many possible interest rates that could be used as explanatory variables (e.g. the bank prime rate, the Treasury bill rate, etc.). These interest rates are very similar to one another and will be highly correlated. If you include more than one of them you will likely run into a multicollinearity problem. The solution to this problem is clear: include only one of the interest rates. Since the various interest rates are essentially measures of the same phenomenon, common sense says that throwing out all but one of the interest rate variables will not cause any loss in explanatory power and will address the multicollinearity problem. However, we will not give a numerical example here since interest rates and exchange rates are time series data. As we shall see in future chapters, a naive use of multiple regression techniques with time series data can yield misleading results.

Example: Multicollinearity illustrated using artificial data

To illustrate the multicollinearity problem and how to address it, we first artificially generate $N = 50$ data points from the regression model:

$$Y = 0.5X_1 + 2X_2 + e.$$

We expect OLS estimates to be roughly $\hat{\alpha} = 0$, $\hat{\beta}_1 = 0.5$ and $\hat{\beta}_2 = 2$ since these values were used to create the data. However, the data generated have a correlation between X_1 and X_2 that is extremely high. In fact, it equals 0.98, indicating multicollinearity is a likely problem. Table 6.5 gives regression results using this data.

These results are very different from those we had hoped to get. The OLS point estimates are very different from those used to generate the data. For instance, $\hat{\beta}_1 = 2.08$ even though $\beta_1 = 0.5$ was used to generate the data. In fact, the OLS estimate for β_1 is almost exactly the same as the true value for β_2! This result illustrates how OLS can get "confused" about the role played by individual explanatory variables when they are highly correlated. Note also that one

Table 6.5   Regression results using artificial data.

	Coefficient	Standard error	*t*-stat	P-value	Lower 95%	Upper 95%
Intercept	0.166191	0.1025278	1.57859	0.121137	−0.045601	0.377983
X1	2.083733	0.952938	2.18664	0.033782	0.16667	4.00080
X2	0.147775	0.965767	0.153013	0.879043	−1.7951	2.09065

$R^2 = 0.76$ and the P-value for testing $R^2 = 0$ is $1.87\text{E} - 15$.

Table 6.6   Regression results using artificial data omitting X_2.

	Coefficient	Standard error	t-stat	P-value	Lower 95%	Upper 95%
Intercept	0.166715	0.104146	1.60078	0.115989	−0.042685	0.376115
X1	2.22690	0.178806	12.4543	1.2E − 16	1.86739	2.58641

$R^2 = 0.76$ and the P-value for testing whether it equals zero is 1.2E − 16.

of the explanatory variables is not statistically significant at the 5% level and that the other is only marginally significant. Furthermore, 95% confidence intervals for all coefficients are very large. These results suggest that the explanatory variables have only weak explanatory power. In contrast, the R^2 is very large and strongly statistically significant, suggesting that the explanatory variables have excellent explanatory power.

Given the problem of multicollinearity, many researchers would advocate omitting X_2 from the regression. If we follow their advice and rerun the regression, we obtain the results shown in Table 6.6.

Note that these results look much better from a statistical point of view. β_1 is strongly statistically significant and the confidence interval indicates it is estimated quite precisely. So, in one sense, omitting X_2 has solved the multicollinearity problem. The only problem is that $\hat{\beta}_1$ is nowhere near the true value of 0.5 (and the confidence interval does not contain 0.5). Generally, since X_2 is omitted from the model, X_1 attempts to take its place. Since X_1 is so highly correlated with X_2, the former can proxy for the latter quite well. Hence β_1 combines the effects of both explanatory variables. In other words, just as omitting important explanatory variables in the house price example gave us a biased view of the effect of bedrooms on house prices, omitting X_2 here gives us a biased view of the effect of X_1 on Y. There is nothing you can really do about this other than to note that it may occur if multicollinearity is present and interpret your results with caution.

Note that multicollinearity involves correlations between explanatory variables, not the dependent variable. For it to be a problem, the correlations between variables must be extremely high. If we return to the house pricing example, we can see that the explanatory variables are moderately correlated with one another (e.g. some correlations are around 0.3 or 0.4). But this moderate correlation does not lead to a multicollinearity problem since all the coefficients are significantly different from zero (see the P-values in Table 6.1).

Exercise 6.3

For this question, use data set EXECUTIVE.XLS with Y = executive compensation, X = profits, W = change in sales and Z = change in debt. Carry out a multiple regression analysis of this data set addressing the issues raised in this chapter. For instance, you may want to:

(a) Regress Y on X_1, X_2 and X_3 and verbally interpret the coefficient estimates you obtain.
(b) Discuss the statistical significance of the coefficients. Are there explanatory variables that can be dropped?
(c) Discuss the fit of the regression.
(d) Calculate a correlation matrix. Through consideration of this and regression results, discuss the issue of multicollinearity.

Chapter summary

1. The multiple regression model is very similar to the simple regression model. The chapter emphasized only differences between the two.
2. The interpretation of regression coefficients is subject to *ceteris paribus* conditions. For instance, β_j measures the marginal effect of X_j on Y, **holding the other explanatory variables constant**.
3. If important explanatory variables are omitted from the regression the estimated coefficients can be misleading, a condition known as the omitted variables bias. The problem gets worse if the omitted variables are strongly correlated with the included explanatory variables.
4. If the explanatory variables are highly correlated with one another, coefficient estimates and statistical tests may be misleading. This is referred to as the multicollinearity problem.

Appendix 6.1: Mathematical interpretation of regression coefficients

Readers who know some calculus can use this knowledge to obtain some mathematical intuition of the difference between simple and multiple regression. In the case of the simple regression model, basic calculus can be used to derive the relationship:

$$\frac{dY}{dX} = \beta.$$

That is, the regression coefficient, β, can be interpreted as a measure of how much Y changes when X is changed a small amount. This is a **total derivative**.

In the case of the multiple regression model, we can say:

$$\frac{\partial Y}{\partial X_j} = \beta_j.$$

In other words, the coefficients are **partial derivatives** rather than total derivatives. This partial derivative can be interpreted as measuring the effect of a small change in X_j on Y, **treating all the other explanatory variables as though they are constant**.

Endnotes

1. Formally, we should put an "i" subscript on all the variables to indicate each observation. In other words, we should have written: $Y_i = \alpha + \beta_1 X_{1i} + \beta_2 X_{2i} + \ldots + \beta_k X_{ki} + e_i$. However, adding so many subscripts is messy and makes the equation hard to read. So here, and throughout this book, we will often drop the "i" subscript (or "t" subscript with time series data) unless it is important to specify the individual observation.

2. Readers familiar with calculus should note that we can find OLS estimates in the multiple regression model in the usual way. That is, we can take first derivatives with respect to α and $\hat{\beta}_1, \hat{\beta}_2, \ldots, \hat{\beta}_k$, set these derivatives to zero, and then solve.

3. Matrix algebra is essential for theoretical derivations or proofs involving the multiple regression model, since the formulae can be extremely complex without it. Matrix algebra is beyond the scope of this book, but if you do further study in financial econometrics you will come to see the value of its use.

4. The methods described for one explanatory variable in Appendix 5.1 also apply to the case of many explanatory variables. That is, each coefficient will have a t-statistic that can be compared to the critical value of 1.96 if the sample size is large. In cases where there are many explanatory variables you might also want to test complicated hypotheses involving several coefficients (e.g. H_0: $\beta_1 + \beta_2 = \beta_3$). These tests are more difficult to carry out than those covered here. However, you may wish to consult Appendix 11.1, which has some discussion of hypothesis testing in such cases.

5. If you find this reasoning confusing, think back to the chapter on correlation. There we considered an example involving the variables cigarette smoking, alcohol drinking and lung cancer. We pointed out there that scientific studies indicate that it is smoking which causes lung cancer. However, smokers also tend to drink more alcohol than non-smokers. Hence, the correlation between drinking and lung cancer is positive even though drinking does not cause lung cancer. This type of issue is exactly of the sort we are getting at in this example. That is, a simple regression involving only the lung cancer and drinking variables would

indicate that the effect of drinking on lung cancer is large, even though drinking does not cause lung cancer. Why does this occur? Because we have left out the smoking variable which is an important explanatory variable for lung cancer. This left-out explanatory variable is correlated with the explanatory variable being used in the simple regression (i.e. drinking).

6. But, if you put in too many irrelevant explanatory variables to begin with, you could find virtually all explanatory variables to be insignificant. Hence, some common sense is required about what a good initial regression might be.

CHAPTER 7

Regression with dummy variables

Previous chapters used quantitative data to demonstrate important statistical concepts. However, some of the data financial analysts use is qualitative (see Chapter 2 for a discussion of the distinction between qualitative and quantive data). Dummy variables, briefly described in Chapter 2, are a way of turning qualitative variables into quantitative variables. Once the variables are quantitative, then the correlation and regression techniques described in previous chapters can be used. Formally, a dummy variable is a variable that can take on only two values, 0 or 1. We will demonstrate how regression works when some of the explanatory variables are dummies using the following examples.

Example: The determinants of market capitalization

We have discussed this example in previous chapters. However, an important issue involving this data set was not discussed previously since it involved a dummy explanatory variable. By way of motivating this issue, note that most of the shares traded on the stock market are old shares in existing firms. However, many old firms will issue some new shares in addition to those already trading – what are referred to as "seasoned equity offerings" or SEOs. Furthermore, some firms that have not traded shares on the stock market in the past may decide to now issue such shares (e.g. a computer software firm owned by one individual may decide to "go public" and sell shares in order to raise money for future investment or expansion). Such shares are called "initial public offerings" or IPOs. Some researchers have argued on the basis of empirical evidence that IPOs are undervalued relative to SEOs. Accordingly, in addition to all the company characteristics we have used before, we also have a dummy variable used to investigate this possibility.

To be precise, Excel file EQUITY.XLS contains data on $N = 309$ US firms in 1996. All variables except the dummy variable are measured in millions of US dollars.

- MARKETCAP = the total value of all shares (new and old) outstanding just after the firm issued the new shares. This is calculated as the price per share times the number of shares outstanding.
- DEBT = the amount of long-term debt held by the firm.
- SALES = total sales of the firm.
- INCOME = net income of the firm.
- ASSETS = book value of the assets of the firm.
- SEO = a dummy variable that equals 1 if the new share issue is an SEO and equals 0 if it is an IPO.

Example: Explaining house prices

In the previous chapter, we worked through an extended example that investigated the factors influencing housing prices in Windsor, Canada. Recall that the explanatory variables we used in that chapter were all quantitative (e.g. lot size of property measured in square feet, the number of bathrooms). However, there are other factors that might influence housing prices that are not directly quantitative. Examples include the presence of: a driveway, air conditioning, a recreation room, a basement, and gas central heating. All these variables are Yes/No qualitative variables (e.g. Yes = the house has a driveway/No = the house does not have a driveway).

In order to carry out a regression analysis using these explanatory variables, we first need to transform them into dummy variables by changing the Yes/No into 1/0. Using the letter D to indicate dummy explanatory variables, we can define:

- $D_1 = 1$ if the house has a driveway (= 0 if it does not).
- $D_2 = 1$ if the house has a recreation room (= 0 if not)
- $D_3 = 1$ if the house has a basement (= 0 if not)
- $D_4 = 1$ if the house has gas central heating (= 0 if not)
- $D_5 = 1$ if the house has air conditioning (= 0 if not)

For instance, a house with a driveway, basement and gas central heating, but no air conditioning nor recreation room would have values for these variables of $D_1 = 1$, $D_2 = 0$, $D_3 = 1$, $D_4 = 1$ and $D_5 = 0$. These variables (and many others) are in data set HPRICE.XLS.

Once qualitative explanatory variables have been transformed into dummy variables, regression can be carried out in the standard way and all the theory and intuition developed in previous chapters can be used.

Why, then, are we allocating an entire chapter to this topic? There are two answers to this question. First, regression with dummy explanatory variables is quite common and the interpretation of coefficient estimates is somewhat different. For this reason it is worthwhile discussing the interpretation in detail. Second, regression with dummy explanatory variables is closely related to another set of techniques called Analysis of Variance (or ANOVA for short). ANOVA is not used that often by financial researchers (although in the field of corporate finance it is sometimes used), but it is an extremely common tool in other social and physical sciences such as sociology, education, medical statistics and epidemiology.

While most computer software packages such as Excel have ANOVA capabilities, the terminology of ANOVA is quite different from that used by financial analysts, so ANOVA may seem confusing and unfamiliar to you (e.g. the Excel Tools/Data Analysis menu has several ANOVA choices referring to "Single factor", "Two-factor with replication", "Two-factor without replication"). What we should note here, however, is that *regression with dummy explanatory variables can do anything ANOVA can.* In fact, regression with dummy variables is a more general and more powerful tool than ANOVA. For instance, the terms "Single factor ANOVA" or "Two-factor ANOVA" refer to the number of dummy explanatory variables. Excel (and most common computer packages that perform ANOVA), can handle no more than two. However, Excel allows for up to 16 explanatory variables in its multiple regression facilities and, thus, can handle very complicated ANOVA models. In short, if you know how to use and understand regression, then you have no need to learn about ANOVA.

Exercise 7.1

Using the data set HPRICE.XLS, calculate and interpret descriptive statistics and a correlation matrix for the five dummy variables listed in the example above. How can you interpret the mean of a dummy variable?

Simple regression with a dummy variable

We begin by considering a regression model with one dummy explanatory variable, D:

$$Y = \alpha + \beta D + e.$$

If we carry out OLS estimation of the above regression model, we obtain $\hat{\alpha}$ and $\hat{\beta}$. We can look at confidence intervals for α or β; examine P-values to test whether the coefficients are statistically significant; calculate R^2; perform an F-test for the significance of the regression; etc., exactly as before. Refer back to Chapters 4, 5 and 6 if you are still unfamiliar with any of this material. An important topic at this stage for discussion, however, is the interpretation of the coefficients.

The straight-line relationship between Y and D gives a fitted value for the ith observation of:

$$\hat{Y}_i = \hat{\alpha} + \hat{\beta} D_i.$$

Note, since D_i is either 0 or 1, $\hat{Y}_i = \hat{\alpha}$ or $\hat{Y}_i = \hat{\alpha} + \hat{\beta}$. Two examples will serve to illustrate how this fact can be used to interpret regression results.

Example: Explaining house prices (continued from page 111)

Table 7.1 gives computer output from a regression of Y = house prices on D = air conditioning dummy using data from HPRICE.XLS. Note that an examination of the P-value or the confidence interval (i.e. Upper 95%, Lower 95%) shows us that β is strongly significant. Furthermore, $\hat{\alpha} = 59,885$ and $\hat{\beta} = 25,996$. How can we interpret these numbers? We can, of course, use the same marginal effect intuition as we used in Chapter 4. That is, we can say that β is a measure of how much Y tends to change when X is changed by one unit. But, with the present dummy explanatory variable a "one unit" change implies a change from "No air conditioner" to "Having an air conditioner". That is, we can say "houses with an air conditioner tend to be worth $25,996 more than houses without an air conditioner".

Table 7.1   Regression of house prices on air conditioning dummy.

	Coefficient	Standard error	t-stat	P-value	Lower 95%	Upper 95%
Intercept	59884.85	1233.50	48.55	7.1E − 200	57461.84	62307.86
D	25995.74	2191.36	11.86	4.9E − 29	21691.18	30300.32

However, there is another, closely related, way of thinking about regression results when the explanatory variable is a dummy. In the case of houses without air conditioning $D_i = 0$ and hence $\hat{Y}_i = 59{,}885$. In other words, our regression model finds that houses without air conditioning are worth on average $59,885. In the case of houses with air conditioning, $D_i = 1$ and the regression model finds that $\hat{Y}_i = \hat{\alpha} + \hat{\beta} = 85{,}881$. Thus, houses with air conditioning are worth on average $85,881. This is one attractive way of presenting the information provided by the regression. Alternatively, we could focus on $\hat{\beta}$ directly and say that houses with air conditioners tend to be worth $25,996 more than houses without them.

To provide more intuition, note that if we had not carried out a regression, but simply calculated the average price for houses with air conditioning, we would have found this figure to be $85,881. If we had then calculated the average price for houses without air conditioning, we would have found them to be worth $59,885. That is, we would have found exactly the same results as in the regression analysis.

Remember, however, the discussion of the omitted variables bias in Chapter 6. The simple regression in this example is omitting many important explanatory variables. We definitely cannot use the results of this simple regression to make statements like "Adding an air conditioner to your house will raise its value by $25,996". Since air conditioners cost a few hundred dollars, the previous statement is clearly ridiculous.

Example: The determinants of market capitalization (continued from page 110)

Table 7.2 gives computer output from a regression of Y = market capitalization on SEO = the dummy variable which equals 1 for SEOs (= 0 for IPOs) from EQUITY.XLS.

Using similar reasoning as for the house price example, we can say that the companies issuing SEOs do tend to be worth more ($637.78 million more) than

Table 7.2   Regression of market capitalization on SEO.

	Coefficient	Standard error	*t*-stat	P-value	Lower 95%	Upper 95%
Intercept	191.795	253.642	0.756	0.450	−307.301	690.891
SEO	637.780	296.583	2.150	0.032	54.188	1221.371

IPO companies and that this result is statistically significant (since the P-value is less than 0.05). However, this regression may too suffer from omitted variables bias. It is possible that the companies issuing SEOs have a greater market capitalization simply because they tend to be bigger, more established and more profitable than the IPO companies.

Multiple regression with dummy variables

Now, consider the multiple regression model with several dummy explanatory variables:

$$Y = \alpha + \beta_1 D_1 + \ldots + \beta_k D_k + e.$$

OLS estimation of this regression model and statistical analysis of the results can be carried out in the standard way. To aid in interpretation, we return to the house-pricing example.

Example: Explaining house prices (continued from page 113)

Consider the case where we have two dummy explanatory variables, $D_1 = 1$ if the house has a driveway (= 0 if not) and $D_2 = 1$ if the house has a recreation room (= 0 if not). These dummy variables implicitly classify the houses in the data set into four different groups:

1. Houses with a driveway and recreation room ($D_1 = 1$ and $D_2 = 1$).
2. Houses with a driveway, but no recreation room ($D_1 = 1$ and $D_2 = 0$).
3. Houses with no driveway, but with a recreation room ($D_1 = 0$ and $D_2 = 1$).
4. Houses with no driveway and no recreation room ($D_1 = 0$ and $D_2 = 0$).

Keep this classification in mind as we interpret Table 7.3, which contains results from a regression of house price (Y), on D_1 and D_2.

Table 7.3   Regression of house price on driveway and recreation room dummies.

	Coefficient	Standard error	*t*-stat	P-value	Lower 95%	Upper 95%
Intercept	47099.08	2837.62	16.60	2.42E − 50	41525.02	52673.14
D1	21159.91	3062.44	6.91	1.37E − 11	15144.22	27175.60
D2	16023.69	2788.63	5.75	1.52E − 08	10545.86	21501.51

Putting in either 0 or 1 values for the dummy variables, we obtain the fitted values for Y for the four categories of houses:

1. If $D_1 = 1$ and $D_2 = 1$, then $\hat{Y} = \hat{\alpha} + \hat{\beta}_1 + \hat{\beta}_2 = 47,099 + 21,160 + 16,024 = 84,283$. In other words, the average price of houses with a driveway and recreation room is \$84,283.
2. If $D_1 = 1$ and $D_2 = 0$, then $\hat{Y} = \hat{\alpha} + \hat{\beta}_1 = 47,099 + 21,160 = 68,259$. In other words, the average price of houses with a driveway but no recreation room is \$68,259.
3. If $D_1 = 0$ and $D_2 = 1$, then $\hat{Y} = \hat{\alpha} + \hat{\beta}_2 = 47,099 + 16,024 = 63,123$. In words, the average price of houses with a recreation room but no driveway is \$63,123.
4. If $D_1 = 0$ and $D_2 = 0$, then $\hat{Y} = \hat{\alpha} = 47,099$. In words, the average price of houses with no driveway and no recreation room is \$47,099.

In short, multiple regression with dummy variables may be used to classify the houses into different groups and to find average house prices for each group. Alternatively, results may be presented directly as coefficient estimates. For instance, $\hat{\beta}_1$ is a measure of the extra value of a house with a driveway relative to a house with no driveway holding the other features of the house (in this case the presence or absence of a recreation room) constant.

Exercise 7.2

Interpret the statistical information in the above example. Are all of the explanatory variables statistically significant?

Exercise 7.3

For this question use $Y =$ the price of a house and the dummy variables $D_1 = 1$ if the house has a driveway ($= 0$ otherwise) and $D_2 = 1$ if the house has a recreation room ($= 0$ otherwise) from the house price example (it can be obtained from HPRICE.XLS). Without using regression techniques, calculate the average price of the four types of houses listed in the previous example (e.g. a house with a driveway and a rec. room, etc.). Hint: What do you obtain if you multiply a dummy variable by Y? How do these average price numbers relate to the regression coefficients and results in the previous example?

Exercise 7.4

For this question use data set HPRICE.XLS and the five dummy variables, D_1 to D_5, listed at the beginning of the chapter (i.e. the dummy variables for whether a house has a driveway, recreation room, basement, gas central heating and air conditioning).

(a) With five dummy variables, how many classes of houses are possible? (e.g. houses with a driveway, recreation room, basement and gas central heating but no air conditioning comprise one class.) What implications does this have for interpreting regression results as in the previous example?

(b) How would you calculate the number of houses in each group using a computer package like Excel? For instance, of the 546 houses in the data set, how many have a driveway, gas central heating and air conditioning, but no recreation room and no basement?

(c) Run a regression of Y = house price on the five dummies.

(d) Discuss the statistical significance of the explanatory variables.

(e) Calculate the average price for a few chosen types of housing (e.g. those with a driveway, recreation room and basement but no gas central heating and no air conditioning).

(f) Which house characteristic tends to raise the price of a house the most?

Multiple regression with both dummy and non-dummy explanatory variables

In the previous discussion, we have assumed that all the explanatory variables are dummies but, in practice, you may often have a mix of different types of explanatory variables. The simplest such case is one where there is one dummy variable (D) and one quantitative explanatory variable (X) in a regression:

$$Y = \alpha + \beta_1 D + \beta_2 X + e.$$

The interpretation of results from such a regression can be illustrated in the context of an example.

Example: Explaining house prices (continued from page 115)

If we regress Y = house price on D = air conditioner dummy and X = lot size, we obtain $\hat{\alpha} = 32,693$, $\hat{\beta}_1 = 20,175$ and $\hat{\beta}_2 = 5.638$. Above we noted that the dummy can take on only the values 0 or 1, and demonstrated that the fitted value for Y can take on a different value for each group of houses. Hence regression results could be interpreted as revealing the average price of a house in each possible group.

Here things are not quite so simple since we obtain $\hat{Y}_i = 52,868 + 5.638X_i$ if $D_i = 1$ (i.e. the *i*th house has an air conditioner) and $\hat{Y}_i = 32,693 + 5.638X_i$ if $D_i = 0$ (i.e. the house does not have an air conditioner). In other words, there are two different regression lines depending on whether the house has an air conditioner or not. Contrast this point with the discussion in example above where we had only one dummy explanatory variable. In that case, the regression implied that the average price of the house differed between houses with and without air conditioners. Here we are saying a wholly different regression line exists. In other words, we cannot simply state (as we did in examples in previous examples in this chapter) what the average value of different groups of houses will be.

We can, however, say that $\hat{\beta}_1 = 20,175$ is a measure of the extra value that an air conditioner will add to the value of a house, *ceteris paribus*. In other words, if we compare two houses with the same value of X (in this case, lot size), $\hat{Y}_i$ will always be $20,175 higher for the house with an air conditioner relative to a house with no air conditioner.

It is worthwhile to examine more closely the two different regression lines that exist for houses with and without air conditioners. Note that they both have the same slope, $\hat{\beta}_2 = 5.638$ and differ only in the intercept (i.e. if $D_i = 1$ the intercept is 52,868, if $D_i = 0$ the intercept is 32,693). Since they have the same slope (and the slope is the marginal effect), the marginal effect of lot size on house price is the same for houses with and without air conditioning. For instance, we can say "An extra square foot of lot size is associated with adding an extra $5.63 on the price of a house".

We can extend the previous discussion to the case of many dummy and non-dummy explanatory variables. An example having two dummy and two non-dummy explanatory variables is the following regression model:

$$Y = \alpha + \beta_1 D_1 + \beta_2 D_2 + \beta_3 X_1 + \beta_4 X_2 + e.$$

The interpretation of results from this regression model combines elements from all the previous examples in this chapter.

Example: Explaining house prices
(continued from page 117)

If we regress Y = house price on D_1 = dummy variable for driveway, D_2 = dummy variable for recreation room, X_1 = lot size and X_2 = number of bedrooms we obtain: $\hat{\alpha} = -2736$, $\hat{\beta}_1 = 12{,}598$, $\hat{\beta}_2 = 10{,}969$, $\hat{\beta}_3 = 5.197$ and $\hat{\beta}_4 = 10{,}562$. We can interpret these results by figuring out what the fitted regression lines (i.e. $\hat{Y}$) are for the different possible values of the dummy variables.

1. If $D_1 = 1$ and $D_2 = 1$, then $\hat{Y} = \hat{\alpha} + \hat{\beta}_1 + \hat{\beta}_2 + \hat{\beta}_3 X_1 + \hat{\beta}_4 X_2 = 20{,}831 + 5.197 X_1 + 10{,}562 X_2$. This is the regression line for houses with a driveway and recreation room.
2. If $D_1 = 1$ and $D_2 = 0$, then $\hat{Y} = 9{,}862 + 5.197 X_1 + 10{,}562 X_2$. This is the regression line for houses with a driveway but no recreation room.
3. If $D_1 = 0$ and $D_2 = 1$, then $\hat{Y} = 8{,}233 + 5.197 X_1 + 10{,}562 X_2$. This is the regression line for houses with a recreation room but no driveway.
4. If $D_1 = 0$ and $D_2 = 0$, then $\hat{Y} = -2{,}736 + 5.197 X_1 + 10{,}562 X_2$. This is the regression line for houses with no driveway and no recreation room.

That is, with two dummy variables we have four different regression lines. All of these lines have the same slopes but different intercepts. The coefficients on the dummy variables, $\hat{\beta}_1$ and $\hat{\beta}_2$, measure the additional value associated with having a driveway and a recreation room, respectively. The coefficients on the non-dummy variables, $\hat{\beta}_3$ and $\hat{\beta}_4$, can be interpreted as the marginal effects of lot size and of number of bedrooms, respectively.

The following are a few of the types of verbal statements that we can make about the regression results:

1. "Houses with driveways tend to be worth $12,598 more than similar houses with no driveway".
2. "If we consider houses with the same number of bedrooms, then adding an extra square foot of lot size will tend to increase the price of a house by $5.20".
3. "An extra bedroom will tend to add $10,562 to the value of a house, *ceteris paribus*".

We should stress, however, that all such statements assume that omitted variables bias is not a problem in the regression. Furthermore, statements which imply causality (e.g. "adding an extra square foot of lot size will *tend to increase* the price of the house by $5.20") are only valid if it is truly the case that the explanatory variable causes the dependent variable (see Chapters 4 and 6 for further discussion of causality in regression).

Exercise 7.5

For this question use data set HPRICE.XLS, the five dummy variables, D_1 to D_5, listed in Exercise 7.4 and the following four non-dummy explanatory variables:

- X_1 = the lot size of the property (in square feet)
- X_2 = the number of bedrooms
- X_3 = the number of bathrooms
- X_4 = the number of storeys (excluding the basement).

(a) Run a regression of Y on $D_1, \ldots, D_5, X_1, \ldots, X_4$.
(b) Discuss which variables are statistically significant.
(c) Which of the characteristics measured by the dummies has the largest effect on housing prices?
(d) Choose particular configurations of the dummy variables (e.g. one indicating a house with: a driveway, no recreation room, a basement, no gas central heating and no air conditioner) and write out the formula for the regression line.
(e) Discuss results relating to the non-dummy explanatory variables, paying particular reference to the *ceteris paribus* conditions.

Example: The determinants of market capitalization (continued from page 114)

Table 7.4 presents results from a regression of market capitalization on a regular explanatory variable, ASSETS and the SEO dummy variable. Somewhat surprisingly, it seems that the book value of assets has little effect on market capitalization (since this variable is statistically insignificant). The SEO dummy variable is positive and significant. Hence, our finding from the simple regression that IPOs did seem to be undervalued is holding up in this multiple regression.

Table 7.4 Regression of house price on ASSETS and SEO.

	Coefficient	Standard error	t-stat	P-value	Lower 95%	Upper 95%
Intercept	191.728	254.047	0.755	0.451	−308.172	691.628
ASSETS	0.0008	0.006	0.153	0.879	−0.01	0.012
SEO	635.79	297.340	2.138	0.033	50.7	1220.881

Interacting dummy and non-dummy variables

We used the dummy variables above in a way that allowed for different intercepts in the regression line, but the slope of the regression line was always the same. We can, however, allow for different slopes by interacting dummy and non-dummy variables. To understand this consider the following regression model:

$$Y = \alpha + \beta_1 D + \beta_2 X + \beta_3 Z + e.$$

D and X are dummy and non-dummy explanatory variables, as above. However, here we have added a new variable Z into the regression and we define $Z = DX$.

How do we interpret results from a regression of Y on D, X and Z? This question can be answered by noting that Z is either 0 (for observations with $D = 0$) or X (for observations with $D = 1$). If, as before, we consider the fitted regression lines with $D = 0$ and $D = 1$ we obtain:

- If $D = 1$ then $\hat{Y} = (\hat{\alpha} + \hat{\beta}_1) + (\hat{\beta}_2 + \hat{\beta}_3)X$.
- If $D = 0$, then $\hat{Y} = \hat{\alpha} + \hat{\beta}_2 X$.

In other words, two different regression lines corresponding to $D = 0$ and $D = 1$ exist and have different intercepts and slopes. One implication is that the marginal effect of X on Y is different for $D = 0$ and $D = 1$. In a written report, you could write up each of the regression lines separately using the terminology and interpretation of Chapters 4 and 6.

Example: Explaining house prices (continued from page 118)

If we regress Y = house price on three explanatory variables: D = air conditioner dummy, X = lot size and $Z = DX$, we obtain $\hat{\alpha} = 35,684$, $\hat{\beta}_1 = 7,613$, $\hat{\beta}_2 = 5.02$ and $\hat{\beta}_3 = 2.25$. This implies that the marginal effect of lot size on housing is 7.27 (i.e. adding an extra square foot of lot size is associated with a $7.27 increase in house prices) for houses with air conditioners and only $5.02 for houses without. Furthermore, since the p-value corresponding to $\hat{\beta}_3$ is 0.02, the difference in marginal effects is statistically significant. This finding indicates that increasing lot size will tend to add more to the value of a house if it has an air conditioner than if it does not.

Exercise 7.6

For this question use data set HPRICE.XLS, the five dummy variables, D_1 to D_5 and the four non-dummies $X_1, \ldots, X_4$ discussed in Exercise 7.4. Experiment with different configurations of these explanatory variables with some interaction terms (e.g. try including 10 explanatory variables: D_1 to D_5 and the four non-dummies $X_1, \ldots, X_4$ plus an interaction term $D_1 X_2$, say). Can you find any interaction terms (i.e. Zs) that are statistically significant? Explain in words what your findings are.

Exercise 7.7

For this question use data set EQUITY.XLS containing the SEO dummy DEBT, SALES, INCOME and ASSETS (see the example at the beginning of this chapter for precise definitions of variables). Construct four new explanatory variables which interact the SEO dummy with each of the four other explanatory variables. Using these nine explanatory variables (i.e. the original five explanatory variables and four interactions), construct and justify a regression model. Begin by running a regression with all explanatory variables, then experiment with dropping out insignificant variables until you find a specification where all explanatory variables are significant (and you are not omitting any significant variables). Write a short report interpreting the results from the regression model you end up with.

What if the dependent variable is a dummy?

Thus far, we have focussed on the case where the explanatory variables can be dummies. However, in some cases the dependent variable may be a dummy. For instance, a researcher in the field of corporate finance might be interested in investigating why some companies go bankrupt and others do not, or why some raise money by issuing equity and others use debt, etc. An empirical analysis might involve collecting data from many different companies. Potential explanatory variables might include company characteristics such as debt, sales, profit, and so on. The dependent variable, however, would be qualitative (e.g. for each company data would be of the form "It went bankrupt"/"It did not go bankrupt" or "The company expanded through debt financing"/"The company did not use debt to finance its expansion") and the researcher would have to create a dummy dependent variable.

The techniques for working with dummy dependent variables[1] are beyond the scope of this book. However, there are two facts worth noting:

1. There are some problems with using OLS estimation in this case. However, these problems are not enormous, so that OLS estimation might be adequate in many circumstances.
2. Nevertheless, there are better estimation methods than OLS. The two main alternatives are termed Logit and Probit. Computer software packages with only basic statistical capabilities (e.g. Excel) do not have the capability to perform these estimation methods. Thus, if you ever need to do extensive work with dummy dependent variable models, you will have to use another software package (e.g. Stata).

Chapter summary

1. Dummy variables can take on a value of either 0 or 1. They are often used with qualitative data.
2. The statistical techniques associated with the use of dummy explanatory variables are exactly the same as with non-dummy explanatory variables.
3. A regression involving **only** dummy explanatory variables implicitly classifies the observations into various groups (e.g. houses with air conditioning and those without). Interpretation of results is aided by careful consideration of what the groups are.
4. A regression involving dummy and non-dummy explanatory variables implicitly classifies the observations into groups and says that each group will have a regression line with a different intercept. All these regression lines have the same slope.
5. A regression involving dummy, non-dummy and interaction (i.e. dummy times non-dummy variables) explanatory variables implicitly classifies the observations into groups and says that each group will have a different regression line with a different intercept and slope.
6. If the dependent variable is a dummy, then other techniques which are not covered in this book should be used.

Endnote

1. To introduce some jargon, such models are called "limited dependent variable" models. That is, the dependent variable can take on a limited range of values.

CHAPTER 8

Regression with lagged explanatory variables

Most applications in finance are concerned with the analysis of time series data. However, most of the examples in Chapters 3 to 7 used cross-sectional data. This allowed us to build up the basic ideas underlying regression, including statistical concepts such as hypothesis testing and confidence intervals, in a simple manner. When working with time series variables, knowledge of such ideas is essential. However, some additional issues arise when working with time series data. The purpose of this chapter is to offer an introduction to these issues and to familiarize the reader with some concepts and notation used with time series models. After this introductory material, we take one step away in the direction of developing the models and methods that are used with financial time series.

The goal of the researcher working with time series data does not differ too much from that of the researcher working with cross-sectional data: both aim to develop a regression relating a dependent variable to some explanatory variables. However, the analyst using time series data will face two problems that the analyst using cross-sectional data will not encounter: (1) one time series variable can influence another with a time lag; and (2) if the variables are **nonstationary**, a problem known as **spurious regression** may arise.

At this stage, you are not expected to understand the second of these problems. The terms **nonstationary, stationary** and **spurious regression** will be discussed in detail in subsequent chapters of this book. But keep in mind this general rule: **If you have nonstationary time series variables then you should not include them in a regression model.** The appropriate route is to transform the variables before running a regression in order to make them stationary. There is one exception to this general rule, which we shall discuss later, and which occurs where the variables in a regression model are **cointegrated**. We will elaborate on what we mean by these terms later. If you find it confusing for them to be introduced now without definitions, just think in the following terms: Some problems arise with time series data that do not arise with cross-sectional data. These problems make it risky to naively use multiple regression in the manner of Chapters 4 to 7. The purpose of this and the following chapters is to show you how to correctly modify regression techniques with time series data.

In this chapter, we will assume all variables in the regression are **stationary**. The next chapter explains what this means. At this point, note only that the second problem will not occur and that we can therefore focus on the first problem.

The first problem can be understood intuitively with some simple examples. When we estimate a regression model we are interested in measuring the effect of one or more explanatory variables on the dependent variable. In the case of time series data we have to be very careful in our choice of explanatory variables since their effect on the dependent variable may take time to manifest itself.

For instance, in previous chapters we worked with cross-sectional regressions involving company data. In one example, our dependent variable was market capitalization and explanatory variables were company characteristics (e.g. income, assets, sales, etc.). In another, our dependent variable was executive compensation which we sought to explain using variables like profits and debt. However, all our dependent and explanatory variables referred to the same year. In practice, this may not be reasonable. The value that the stock market places on a firm might depend not only on current income, but on historical income as well. After all, current income could be affected by short-term factors and may not be a totally reliable guide to long-run performance. For instance, an ice cream company might suffer a short-term fall in income due to an unusually cold summer. Looking at data based on this one unusual event could give an unreliable view of the long-run potential of this company. Similar considerations hold for our executive compensation example where compensation might be determined not only on current profits, but also on past profits. In short, there are good reasons to include not only current values of explanatory variables, but also past values.

To put this concept in the language of regression, we say that the value of the dependent variable at a given point in time should depend not only on the value of the explanatory variable at that time period, but also on values of the explanatory variable in the past. A simple model to incorporate such **dynamic** effects has the form:[1]

$$Y_t = \alpha + \beta_0 X_t + \beta_1 X_{t-1} + \ldots + \beta_q X_{t-q} + e_t.$$

This is precisely the same as the multiple regression model in Chapter 6, with the exception that the "explanatory variables" are not entirely different (e.g. lot size, number of bathrooms, number of bedrooms, etc.) but are just one explanatory variable that is observed at different time periods. In this model, the right-hand side variables are referred to as **lagged variables** and q, the **lag order** or **lag length**. We will focus on the case where the dependent variable depends on one explanatory variable and its lags. However, everything we say can be generalized in a straightforward fashion to several explanatory variables, all having time lags. Since the effect of the explanatory variable on the dependent variable does not happen all at once, but rather is distributed over several time periods, this model is sometimes referred to as a **distributed lag model**.

Since the regression model with time lags is a regression model, everything we said in Chapters 4 to 6 about regression is relevant here. For instance, computer packages like Excel can provide OLS estimates of coefficients, confidence intervals and P-values for testing whether coefficients are equal to zero. Coefficients can be interpreted as measures of the influence of the explanatory variable on the dependent variable. In this case, we have to be careful with timing. For instance, we interpret results as: "β_2 measures the effect of the explanatory variable **two periods ago** on the dependent variable, *ceteris paribus*". Other than these minor differences, both the statistical methods and interpretation are very similar to the tools we described previously. Nevertheless, it is worth discussing this class of models separately, as it will help us to develop some time series terminology and introduce ideas that we will build on in subsequent chapters.

Before turning to an illustrative example of how to work with regression models with lagged variables, we will make two brief detours. One of these describes what lagged variables are and how to calculate them in a spreadsheet software package. The other clarifies the notation that will be used in this and subsequent chapters.

Aside on lagged variables

The concept of a lagged variable is fundamental to time series data, so we will describe in some detail what it means and how to construct and work with lagged variables on a computer spreadsheet. We do this mostly because it really helps to understand what lagged variables are by seeing how they are constructed. However, we partly work with a spreadsheet to begin to show you that it is awkward to work with spreadsheets when you have time series variables. It is possible to do almost everything in this book (with the exception of models involving volatility which we will discuss later) with a spreadsheet such as Excel. However, it is much more convenient to use a specialized computer package for financial econometrics such as E-views, MicroFit or Stata.

Suppose we have time series data for $t = 1, \ldots, T$ periods on a variable X. As before, we denote individual observations by X_t for $t = 1, \ldots, T$. Consider creating a new variable W which has observations $W_t = X_t$ for $t = 2, \ldots, T$ and a new variable Z which has observations $Z_t = X_{t-1}$ for $t = 2, \ldots, T$. Why do we write $t = 2, \ldots, T$ instead of $t = 1, \ldots, T$? If we had written $t = 1, \ldots, T$ then the first observation of the variable Z, Z_1, would be set equal to X_0. Yet we do not know what X_0 is since variable X is observed only from $t = 1, \ldots, T$. In other words, W and Z have only $T - 1$ observations. Note also that had we written $Z_t = X_{t-2}$ then the new variable Z would have observations from $t = 3, \ldots, T$ and only $T - 2$ observations.

The new variables W and Z both have $T - 1$ observations. If we imagine W and Z as two columns containing $T - 1$ numbers each (as in an Excel spreadsheet), we can see that the first element of W will be X_2 and the first element of Z will be X_1. The second element of W and Z will be X_3 and X_2, etc. In words, we say that W contains X and Z contains X one period ago or **lagged one period**. In general, we can create variables "X lagged one period – or "lagged X" for short – "X lagged two periods" – or, in general, "X lagged j periods".

You can think of "X", "X lagged one period", "X lagged two periods", etc. as different explanatory variables in the same way as you can of "house price", "lot size", or "number of bedrooms" as different explanatory variables.

Note, however, that if you want to include several explanatory variables in a multiple regression model, all variables must have the same number of observations. Let us consider the implication of this statement, in the present context. Suppose a regression includes $X = $ the interest rate lagged j periods as an explanatory variable. If you began with $t = 1, \ldots, T$ observations on the interest rate, then X lagged j periods will contain only $T - j$ observations. Since this variable contains only $T - j$ observations you must make sure that all the other variables in the model also contain exactly $T - j$ observations. In words, each variable in a time series regression must contain the number of observations equal to T minus the maximum number of lags that any variable has.

Many of the more sophisticated statistical software packages (e.g. E-views, Stata or MicroFit,) will create lagged variables automatically with a simple command, but not most spreadsheet packages like Excel. This is a key reason why, when working with time series data, you might want to learn such a software package and not work with a spreadsheet such as Excel. When working with a spreadsheet you will have to create lagged variables yourself before running a regression involving them. A brief explanation of how to do this will be both useful when you work with spreadsheets and will provide a practical way to illustrate the material above.

As an example, suppose we have 10 observations on variables Y and X (i.e. $t = 1, \ldots, 10$) and we wish to run a regression model that includes X, lagged X, X lagged two periods and X lagged 3 periods. That is, we wish to estimate the regression model:

$$Y_t = \alpha + \beta_1 X_t + \beta_2 X_{t-1} + \beta_3 X_{t-2} + \beta_4 X_{t-3} + e_t.$$

Table 8.1 shows how the data would look in a spreadsheet format.

Note that spreadsheets label each observation by row and column, as in Table 8.1. Each column contains a variable (e.g. Column C contains the variable X lagged one period) and each row contains observations. Note that each of the variables contains 7 observations, which is T minus maximum number of lags (i.e. $10 - 3 = 7$). Looking across any row (e.g. Row 4) you can see that: (a) Y and X contain data at a particular

Table 8.1   Creating lagged variables.

	Column A Y	Column B X	Column C X lagged one period	Column D X lagged two periods	Column E X lagged three periods
Row 1	Y_4	X_4	X_3	X_2	X_1
Row 2	Y_5	X_5	X_4	X_3	X_2
Row 3	Y_6	X_6	X_5	X_4	X_3
Row 4	Y_7	X_7	X_6	X_5	X_4
Row 5	Y_8	X_8	X_7	X_6	X_5
Row 6	Y_9	X_9	X_8	X_7	X_6
Row 7	Y_{10}	X_{10}	X_9	X_8	X_7

point in time (e.g. Y_7 and X_7 or $t = 7$); (b) X lagged will contain the observation from one period previously (e.g. X_6); (c) X lagged two periods will contain the observation from two periods previously (e.g. X_5); and (d) X lagged three periods will contain the observation from three periods previously (e.g. X_4).

You can create this table in Excel. First use the Cut/Paste commands in the spreadsheet containing the original data on Y and X (i.e. the one that contained the 10 original observations on the two variables) to create a spreadsheet that looks like Table 8.1. Then run the regression by using the Excel regression menu in the standard way and specifying A1:A7 in the box labeled "Input Y-range", and B1:E7 in the box labeled "Input X-range".

This section on lagged variables may seem of little direct relevance for understanding and interpreting results. However, it is important not to forget this material if you are at the computer, working with a spreadsheet.

Aside on notation

It is also important to make sure that our notation is clear. Consider a variable, X (e.g. executive compensation). After collecting data on X we will have observations X_i for $i = 1, \ldots, N$ for cross-sectional data and X_t for $t = 1, \ldots, T$ for time series data (see Chapter 2).

In other words, X is a generic notation for the variable and X_i or X_t indicates a particular observation of the variable (e.g. X_i = executive compensation in the ith company or X_t = executive compensation in the tth time period). In our discussion of regression in Chapters 4 to 7 we often wrote equations of the form:

$$Y = \alpha + \beta X + e.$$

Expressed in words, the above implies that "the dependent variable Y depends on the explanatory variable X in a linear fashion". When we have actual data we can write,

$$Y_i = \alpha + \beta X_i + e_i.$$

Expressed in words, "observation i of Y depends on observation i of X". For instance, "executive compensation **in company** i depends on profits **in company** i". Both of these equations are perfectly correct. But, since the subscript i in the latter equation is a little obvious (e.g. it is obvious that executive compensation in Company A depends on profits in Company A – it certainly will not depend on profits in Company B), you often see the i subscript dropped out from the latter equation for simplicity's sake.

We complicated our notation even more in Chapter 6 in our discussion of multiple regression, in which $X_1, X_2, \ldots, X_k$ were k different explanatory variables. Here the subscript on X indicated which explanatory variable we were referring to, not which observation. In the rare cases when we wanted to be more explicit we wrote, for example, X_{2i}, to indicate the ith observation of the second explanatory variable. However, since it is usually obvious in the multiple regression case that Y_i (e.g. executive compensation **in company** i) depends on X_{1i} (e.g. profits **in company** i) and on X_{2i} (e.g. change in sales **in company** i), the i subscript was often dropped from the equation.

In short, throughout this book our subscript notation, which distinguishes between a variable and a particular observation of a variable, has been a little loose. This is okay (and common in textbooks), since the meaning is fairly obvious from the context and the alternative is to clutter up equations with numerous subscripts. In the time series chapters of this book, we will show similar informality, using the notation X_{t-j} to indicate both a particular observation (e.g. if $t = 1968$ and $j = 3$, then X_{t-j} is the value of variable X in 1965) and the variable X lagged j periods. It will be obvious from the context which is which. Quite frankly, in virtually any equation in this book it will not matter which way you interpret it.

Example: Long-run prediction of a stock market price index

The issue of whether stock market returns are predictable is a very important one in finance. After all, if an investor could predict stock market behavior, she could make a lot of money. Of course, in practice, predicting which stocks will increase in value tomorrow is extremely difficult. We will return to the issue of short-run prediction of stock prices in the next chapter, when we discuss random walk behavior. In this example, we focus on long-run prediction of the stock market.

This is not a book on financial theory and, hence, we will not describe the theoretical model which motivates the regressions we will run in any detail. In general, many researchers have studied the relationship between stock prices, dividends and returns. The basic equation relating these three concepts was given in Chapter 2 as:

$$\text{Return} = R_t = \frac{(P_t - P_{t-1} + D_t)}{P_{t-1}} \times 100,$$

where R_t is the return on holding a share from period $t-1$ through t, P_t is the price of the stock at the end of period t and D_t is the dividend earned between period $t-1$ and t. This basic relationship, along with various assumptions about how these variables might evolve in the future, can be used to develop various theoretical financial models.[2] A particularly useful such model implies that the ratio of dividends to stock price should have some predictive power for future returns, particularly at long horizons.

How does such a theory relate to our regression model with lagged explanatory variables? It implies a model where the dependent variable (Y) is the total return on the stock market index over a future period (let us say h months, where h denotes the forecasting horizon) but the explanatory variable (X) is the current dividend-price ratio. Thus, we have a regression model of the form:

$$Y_{t+h} = \alpha + \beta X_t + e_{t+h},$$

where the dependent variable, Y_{t+h}, is calculated using the returns R_{t+1}, $R_{t+2}, \ldots, R_{t+h}$. Or, equivalently, we can write this regression as:

$$Y_t = \alpha + \beta X_{t-h} + e_t.$$

This is a specialized version of our general regression with lagged explanatory variables described above.

The theory developed by financial researchers suggests that the explanatory power for this regression should be poor at short horizons (e.g. $h = 1$ or 2) but improve at longer horizons. The file LONGRUN.XLS contains monthly data for a hundred years on $Y = 12$ month returns (i.e. $h = 12$) from a stock market along with X the dividend-price ratio (12 months ago).

Table 8.2 contains results from the regression. Since the P-value for the coefficient on X_{t-12} is less than 0.05, the coefficient is significant. We can conclude that the dividend-price ratio does have explanatory power for 12 month returns. This supports the theory that the dividend-price ratio does have some predictive power for long-run returns. However, we also find $R^2 = 0.019$ indicating that this predictive power is weak (although it is statistically significant). Only 1.9% of the variation in 12 month returns can be explained by the dividend-price ratio.

Table 8.2 Regression results for the long-run prediction of stock returns example.

	Coefficient	Standard error	t-stat	P-value	Lower 95%	Upper 95%
Intercept	−0.003	0.005	−0.662	0.508	−0.013	0.006
X_{t-12}	0.022	0.005	4.833	1.5E − 6	0.013	0.032

Example: The effect of bad news on market capitalization

The share price of a company can be sensitive to bad news. Suppose that Company B is in an industry which is particularly sensitive to the price of oil. If the price of oil goes up, then the profits of Company B will tend to go down and some investors, anticipating this, will sell their shares in Company B driving its price (and market capitalization) down. However, this effect might not happen immediately. For instance, if Company B holds large inventories produced with cheap oil, it can sell these and maintain its profits for a while. But when new production is required, the higher oil price will lower profits. Furthermore, the effect of the oil price might not last forever, since Company B also has some flexibility in its production process and can gradually adjust to higher oil prices. Hence, news about the oil price should affect the market capitalization of Company B, but the effect might not happen immediately and might not last too long.

The file BADNEWS.XLS contains data collected on a monthly basis over five years (i.e. 60 months) on the following variables:

- Y = market capitalization of Company B ($000)
- X = the price of oil (dollars per barrel).[3]

Since this is time series data[4] and it is likely that previous months' news about the oil price will affect current market capitalization, it is necessary to include lags of X in the regression. Table 8.3 contains OLS estimates of the coefficients in a distributed lag model in which market capitalization is allowed to depend on present news about the oil price and news up to four months ago. That is,

$$Y_t = \alpha + \beta_0 X_t + \beta_1 X_{t-1} + \beta_2 X_{t-2} + \beta_3 X_{t-3} + \beta_4 X_{t-4} + e_t.$$

What can we conclude about the effect of news about the oil price on Company B's market capitalization? Increasing the oil price by one dollar per barrel in a given month is associated with:

Table 8.3 Regression results for the effect of news on market capitalization example.

	Coefficient	Standard error	t-stat	P-value	Lower 95%	Upper 95%
Intercept	92001.51	2001.71	45.96	5.86E − 42	87978.91	96024.11
X_t	−145.00	47.62	−3.04	0.0037	−240.70	−49.30
X_{t-1}	−462.14	47.66	−9.70	5.52E − 13	−557.91	−366.38
X_{t-2}	−424.47	46.21	−9.19	3.12E − 12	−517.33	−331.62
X_{t-3}	−199.55	47.76	−4.18	0.00012	−295.52	−103.58
X_{t-4}	−36.90	47.45	−0.78	0.44	−132.25	58.45

1. An immediate reduction in market capitalization of $145,000, *ceteris paribus*.
2. A reduction in market capitalization of $462,140 one month later, *ceteris paribus*.
3. A reduction in market capitalization of $424,470 two months later, *ceteris paribus*.
4. A reduction in market capitalization of $199,550 three months later, *ceteris paribus*.
5. A reduction of market capitalization of $36,900 four months later, *ceteris paribus*.

Confidence intervals can be interpreted in the standard way. For instance, we are 95% confident that the immediate reduction in market capitalization is at least $49,300 and at most $240,700, *ceteris paribus*.

To provide some intuition about what the *ceteris paribus* condition implies in this context note that, for example, we can also express the second of these statements as: "Increasing the oil price by one dollar in a given month will tend to reduce market capitalization in the following month by $462,120, **assuming that no other change in the oil price occurs**".

If we examine the statistical results in the preceding table, we can see that all of the coefficients are statistically significant, except for β_4. The P-value for this last coefficient is 0.44 which is **not** less than 0.05. Also we note that the confidence interval for β_4 includes zero. Hence we cannot reject the hypothesis that $\beta_4 = 0$. In words, we cannot reject the hypothesis that changes in the oil price four months ago have no effect on current market capitalization.

In general the effect of changes in the oil price on market capitalization exhibits a hump-shaped pattern over time: the immediate effect is fairly small ($145,000). The effect then increases to over $400,000 for each of the two subsequent months, falls to roughly $200,000 three months later, and then drops to about zero four months later. If we add up the effects of an increase of one dollar in the oil price in each period (i.e. $145,000 + $462,140 + $424,470 +

$199,550 + $36,900 = $1,268,060)[5] we receive a measure of the total effect of this increase on market capitalization. In other words, we can say that: "After four months, the effect of adding one dollar to the price of oil is to decrease market capitalization by $1,268,060".

By calculating this total effect and examining the pattern of the coefficients over time, the company and the investor gain important information. Such results, however, assume that the distributed lag model is not missing any explanatory variables. For instance, we are implicitly assuming that X_{t-5} has no effect on current market capitalization. If this assumption is incorrect, our estimates of the total effect of a change in oil prices may be incorrect. This issue relates closely to the problem of omitted variables bias discussed in Chapter 6, and emphasizes the importance of correct choice of lag length (i.e. q in the distributed lag model), a topic to which we now turn.

Exercise 8.1

Use the data set, BADNEWS.XLS, discussed in the previous example for this question. This data set contains $T = 60$ observations on $Y =$ market capitalization and $X =$ oil price.

(a) Create the explanatory variables you would use in a distributed lag model with lag length equal to 4. How many observations do the explanatory variables have?

(b) Using your answer to (a), recreate Table 8.3 in the example above.

(c) Create the explanatory variables you would use in a distributed lag model with lag length equal to 2. How many observations do the explanatory variables have?

(d) Using your answer to (c), estimate the distributed lag model with $q = 2$.

(e) Compare your answers to part (d) and part (b). Discuss why they differ, paying particular attention to the question of omitted variables bias (see Chapter 6 if you have forgotten what this is).

Selection of lag order

When working with distributed lag models, we rarely know *a priori* exactly how many lags we should include. In the previous example, why did we assume that market capitalization depends on movements in the oil price up to four months ago? Why not three or six or even eight? That is, unlike most of the regression models considered in Chapters 4 to 7, we don't know which explanatory variables in a distributed lag model belong in the regression before we actually sit down at the computer and start working with the data. Appropriately, the issue of lag length selection becomes a data-based one where we use statistical means to decide how many lags to include.

There are many different approaches to lag length selection in the econometrics literature. Here we outline a common one that does not require any new statistical techniques beyond those developed in Chapter 5. This method uses t-tests for whether $\beta_q = 0$ to decide lag length. A common strategy is to: (a) Begin with a fairly large lag length,[6] q_{max}, and test whether the coefficient on the maximum lag is equal to zero (i.e. test whether $\beta_{q_{max}} = 0$). (b) If it is, drop the highest lag and re-estimate the model with maximum lag equal to $q_{max} - 1$. (c) If you find $\beta_{q_{max}-1} = 0$ in this new regression, then lower the lag order by one and re-estimate the model. (d) Keep on dropping the lag order by one and re-estimating the model until you reject the hypothesis that the coefficient on the longest lag is equal to zero.

This informal description of lag length selection can be formalized in the following series of steps:

Step 1. Choose the maximum possible lag length, q_{max}, that seems reasonable to you.
Step 2. Estimate the distributed lag model:

$$Y_t = \alpha + \beta_0 X_t + \beta_1 X_{t-1} + \ldots + \beta_{q_{max}} X_{t-q_{max}} + e_t.$$

If the P-value for testing $\beta_{q_{max}} = 0$ is less than the significance level you choose (e.g. 0.05) then go no further. Use q_{max} as lag length. Otherwise go on to the next step.
Step 3. Estimate the distributed lag model:

$$Y_t = \alpha + \beta_0 X_t + \beta_1 X_{t-1} + \ldots + \beta_{q_{max}-1} X_{t-q_{max}+1} + e_t.$$

If the P-value for testing $\beta_{q_{max}-1} = 0$ is less than the significance level you choose (e.g. 0.05) then go no further. Use $q_{max} - 1$ as lag length. Otherwise go on to the next step.
Step 4. Estimate the distributed lag model:

$$Y_t = \alpha + \beta_0 X_t + \beta_1 X_{t-1} + \ldots + \beta_{q_{max}-2} X_{t-q_{max}+2} + e_t.$$

If the P-value for testing $\beta_{q_{max}-2} = 0$ is less than the significance level you choose (e.g. 0.05) then go no further. Use $q_{max} - 2$ as lag length. Otherwise go on to the next step, etc.

As an aside of practical relevance to note when you are working with a spreadsheet, the number of observations used in a distributed lag model is equal to the original number of observations, T, minus the maximum lag length. This means that, in Step 2, we are working with $T - q_{max}$ observations; in Step 3, with $T - q_{max} + 1$ observations; in Step 4 with $T - q_{max} + 2$, observations; etc. Each step will require some cutting and pasting in the spreadsheet to create variables with the appropriate number of observations. Alternatively, some researchers simply use $T - q_{max}$ observations for all regressions. This has the advantage that, at each step, the researcher uses the same observations. However, this strategy may mean using a smaller data set than necessary. Remember from Chapter 5 that having more observations increases the accuracy of OLS estimates.

Example: The effect of bad news on market capitalization (continued from page 132)

(continued from page 132)

Suppose we have selected $q_{max} = 4$ in the regression of market capitalization on oil prices. In other words, we believe that four months is the maximum time period that we can reasonably expect news about the oil price to impact on market capitalization. The strategy outlined above says we should begin by estimating a distributed lag model with lag length equal to 4. Results are given in Table 8.3. Since the P-value corresponding to the explanatory variable X_{t-4} is greater than 0.05 we cannot reject the hypothesis that $\beta_4 = 0$ at the 5% level of significance. Accordingly, we drop this variable from the model and re-estimate with lag length set equal to 3, yielding the results in Table 8.4.

Table 8.4   Lag length set equal to 3.

	Coefficient	Standard error	*t*-stat	P-value	Lower 95%	Upper 95%
Intercept	90402.22	1643.18	55.02	9.19E − 48	87104.94	93699.51
X_t	−125.90	46.24	−2.72	0.0088	−218.69	−33.11
X_{t-1}	−443.49	45.88	−9.67	3.32E − 13	−535.56	−351.42
X_{t-2}	−417.61	45.73	−9.13	2.18E − 12	−509.38	−325.84
X_{t-3}	−179.90	46.25	−3.89	0.0003	−272.72	−87.09

The P-value for testing $\beta_3 = 0$ is 0.0003, which is much less than 0.05. We therefore conclude that the variable X_{t-3} does indeed belong in the distributed lag model. Hence $q = 3$ is the lag length we select for this model. In a formal report, we would present this table of results. Since these results are similar to those discussed above, we will not repeat the interpretation of them.

Exercise 8.2

Use the data set, BADNEWS.XLS. Suppose you believe that six months is the maximum time that the oil price might affect market capitalization and accordingly, you set $q_{max} = 6$. Using the strategy described above, select the lag length of the distributed lag model.

Chapter summary

1. Regressions with time series variables involve two issues we have not dealt with in the past. First, one variable can influence another with a time lag. Second, if the variables are non-stationary, the spurious regressions problem can result. The latter issue will be dealt with in Chapter 10.
2. Distributed lag models have the dependent variable depending on an explanatory variable and time lags of the explanatory variable.
3. If the variables in the distributed lag model are stationary, then OLS estimates are reliable and the statistical techniques of multiple regression (e.g. looking at P-values or confidence intervals) can be used in a straightforward manner.
4. The lag length in a distributed lag model can be selected by sequentially using *t*-tests beginning with a reasonably large lag length.

Endnotes

1. We can, of course, label our coefficients using any convention we want. The convention chosen here relates the subscript on β to the number of periods ago to which the explanatory variables refers. For instance, β_1 is the coefficient on X_{t-1}, which is the value of the explanatory variable one period ago.
2. The interested reader is referred to Chapter 7 of Campbell, Lo and MacKinlay, *The Econometrics of Financial Markets*, for details.
3. Formally, this is a price relative to a benchmark price which accounts for the zeros in the data set.
4. Note that we are assuming this data to be stationary. In a real empirical exercise involving market capitalization, this may be a poor assumption. However, this data set is a fictitious one, created so as to be stationary, so we will not worry about this issue here.
5. The value $1,268,060 is the estimate of the total effect. It is possible to calculate a confidence interval as well, but this would require a more complicated formula and is beyond the scope of this book.
6. Although not too large! Remember that each variable in a distributed lag model will have number of observations equal to T minus the maximum number of lags. If you set the maximum number of lags too large, you will be left with very few observations.

CHAPTER 9

Univariate time series analysis

[handwritten: Y = dependant]
[handwritten: X = independent]

In the previous chapter we discussed regression models with lagged explanatory variables. Remember that they assume that the dependent variable, Y_t, depends on an explanatory variable, X_t, and lags of the explanatory variable, $X_{t-1}, \ldots, X_{t-q}$. Such models are a useful first step in understanding important concepts in time series analysis.

In many cases, distributed lag models can be used without any problems; however, they can be misleading in cases where either: (1) the dependent variable Y_t depends on lags of the dependent variable as well, possibly, as $X_t, X_{t-1}, \ldots, X_{t-q}$; or (2) the variables are nonstationary.

Accordingly, in this chapter and the next, we develop tools for dealing with both issues and define what we mean by "nonstationary". To simplify the analysis, in this chapter we ignore X, and focus solely on Y. In statistical jargon, we will concentrate on **univariate time series** methods. As the name suggests, these relate to one variable or, in the jargon of statistics, one **series** (e.g. Y = a stock price index). As we shall see, the properties of individual series are often important in their own right (e.g. as relating to market efficiency). Furthermore, it is often important to understand the properties of each individual series before proceeding to regression modeling involving several series.

Example: Stock prices on the NYSE

NYSE.XLS contains monthly data from 1952 through 1995 on a major stock price index provided by the New York Stock Exchange (NYSE). The price index is a value-weighted one (see Chapter 2 for a discussion of index numbers). Figure

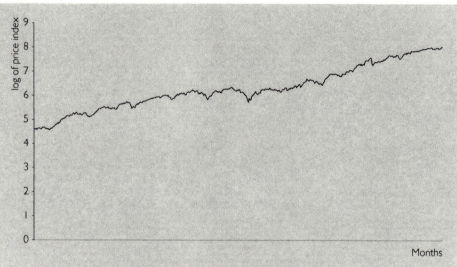

Fig. 9.1 Log of stock price index.

9.1 is a time series plot of the natural logarithm of this series.[1] In other words, Y_t is the stock price index for $t = 1952M1, \ldots, 1995M12$. The data is available in Excel file NYSE.XLS.

Note that the stock price index tends to be increasing over time. You can see some variation (e.g. there are some falls in the stock price index corresponding to the bear market of the mid-1970s), but overall, the time series plot is roughly a straight line with a positive slope. This sustained (in this case upward) movement is referred to as a **trend**. Many financial variables (e.g. stock prices, the price level, measures of personal income and wealth, etc.) exhibit trends of this sort.

It is convenient at this point to introduce the concept of **differencing**. Formally, if Y_t $(t = 1, \ldots, T)$ is a time series variable, then $\Delta Y_t = Y_t - Y_{t-1}$ is the first difference of Y_t.[2] ΔY_t measures the change or growth in a variable over time. If we take natural logarithms of the original series, Y_t, then ΔY_t measures the percentage change in the original variable between time $t-1$ and t. ΔY_t is often called "ΔY", "delta Y" or "the change in Y". Moreover, it is common to refer to Y_{t-1} as "Y_t lagged one period" or "the stock price lagged one period" or "lagged Y", and so on. Figure 9.2 plots the change in the log of the stock price index using the data in NYSE.XLS. Note that this can be interpreted as the return on the stock market (exclusive of dividends).

Note that Figure 9.2 looks very different from Figure 9.1. The trend behavior noted in Figure 9.1 has disappeared completely (we will return to this point later). The figure indicates that the change in the stock price each month tends

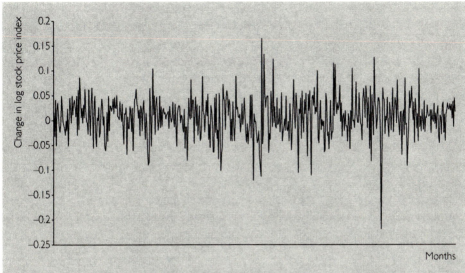

Fig. 9.2 Stock price return.

to be small, although there is considerable variability to this growth rate over time. In some of the months, the NYSE stock price index increased by over 5%. In October 1987, it fell by over 20%.

Exercise 9.1

The file INTERESTRATES.XLS contains data on a long-term and a short-term interest rate (measured as a percentage).

(a) Calculate and interpret descriptive statistics for both the long-term interest rate and its change. Do the same for the short-term interest rate and its change.
(b) Plot and interpret figures analogous to Figures 9.1 and 9.2 using both of these interest rates and their changes.

Another property of time series data, not usually present in cross-sectional data, is the existence of correlation across observations. The stock price index today, for example, is highly correlated with its value last month.[3] In the jargon of Chapter 8, the variable "stock price" is correlated with the variable "stock price lagged one period". In fact, if we calculate the correlation between the stock price and lagged stock price we obtain 0.999044. Yet, if we calculate the correlation between the **change** in the stock price index and the **change** in the stock price index lagged once, we obtain 0.039. These findings make intuitive sense. Stock markets change only slowly over time; even in bear markets they rarely fall by more than a few percent per month. Consequently, this month's stock price tends to be quite similar to last month's and both are highly correlated. Yet, the return on the stock market is more erratic. This month's and last month's return can be quite different, as reflected in the near-zero correlation between them.

Figures 9.1 and 9.2 and the correlation results discussed in the previous paragraph were calculated using a stock market index. But other financial time series exhibit very similar types of behavior. Y, in other words, tends to exhibit trend behavior and to be highly correlated over time, but ΔY tends to the opposite, i.e. exhibits no trend behavior and is not highly correlated over time. These properties are quite important to regression modeling with time series variables as they relate closely to the issue of nonstationarity. Appropriately, we will spend the rest of this chapter developing formal tools and models for dealing with them.

The autocorrelation function

The correlations discussed above are simple examples of **autocorrelations** (i.e. correlations involving a variable and a lag of itself). The **autocorrelation function** is a common tool used by researchers to understand the properties of a time series. Based on the material in the "Aside on lagged variables" and the "Aside on notation" from Chapter 8, we will use expressions like "the correlation between Y and lagged Y". We denote this as r_1.

Exercise 9.2

The file INTERESTRATES.XLS contains data on a long-term and a short-term interest rate.

(a) For each of these two series individually create an XY-plot between the variable and the variable lagged one period.

(b) For each of these variables, calculate r_1.

(c) First difference each of these variables and repeat (a) and (b). How would you interpret the data you have constructed and the correlations and XY-plots?

In general, we may be interested in the correlation between Y and Y lagged p periods. For instance, our stock market data is observed monthly, so the correlation between Y and Y lagged $p = 12$ periods is the correlation between the stock price now and the stock price a year ago (i.e. a year is 12 months). We will denote this correlation by r_p and refer to it as "the autocorrelation at lag p". The **autocorrelation function** treats r_p as a function of p (i.e. it calculates r_p for $p = 1, \ldots, P$). P is the maximum lag length considered and is typically chosen to be quite large (e.g. $P = 12$ for monthly data). The autocorrelation function is one of the most commonly used tools in univariate time series analysis, precisely because it reveals quite a bit of information about the series.

Aside

1. r_p is the correlation between a variable (say, Y) and Y lagged p periods. In our discussion of r_1 we noted Y_t lagged one period was Y_0, which did not exist. For this reason, we used data from $t = 2, \ldots, T$ to define lagged Y and calculate r_1. An even more extreme form of the problem occurs in the calculation of r_p. Consider creating a new variable W which has observations $W_t = Y_t$ for $t = p + 1, \ldots, T$ and a new variable Z which has observations $Z_t = Y_{t-p}$ for $t = p + 1, \ldots, T$. The correlation between W (i.e. Y) and Z (i.e. Y lagged p periods) is r_p. Note that each of the new variables contains $T - p$ observations. So when we calculate r_p we are implicitly "throwing away" the first p observations. If we considered extremely long lags, we would be calculating autocorrelations with very few observations. In the extreme case, if we set $p = T$ we have no observations left to use. This is a justification for not letting p get too big. The issues raised in this paragraph are very similar to those raised in distributed lag models (see Chapter 8, "Aside on lagged variables").

2. The autocorrelation function involves autocorrelations with different lag lengths. In theory, we can use data from $t = 2, \ldots, T$ to calculate r_1; data from $t = 3, \ldots, T$ to calculate r_2; etc., ending with data from $t = P + 1, \ldots, T$ to calculate r_P. But, note that this means that each autocorrelation is calculated with a different number of data points. For this reason, it is standard practice to select a maximum lag (P) and use data from $t = P + 1, \ldots, T$ for calculating **all** of the autocorrelations.

Example: Stock prices on the NYSE (continued from page 139)

Table 9.1 presents the autocorrelation functions for Y = stock price index and ΔY = the return to the stock price index (using data from NYSE.XLS) using a maximum lag of 12 (i.e. $P = 12$). This information can also be presented graphically by making a bar chart with the lag length on the X-axis and the autocorrelation on the Y-axis, as in Figures 9.3 and 9.4.

A striking feature of Table 9.1 and Figures 9.3 and 9.4 is that autocorrelations tend to be virtually one for stock price variable even in the case of high lag lengths. In contrast, the autocorrelations for the change in the stock price

Table 9.1 Autocorrelation functions.

Lag length (p)	Stock price	Change in stock price
1	0.9990	0.0438
2	0.9979	−0.0338
3	0.9969	0.0066
4	0.9958	0.0297
5	0.9947	0.0925
6	0.9934	−0.0627
7	0.9923	−0.0451
8	0.9912	−0.0625
9	0.9902	−0.0113
10	0.9893	−0.0187
11	0.9885	−0.0119
12	0.9876	0.0308

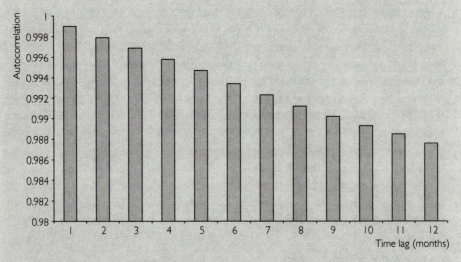

Fig. 9.3 Autocorrelation function for stock prices.

are very small and exhibit a pattern that looks more or less random; the auto-correlations, in other words, are essentially zero. This pattern is common to many financial time series: the series itself has autocorrelations near one, but the change in the series has autocorrelations that are much smaller (often near zero). Below are a few ways of thinking about these autocorrelations:

1. *Y* is highly correlated over time. Even the stock price index a year ago (i.e. $p = 12$) is highly correlated with the stock price index today. ΔY does not exhibit this property. Stock returns this month are essentially uncorrelated with returns in previous months.

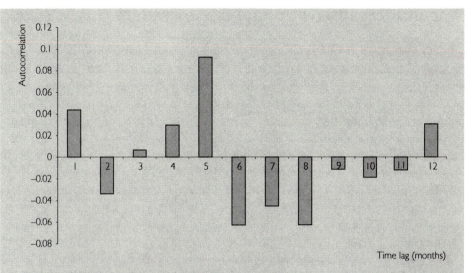

Fig. 9.4 Autocorrelation function for stock returns.

2. If you knew past values of the stock price index, you could make a very good estimate of what the stock price index was this month. However, knowing past values of stock returns will not help you predict the return this month.

3. Y "remembers the past" (i.e. it is highly correlated with past values of itself). This is an example of **long memory** behavior. ΔY does not have this property.

4. Y is a **nonstationary** series while ΔY is **stationary**. We have not formally defined the words "nonstationary" and "stationary", but they are quite important in time series econometrics. We will have more to say about them later, but note for now that the properties of the autocorrelation function for Y are characteristic of nonstationary series.

Exercise 9.3

Use the data on $Y =$ the long-term interest rate given in INTERESTRATES.XLS.

(a) Calculate the autocorrelation function for Y and ΔY with a maximum lag of 4 (i.e. $P = 4$).

(b) Plot these autocorrelation functions in a bar chart.

(c) Interpret the results you have obtained in (a) and (b).

The autoregressive model for univariate time series

The autocorrelation function is a useful tool for summarizing the properties of a time series. Yet, in Chapters 3 and 4, we argued that correlations have their limitations and that regression was therefore a preferable tool. The same reasoning holds here: auto-correlations, in other words, are just correlations, and for this reason it may be desirable to develop more sophisticated models to analyze the relationships between a variable and lags of itself. Many such models have been developed in the statistical literature on univariate time series analysis but the most common model, which can also be interpreted as a regression model, is the so-called **autoregressive model**. As the name suggests, it is a regression model where the explanatory variables are lags of the dependent variable (i.e. "auto" means "self" and hence an autoregression is a regression of a variable on lags of itself). The word "autoregressive" is usually short-ened to "AR".

We begin by discussing the autoregressive model with the explanatory variable being the dependent variable lagged one period. This is called the AR(1) model:

$$Y_t = \alpha + \phi Y_{t-1} + e_t,$$

for $t = 2, \ldots, T$. It looks exactly like the regression model discussed in previous chap-ters,[4] except that the explanatory variable is Y_{t-1}. The value of ϕ in the AR(1) model is closely related to the behavior of the autocorrelation function and to the concept of nonstationarity.

In order to understand the types of behavior characteristic of the AR(1) series, let us artificially simulate three different time series using three different choices for ϕ: $\phi = 0$, 0.8 and 1. All three series have the same values for α (i.e. $\alpha = 0.01$) and the same errors. Figures 9.5, 9.6 and 9.7 provide time series plots of the three data sets.

Note that Figure 9.5 (with $\phi = 0$) exhibits random-type fluctuations around an average of about 0.01 (the value of α). In fact, it is very similar to Figure 9.2, which contains a time series plot of stock returns. Figure 9.7 (with $\phi = 1$) exhibits trend behavior and looks very similar to Figure 9.1, which plots the stock price level. Figure 9.6 (with $\phi = 0.8$) exhibits behavior that is somewhere in-between the random fluc-tuations of Figure 9.5 and the strong trend of Figure 9.7.

Figures 9.5–9.7 illustrate the types of behavior that AR(1) models can capture and show why they are commonly used. For different values of ϕ, these models can allow for the randomly fluctuating behavior typical of growth rates of many financial time series; for the trend behavior typical of the financial series themselves; or for inter-mediate cases between these extremes.

Note also that $\phi = 1$ implies the type of trend behavior we have referred to as non-stationary above, while the other values of ϕ imply stationary behavior. This allows us to provide a formal definition of the concepts of **stationarity** and **nonstation-arity**, at least for the AR(1) model: **For the AR(1) model, we can say that Y is sta-tionary if $|\phi| < 1$ and is nonstationary if $\phi = 1$.** The other possibility, $|\phi| > 1$, is rarely considered in finance. The latter possibility implies that the time series is

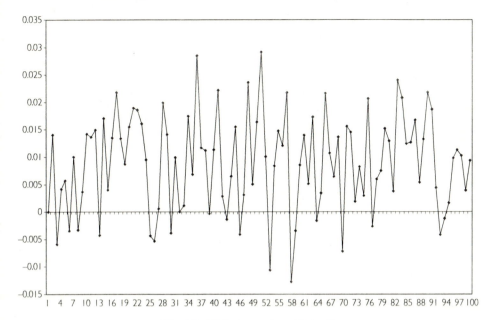

Fig. 9.5 AR(1) time series with $\phi = 0$.

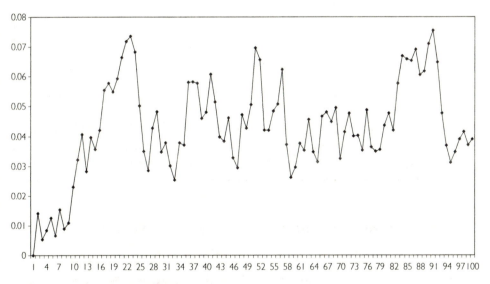

Fig. 9.6 AR(1) time series with $\phi = 0.8$.

exhibiting explosive behavior over time. Since such explosive behavior is only observed in unusual cases, it is of little empirical relevance and we shall not discuss it here. Mathematical intuition for the properties of the AR(1) model and how it relates to the issue of nonstationarity is given in Appendix 9.1.

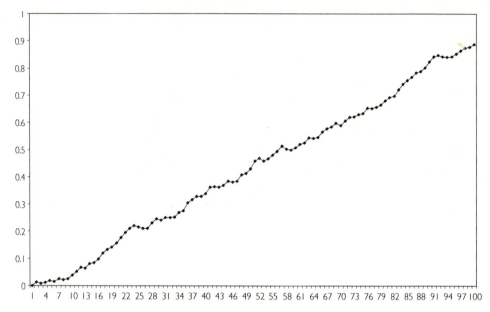

Fig. 9.7 AR(1) time series with $\phi = 1$.

Exercise 9.4

Use the data in files FIG95.XLS, FIG96.XLS and FIG97.XLS, which were used to create Figures 9.5–9.7, respectively.

(a) Calculate the autocorrelation function for each time series using a maximum lag of 4.
(b) Relate your findings in (a) to your answers to Exercise 9.3. Focus in particular on the question of whether the AR(1) model is capable of generating the types of behavior observed in the financial time series.

Nonstationary versus stationary time series

Above we introduced the terms "nonstationary" and "stationary" without providing any formal definition (except for the AR(1) model). As we shall see, the distinction between stationary and nonstationary time series is an extremely important one. To formally define these concepts requires that we get into statistical issues that are beyond the scope of this book. But we provide some general intuition for these concepts below.

Formally, "nonstationary" merely means "anything that is not stationary". Economists usually focus on the one particular type of nonstationarity that seems to be present in many financial time series: **unit root** nonstationarity. We will generalize this concept later, but at this stage it is useful to think of a unit root as implying $\phi = 1$ in the AR(1) model. Following are different ways of thinking about whether a time series variable, Y, is stationary or has a unit root:

1. In the AR(1) model, if $\phi = 1$, then Y has a unit root. If $|\phi| < 1$ then Y is stationary.
2. If Y has a unit root then its autocorrelations will be near one and will not drop much as lag length increases.
3. If Y has a unit root, then it will have a long memory. Stationary time series do not have long memory.
4. If Y has a unit root then the series will exhibit trend behavior (especially if α is non-zero).
5. If Y has a unit root, then ΔY will be stationary. For this reason, series with unit roots are often referred to as **difference stationary** series.

The final point can be seen most clearly by subtracting Y_{t-1} from both sides of the equation in the AR(1) model, yielding:

$$\Delta Y_t = \alpha + \rho Y_{t-1} + e_t,$$

where $\rho = \phi - 1$. Note that, if $\phi = 1$, then $\rho = 0$ and the previous equation can be written solely in terms of ΔY_t, implying that ΔY_t fluctuates randomly around α. For future reference, note that we can test for $\rho = 0$ to see if a series has a unit root. Furthermore, a time series will be stationary if $-1 < \phi < 1$ which is equivalent to $-2 < \rho < 0$. We will refer to this as the **stationarity condition**.

By way of providing more intuition (and jargon!) for the AR(1) model, let us consider the case where $\phi = 1$ (or, equivalently, $\rho = 0$). In this case we can write the AR(1) model as:

$$Y_t = \alpha + Y_{t-1} + e_t.$$

This is referred to as the **random walk** model. More precisely, the random walk model has no intercept (i.e. $\alpha = 0$), while the preceding equation is referred to as a **random walk with drift**. The presence of the intercept allows for changes in variables to be, on average, non-zero. So, for instance, if Y is (the log of) a stock price of a particular company then the random walk with drift model can be written as:

$$Y_t - Y_{t-1} = \alpha + e_t.$$

Since the left-hand of this equation is the stock return (exclusive of dividends), then the model says stock returns are equal to α (e.g. a benchmark return relevant for this company taking into account its risk, etc.) plus a random error.

In the random walk model, since $\phi = 1$, Y has a unit root and is nonstationary. This model is commonly thought to hold for phenomena like stock prices, a point we will elaborate on next.

Example: Market efficiency and the random walk hypothesis

A simple version of the random walk hypothesis is that the price of a stock today is the price of a stock yesterday plus an (unpredictable) error term. Thus the return to holding the stock is unpredictable. If stock returns were predictable, then investors would instantly buy up the stocks expected to rise and sell the stocks expected to fall. The price of the former would instantly rise and the latter would instantly fall to the points where returns were no longer predictable. This is an example of a market efficiency argument: that efficient stock markets should not allow for abnormal profits and should instantly adjust to all available news or information relevant for stock prices. There is a huge literature on market efficiency (with different researchers using slightly different definitions of this concept). However, the market efficiency argument outlined in this paragraph is commonly used to argue that stock prices should behave as a random walk with drift and this hypothesis is investigated in many research papers.

Example: Stock prices on the NYSE (continued from page 143)

The AR(1) model is a regression model. Accordingly, we can use OLS to regress the variable Y on lagged Y.[5] If we do this, we find $\hat{\alpha} = 0.00773$ and $\hat{\phi} = 0.99986$. Since the OLS estimate, $\hat{\phi}$, and the true value of the AR(1) coefficient, ϕ, will rarely if ever be identical, it is quite possible that $\phi = 1$ since the OLS estimate is extremely close to one. So the random walk model is plausible for this data set.

If we regress ΔY_t on Y_{t-1}, we obtain an OLS estimate of ρ which is -0.00014. Note that we are finding $\hat{\rho} = \hat{\phi} - 1$, just as we would expect.

Exercise 9.5

Use the data in files FIG95.XLS, FIG96.XLS and FIG97.XLS, which were used to create Figures 9.5–9.7, respectively.

(a) Calculate OLS estimates of ρ and ϕ in the two variants of the AR(1) model.
(b) Relate your results in (a) to the question of whether any of the series contain a unit root.
(c) Repeat (a) and (b) using the short-term interest rate data in INTERESTRATES.XLS.

Extensions of the AR(1) model

We have argued above that the AR(1) model can be interpreted as a simple regression model where last period's Y is the explanatory variable. However, it is possible that more lags of Y should be included as explanatory variables. This can be done by extending the AR(1) model to the autoregressive of order p, AR(p), model:

$$Y_t = \alpha + \phi_1 Y_{t-1} + \ldots + \phi_p Y_{t-p} + e_t,$$

for $t = p + 1, \ldots, T$. We will not discuss the properties of this model, other than to note that they are similar to the AR(1) model but are more general in nature. That is, this model can generate the trend behavior typical of financial time series and the randomly fluctuating behavior typical of their growth rates.

In discussing unit root behavior it is convenient to subtract Y_{t-1} from both sides of the previous equation. With some rearranging[6] we obtain:

$$\Delta Y_t = \alpha + \rho Y_{t-1} + \gamma_1 \Delta Y_{t-1} + \ldots + \gamma_{p-1} \Delta Y_{t-p+1} + e_t,$$

where the coefficients in this regression, $\rho, \gamma_1, \ldots, \gamma_{p-1}$ are simple functions of ϕ_1, $\ldots, \phi_p$. For instance, $\rho = \phi_1 + \ldots + \phi_p - 1$. Note that this is identical to the AR(p) model, but is just written differently. Hence we refer to both previous equations as AR(p) models. In case you are wondering where the Y_{t-p} term from the first equation went to in the second, note that it appears in the second equation in the ΔY_{t-p+1} term (i.e. $\Delta Y_{t-p+1} = Y_{t-p+1} - Y_{t-p}$). Note also that both variants have the same number of coefficients, $p + 1$ (i.e. the first variant has $\alpha, \phi_1, \ldots, \phi_p$ while the second variant has $\alpha, \rho, \gamma_1, \ldots, \gamma_{p-1}$). However, in the second variant the AR(p) model has last coefficient γ_{p-1}. Don't let this confuse you, it is just a consequence of the way we have rearranged the coefficients in the original specification.

The key points to note here are that the above equation is still in the form of a regression model; and $\rho = 0$ implies that the AR(p) time series Y contains a unit root; if $-2 < \rho < 0$, then the series is stationary. Looking at the previous equation with $\rho = 0$ clarifies an important way of thinking about unit root series which we have highlighted previously: if a time series contains a unit root then a regression model involving only ΔY is appropriate (i.e. if $\rho = 0$ then the term Y_{t-1} will drop out of the equation and only terms involving ΔY or its lags appear in the regression). It is common jargon to say that "if a unit root is present, then the data can be differenced to induce stationarity".

As we will discuss in the next chapter, with the exception of a case called cointegration, we do not want to include unit root variables in regression models. This suggests that, if a unit root in Y is present, we will want to difference it and use ΔY. In order to do so, we must know first if Y has a unit root. In the past, we have emphasized that unit root series exhibit trend behavior. Does this mean that we can simply examine time series plots of Y for such trending to determine if it indeed has a unit root? The answer is no. To explain why, let us introduce another model.

We showed previously that many financial time series contain trends and that AR models with unit roots also imply trend behavior. However, there are other models that also imply trend behavior. Imagine that Figure 9.1 (or Figure 9.7) is an XY-plot where the X-axis is labeled time, and that we want to build a regression model using this data. You might be tempted to fit the following regression line:

$$Y_t = \alpha + \delta t + e_t,$$

where the coefficient on the explanatory variable, time, is labeled δ to distinguish it from the ϕ in the AR(1) model. Note that you can interpret the previous regression as involving the variable Y and another variable with observations 1, 2, 3, 4, ..., T. This is another regression model which yields trend behavior. To introduce some jargon, the term δt is referred to as a **deterministic trend** since it is an exact (i.e. deterministic) function of time. In contrast, unit root series contain a so-called **stochastic trend** (justification for the term "stochastic trend" is given in Appendix 9.1).

We can even combine this model with the AR(1) model to obtain:

$$Y_t = \alpha + \phi Y_{t-1} + \delta t + e_t.$$

Figure 9.8 is a time series plot of artificial data generated from the previous model with $\alpha = 0$, $\phi = 0.2$ and $\delta = 0.01$. Note that this series is stationary since $|\phi| < 1$. Yet, Figure 9.8 looks much like Figure 9.7 (or Figure 9.1). Stationary models with a deterministic trend can yield time series plots that closely resemble those from non-

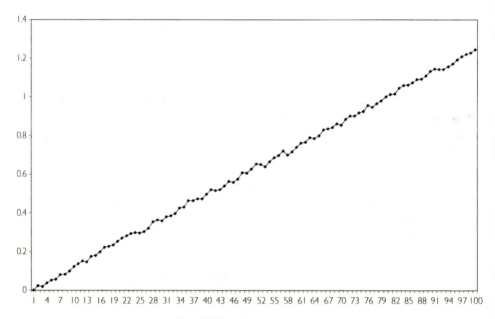

Fig. 9.8 Trend stationary series.

stationary models having a stochastic trend. Thus, you should remember that **look-ing at time series plots alone is not enough to tell whether a series has a unit root**.

The discussion in the previous paragraph motivates jargon that we will use and introduce in the context of the following summary:

1. The **nonstationary** time series variables on which we focus are those containing a **unit root**. These series contain a **stochastic trend**. But if we difference these time series, the resulting time series will be stationary. For this reason, they are also called **difference stationary**.
2. The **stationary** time series on which we focus have $-2 < \rho < 0$ in the AR(p) model. However, these series can exhibit trend behavior through the incorporation of a **deterministic trend**. In this case, they are referred to as **trend stationary**.

Exercise 9.6

The data in FIG98.XLS was used to create Figure 9.8.

(a) Calculate the autocorrelation function for this trend stationary series.
(b) In light of your answer to a), discuss whether the autocorrelation function is a useful tool for testing for a unit root.

If we add a deterministic trend to the AR(p) model, we obtain a very general model that is commonly used in univariate time series analysis:

$$\Delta Y_t = \alpha + \rho Y_{t-1} + \gamma_1 \Delta Y_{t-1} + \ldots + \gamma_{p-1} \Delta Y_{t-p+1} + \delta t + e_t.$$

We refer to the above as the **AR(p) with deterministic trend model** and use it later. You may wonder why we don't just use the original AR(p) specification introduced at the beginning of this section (i.e. the one where the explanatory variables are Y_{t-1}, $\ldots$, Y_{t-p}). There are two reasons. First, we are going to test for a unit root. With the present specification, this is simply a test of $\rho = 0$. Testing for whether regression coefficients are zero is a topic which we have learned previously (refer to Chapter 5). With the original AR(p) model, testing for a unit root is more complicated. Second, $Y_{t-1}, Y_{t-2}, \ldots, Y_{t-p}$ are often highly correlated with each other (see the autocorrelation function in Figure 9.3). If we were to use them as explanatory variables in our regression we might run into serious multicollinearity problems (see Chapter 6). However, in the present model we use $Y_{t-1}, \Delta Y_{t-1}, \ldots, \Delta Y_{t-p+1}$ as explanatory variables, which tend not to be highly correlated (see Figure 9.4), thereby avoiding the problem.

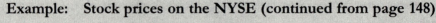

Example: Stock prices on the NYSE (continued from page 148)

The following table contains output from an OLS regression of ΔY_t on Y_{t-1}, ΔY_{t-1}, ΔY_{t-2}, ΔY_{t-3} and a deterministic time trend, created by using the data on stock prices from NYSE.XLS. In other words, it provides regression output for the AR(4) with deterministic trend model. We suspect that stock prices may contain a unit root, a supposition supported somewhat by the table. In particular, a unit root is present if ρ (the coefficient on Y_{t-1}) is zero. As we can see, the estimate of ρ is indeed very small (i.e. $\hat{\rho} = -0.016$).

Table 9.2　AR(4) with deterministic trend model.

	Coefficient	Standard error	t-stat	P-value	Lower 95%	Upper 95%
Intercept	0.082	0.039	2.074	0.039	0.004	0.161
Y_{t-1}	−0.016	0.008	−1.942	0.053	−0.033	0.0002
ΔY_{t-1}	0.051	0.044	1.169	0.243	−0.035	0.138
ΔY_{t-2}	−0.027	0.044	−0.623	0.534	−0.114	0.059
ΔY_{t-3}	0.015	0.044	0.344	0.731	−0.071	0.101
time	1E − 4	5E − 5	1.979	0.048	7E − 7	0.0002

Testing in the AR(p) with deterministic trend model

In Chapters 5 and 6, we described how to test whether regression coefficients were equal to zero. These techniques can be used in the AR(p) with deterministic trend model (i.e. if you wish to omit explanatory variables whose coefficients are not significantly different from zero). In particular, testing is usually done to help choose lag length (p) and to decide whether the series has a unit root. In fact, it is common to first test to select lag length (using hypothesis tests as described in Chapter 8), and then test for a unit root.

However, there is one important complication that occurs in the AR(p) model that was not present in earlier chapters. To understand it, let us divide the coefficients in the model into two groups: (1) α, γ_1, $\ldots$, γ_{p-1}, and δ, and (2) ρ. In other words, we consider hypothesis tests involving ρ separately from those involving the other coefficients.

Testing involving α, γ_1, $\ldots$, γ_{p-1}, and δ

Many sophisticated statistical criteria and testing methods exist to determine the appropriate lag length in an AR(p) model. Nonetheless, simply looking at the t-statistics or P-values in regression outputs can be quite informative. For instance, an examination of Table 9.2 reveals that the P-values associated with the coefficients on the lagged ΔY terms are insignificant, and that they may be deleted from the regression (i.e. the P-values are greater than 0.05). Alternatively, a more common route is to proceed sequentially, as we did in Chapter 8; that is, to choose a maximum lag length, p_{max}, and then sequentially drop lag lengths if the relevant coefficients are insignificant.

More specifically, begin with an AR(p_{max}). If the p_{max}th lag is insignificant, we reduce the model to an AR($p_{max} - 1$). If the ($p_{max} - 1$)th lag is insignificant in the AR($p_{max} - 1$) then drop it and use an AR($p_{max} - 2$), etc. Generally, you should start with a fairly large choice for p_{max}.

In the AR(p) with deterministic trend model we also have to worry about testing whether $\delta = 0$. This can be accomplished in the standard way by checking whether its P-value is less than the level of significance (e.g. 0.05). This test can be done at any stage, but it is common to carry it out after following the sequential procedure for choosing p.

A short summary of this testing strategy is outlined below:

Step 1. Choose the maximum lag length, p_{max}, that seems reasonable to you.

Step 2. Estimate using OLS the AR(p_{max}) with deterministic trend model:

$$\Delta Y_t = \alpha + \rho Y_{t-1} + \gamma_1 \Delta Y_{t-1} + \ldots + \gamma_{pmax-1} \Delta Y_{t-pmax+1} + \delta t + e_t.$$

If the P-value for testing $\gamma_{pmax-1} = 0$ is less than the significance level you choose (e.g. 0.05) then go to Step 5, using p_{max} as lag length. Otherwise go on to the next step.

Step 3. Estimate the AR($p_{max} - 1$) model:

$$\Delta Y_t = \alpha + \rho Y_{t-1} + \gamma_1 \Delta Y_{t-1} + \ldots + \gamma_{pmax-2} \Delta Y_{t-pmax+2} + \delta t + e_t.$$

If the P-value for testing $\gamma_{pmax-2} = 0$ is less than the significance level you choose (e.g. 0.05) then go to Step 5, using $p_{max} - 1$ as lag length. Otherwise go on to the next step.

Step 4. Repeatedly estimate lower order AR models until you find an AR(p) model where γ_{p-1} is statistically significant (or you run out of lags).

Step 5. Now test for whether the deterministic trend should be omitted; that is, if the P-value for testing $\delta = 0$ is greater than the significance level you choose then drop the deterministic trend variable.

Example: Stock prices on the NYSE (continued from page 152)

If we carry out the preceding strategy on the NYSE stock price data, beginning with $p_{max} = 4$, the model reduces to:

$$\Delta Y_t = \alpha + \rho Y_{t-1} + e_t.$$

That is, we first estimated an AR(4) with deterministic trend (see Table 9.2) and found the coefficient on ΔY_{t-3} to be insignificant. Accordingly, we estimated an AR(3) with deterministic trend and found the coefficient on ΔY_{t-2} to be insignificant. We then dropped the latter variable and ran an AR(2), etc. Eventually, after finding the deterministic trend to be insignificant, we settled on the AR(1) model. OLS estimation results for this model are given in Table 9.3.

Table 9.3   AR(1) model.

	Coefficient	Standard error	*t*-stat	P-value	Lower 95%	Upper 95%
Intercept	0.00763	0.0123	0.6188	0.5363	−0.0166	0.0318
Y_{t-1}	−0.00012	0.0019	−0.0631	0.9497	−0.0039	−0.0037

Table 9.3 shows the table of results you might report in a paper or empirical project, including a brief but coherent explanation of the strategy that you used to arrive at this final specification.

These results lead us to the next, most important, testing question: does Y contain a unit root? Remember that, if $\rho = 0$, then Y contains a unit root. In this case, the series must be differenced in the regression model (i.e. it is difference stationary). You may think that you can simply test $\rho = 0$ in the same manner as you tested the significance of the other coefficients. For instance, you might think that by comparing the P-value to a significance level (e.g. 0.05), you can test for whether $\rho = 0$. **SUCH A STRATEGY IS INCORRECT!** In hypothesis testing, ρ is different from other coefficients and, thus, we must treat it differently.

Testing involving ρ

To fully understand why you cannot carry out a unit root test of $\rho = 0$ in the same manner as we would test other coefficients requires that you have knowledge of statistics beyond that covered in this book. Suffice it to note here that most regression packages like Excel implicitly assume that all of the variables in the model are stationary when they calculate P-values. If the explanatory variable Y_{t-1} is nonstationary, its P-value will be incorrect. A correct way of testing for a unit root has been developed by two statisticians named Dickey and Fuller and is known as the **Dickey–Fuller test**.[7] They recommend using the *t*-statistic for testing $\rho = 0$, but correcting the P-value.

We can motivate the Dickey–Fuller test in terms of the following: in Chapter 5, we said that testing could be done by comparing a test statistic (here the *t*-stat) to a critical value to determine whether the former was either "small" (in which case the hypothesis was accepted) or "large" (in which case the hypothesis was rejected). In the standard (stationary) case, the critical values are taken from statistical tables of the Student-*t* distribution. Dickey and Fuller demonstrated that in the unit root case, this is incorrect. They calculated the correct statistical tables from which to take critical values.

The previous paragraphs were meant to motivate why the standard testing procedure was incorrect. Admittedly, they are not very helpful in telling you what to do in practice. If you are going to work extensively with time series data, it is worthwhile to either:

1. Use a computer software package that is more suitable for time series analysis than Excel. Packages such as Stata, E-views, MicroFit or SHAZAM will automatically provide you with correct critical values or P-values for your unit root test. As before, you will reject the unit root if the P-value is less than 0.05 or if the *t*-stat is greater than the critical value (in an absolute value sense).
2. Read further in time series econometrics and learn how to use the Dickey–Fuller statistical tables.[8]

However, a rough rule of a thumb can be used that will not lead you too far wrong if your number of observations is moderately large (e.g. $T > 50$). This approximate rule is given in the following strategy for testing for a unit root:

1. Use the strategy outlined in Steps 1 to 5 above to estimate the AR(p) with deterministic trend model. Record the *t*-stat corresponding to ρ (i.e. the *t*-stat for the coefficient on Y_{t-1}).
2. If the final version of your model **includes a deterministic trend**, the Dickey–Fuller critical value is approximately -3.45. If the *t*-stat on ρ is more negative than -3.45, reject the unit root hypothesis and conclude that the series is stationary. Otherwise, conclude that the series has a unit root.
3. If the final version of your model **does not include a deterministic trend**, the Dickey–Fuller critical value is approximately -2.89. If the *t*-stat on ρ is more negative than -2.89, reject the unit root hypothesis and conclude that the series is stationary. Otherwise, conclude that the series has a unit root.[9]

In the previous example, the final version of the AR(p) model did not include a deterministic trend. The *t*-stat on ρ is -0.063, which is **not** more negative than -2.89. Hence we can **accept** the hypothesis that NYSE stock prices contain a unit root and are, in fact, a random walk. Be careful using this crude rule of thumb when your *t*-stat is close to the critical values listed here.

Example: Long-term interest rates

If we carry out the preceding strategy on the long-term interest rate data (from INTERESTRATES.XLS), beginning with $p_{max} = 4$ and sequentially deleting insignificant lagged variables, we end up with an AR(1) model:

$$\Delta Y_t = \alpha + \rho Y_{t-1} + e_t.$$

OLS estimation results for this model are given in Table 9.4.

We are interested in testing for a unit root and this occurs if $\rho = 0$. A naïve researcher who did not know about the Dickey–Fuller test would incorrectly say: "Since the P-value for ρ (which is 0.035) is less than 0.05, we can conclude that ρ is significant. Thus, the long-term interest rate variable does not contain a unit root". However, a researcher who knew about the Dickey–Fuller test would say: "The final version of the AR(p) model I used did not include a deterministic trend. Hence, I must use the Dickey–Fuller critical value of −2.89. The t-stat on ρ is −2.13, which is *not* more negative than −2.89. Hence we can *accept* the hypothesis that long-term interest rates contain a unit root".

Table 9.4   AR(1) model.

	Coefficient	Standard error	t-stat	P-value	Lower 95%	Upper 95%
Intercept	0.039	0.014	2.682	0.008	0.010	0.067
Y_{t-1}	−0.004	0.002	−2.130	0.035	−0.0077	−0.0003

Exercise 9.7

In this chapter we have recommended a strategy according to which you begin with an AR(p) with deterministic trend model, choose lag length (p), decide whether the deterministic trend should be included or excluded, and then test for a unit root. Carry out this strategy using the following series:

(a) Those in FIG95.XLS and FIG96.XLS (which you know are stationary).
(b) That in FIG97.XLS (which you know has a unit root).
(c) That in FIG98.XLS (which is trend stationary, but exhibits strong trending behavior).
(d) The short term interest rate variable in INTERESTRATES.XLS.

Exercise 9.8

In Exercise 9.7, we tested for unit roots in many series. We noted that if a time series has one unit root, then its difference will be stationary. Verify that this is true for the series having unit roots in Exercise 9.7. That is, discuss how you would test to see if the *change* in the series has a unit root. Then carry out this test.

Some words of warning about unit root testing: The Dickey–Fuller test exhibits what statisticians refer to as **low power**. In other words, the test can make the mistake of finding a unit root even when none exists. Intuitively, trend stationary series can look a lot like unit root series (compare Figures 9.7 and 9.8) and it can be quite hard to tell them apart. Furthermore, other kinds of time series models can also appear to exhibit unit root behavior, when in actuality they do not have unit roots. A prime example is the time series model characterized by abrupt changes or breaks. These **structural breaks** can occur in time series models, and can be precipitated by events such as wars or crises in supply (e.g. the OPEC oil embargo). Stock prices can exhibit structural breaks due to market crashes; and commodity prices, due to droughts and other natural disasters. All in all, structural breaks are potentially a worry for many types of time series data and some caution needs to be taken when interpreting the results of Dickey–Fuller tests. There are many other tests for a unit root. To explain these would require a long technical digression which would distract from the main focus of this book. However, depending on which software package you have available, a little bit of extra study should enable you to use them in practice. Remember the structure of any hypothesis testing procedure involves your knowing the hypothesis being tested (here the unit root hypothesis) as well as a P-value (or a test statistic with critical value to compare it to). Many software packages provide these automatically. For instance, Stata allows you to do another popular unit root test called the Phillips–Perron test (as well as others) in this manner.

Exercise 9.9

This exercise could actually be interpreted as an empirical project and could be short or long, depending on what the student is interested in achieving. The book *Nonlinear Time Series Models in Empirical Finance* by Philip Hans Franses and Dick van Dijk (Cambridge University Press) is one you may use in your future studies. It uses more sophisticated tools in statistics than the present book, so at this stage you might find it difficult. However, it does have a website containing a rich collection of data sets from several countries on stock prices and exchange rates which you can download (see http://www.few.eur.nl/few/

people/djvandijk/nltsmef/nltsmef.htm). In particular, stock price indices from Amsterdam (EOE), Frankfurt (DAX), Hong Kong (Hang Seng), London (FTSE100), New York (S&P500), Paris (CAC40), Singapore (Singapore All Shares) and Tokyo (Nikkei) are provided. The exchange rates are the Australian dollar, British pound, Canadian dollar, German DeutschMark, Dutch guilder, French franc, Japanese yen and the Swiss franc, all expressed as number of units of the foreign currency per US dollar. The sample period for the stock indexes runs from 6 January 1986 until 31 December 1997, whereas for the exchange rates the sample covers the period from 2 January 1980 until 31 December 1997. Investigate the random walk hypothesis using this data. Do stock prices appear to follow a random walk in every country? Do exchange rates?

Note that this data is available at a daily frequency. You may want to work with the data at this frequency or at a weekly (e.g. by just using data every Wednesday) or monthly frequency (e.g. by just using data from the last day of each month). Do your results for the unit root tests depend on whether you use daily, weekly or monthly data?

Chapter summary

1. Many financial time series exhibit trend behavior, while their differences do not exhibit such behavior.
2. The autocorrelation function is a common tool for summarizing the relationship between a variable and lags of itself.
3. Autoregressive models are regression models used for working with time series variables. Such models can be written in two ways: one with Y_t as the dependent variable, the other with ΔY_t as the dependent variable.
4. The distinction between stationary and nonstationary models is a crucial one.
5. Series with unit roots are the most common type of nonstationary series considered in financial research.
6. If Y_t has a unit root then the AR(p) model with ΔY_t as the dependent variable can be estimated using OLS. Standard statistical results hold for all coefficients except the coefficient on Y_{t-1}.[10]
7. The Dickey–Fuller test is a test for the presence of a unit root. It involves testing whether the coefficient on Y_{t-1} is equal to zero (in the AR(p) model with ΔY_t being the dependent variable). Software packages such as Excel do not print out the correct P-value for this test.

Appendix 9.1: Mathematical intuition for the AR(1) model

Mathematical insight into the properties of the AR(1) model can be gained by writing it in a different way. For simplicity, we will set $\alpha = 0$ in order to focus on the role that lagged Y plays. Note that the AR(1) model will hold at any point in time so we can lag the whole AR(1) equation given in the body of the chapter and write:

$$Y_{t-1} = \phi Y_{t-2} + e_{t-1}.$$

If we substitute this expression for Y_{t-1} into the original AR(1) model we obtain:

$$Y_t = \phi^2 Y_{t-2} + e_t + \phi e_{t-1}.$$

Note that the previous expression depends on Y_{t-2}, but we can write:

$$Y_{t-2} = \phi Y_{t-3} + e_{t-2},$$

and substitute this expression for Y_{t-2} in the other equation. If this procedure is repeated we end up with an alternative expression for the AR(1) model:

$$Y_t = \phi^{t-1} Y_1 + \sum_{j=0}^{t-2} \phi^j e_{t-j}.$$

This expression looks complicated, but we can consider two special cases as a means of understanding its implications. In the first of these we assume $\phi = 1$ and the previous equation reduces to:

$$Y_t = Y_1 + \sum_{j=0}^{t-2} e_{t-j}.$$

The important point to note about the two terms on the right hand side of the previous equation is that they illustrate a long memory property; the value of the time series starts at Y_1, which always enters the expression for Y_t, even if t becomes very large. That is, the time series "never forgets" where it started from. It also "never forgets" past errors (e.g. e_1 always enters the above formula for Y_t even if t gets very large). It can be shown that the trending behavior of this model arises as a result of the second term, which says that current Y contains the sum of all past errors. Statisticians view these errors as random or "stochastic" and this model is often referred to as containing a **stochastic trend**. This is a key property of nonstationary series.

A second special case stands in contrast to the properties described above. If we suppose $|\phi| < 1$, we can see that ϕ^{t-1} will be decreasing as t increases (e.g. if $\phi = 0.5$, then $\phi^2 = 0.25$, $\phi^{10} = 0.001$ and $\phi^{100} = 7.89 \times 10^{-31}$, etc.). The influence of Y_1 and past errors on Y_t will gradually lessen as t increases and Y slowly "forgets the past". Y will not exhibit the long memory property we observed for the case where $\phi = 1$. This is a key property of stationary series.

Endnotes

1. Details about logarithms are discussed in Chapters 1, 2 and 4 (see especially the discussion on Nonlinearity in Regression). This footnote is intended to refresh your memory of this material. It is common to take the natural logarithm of the time series if it seems to be growing over time. If a series, Y, is growing at a roughly constant rate, then the time series plot of $\ln(Y)$ will approximate a straight line. In this common case, $\ln(Y)$ will generally be well-behaved. Note also that in regressions of logged variables, the coefficients can be interpreted as elasticities. It can also be shown that $\ln(Y_t) - \ln(Y_{t-1})$ is approximately equal to the percentage change in Y between periods $t - 1$ and t.

   For all these reasons, it is often convenient to work with logged series. Note that this log transformation is so common that many reports and papers will initially explain that the variables are logged, but thereafter drop the explicit mentioning of the log transformation. For instance, an author might refer to "the natural log of wealth" as "wealth" for brevity. We will follow this tradition in the examples in this book.

2. Since Y_0 is not known, ΔY_t runs from $t = 2, \ldots, T$ rather than from $t = 1, \ldots, T$. We focus on the empirically useful case of first-differencing but we can define higher orders of differencing. For instance, the second difference of Y_t is defined as: $\Delta^2 Y_t = \Delta Y_t - \Delta Y_{t-1}$.

3. Put another way, if you knew what the stock price index was today (let's say, in January it is 2,000), you could make a pretty good guess about roughly what it would be next month. That is, it might go up or down a couple percentage points to 2,100 or 1,900, but it is highly unlikely to be, say, 100 or 5,000. This ability to predict well is evidence of high correlation.

4. It is common practice to use Greek letters to indicate coefficients in regression models. We can, of course, use any Greek symbol we want to denote the slope coefficient in a regression. Here we have called it ϕ rather than β. We will reserve β (perhaps with a subscript) to indicate coefficients relating to the explanatory variable X.

5. Some statistical problems arise with OLS estimation of this model, if the model is nonstationary or nearly so (i.e. ϕ is close to one or, equivalently, ρ is close to zero). Nevertheless, OLS is still a very common estimation method for AR models (especially if ϕ is not that close to 1), so you will probably not go far wrong through sticking with OLS when working with AR models. If you take courses in financial econometrics or time series statistics in the future, you will undoubtedly learn about other estimators.

6. Each step in the derivation of this equation involves only simple algebra (e.g. subtracting the same thing from both sides of the equation, etc.). However, there are many steps involved and the derivation of this equation is a bit messy.

7. Some authors use the term "Dickey–Fuller test" for testing for $\rho = 0$ in the AR(1) model and use the term "Augmented Dickey–Fuller test" for testing in the AR(p) model (i.e. the basic unit root test is "augmented" with extra lags).

8. *Undergraduate Econometrics* by Carter Hill, William Griffiths and George Judge (second edition, John Wiley & Sons, Ltd, 2000), chapter 16 is a good place to start.

9. Formally, −3.45 and −2.89 are the critical values for $T = 100$ using a 5% level of significance. Critical values for values of T between 50 and infinity are within 0.05 of these values.

10. Formally, standard hypothesis tests can be conducted on coefficients on stationary variables.

Regression with time series variables

In regression analysis, researchers are typically interested in measuring the effect of an explanatory variable or variables on a dependent variable. As mentioned in Chapter 8, this goal is complicated when the researcher uses time series data since an explanatory variable may influence a dependent variable with a time lag. This often necessitates the inclusion of lags of the explanatory variable in the regression. Furthermore, as discussed in Chapter 9, the dependent variable may be correlated with lags of itself, suggesting that lags of the dependent variable should also be included in the regression.

As we shall see, there are also several theories in finance which imply such a regression model. This is not a book which derives financial theories to motivate our regression models. However, to give you a flavor of the kind of things financial researchers do with time series data, it is useful briefly to mention a few classic articles in finance and the time series data sets they use. An influential paper by Campbell and Ahmer called "What moves the stock and bond markets? A variance decomposition for long-term asset returns"[1] used American data on excess stock returns, various interest rates, the yield spread (defined using the difference between long- and short-term interest rates) and the dividend-price ratio. Another influential paper by Lettau and Ludvigson called "Consumption, aggregate wealth and expected stock returns"[2] investigated an important relationship in financial economics using data on excess stock returns, asset wealth, labor income and consumption. In Chapter 8, we presented an example involving the prediction of long-run stock returns using the dividend-price ratio. Such regressions grew out of influential work such as "Stock prices, earnings and expected dividends" by Campbell and Shiller.[3] Examples such as these abound in finance. Exact details about why these researchers chose the particular variables they did is not important for present purposes (indeed you need not even worry about precisely what all these variables are). The key thing to note is that important financial theories involve several time series variables and imply models such as the ones discussed in this chapter and the next.

These considerations motivate the commonly used autoregressive distributed lag (or ADL) model:

$$Y_t = \alpha + \delta t + \phi_1 Y_{t-1} + \ldots + \phi_p Y_{t-p} + \beta_0 X_t + \beta_1 X_{t-1} + \ldots + \beta_q X_{t-q} + e_t.$$

In this model, the dependent variable, Y, depends on p lags of itself, the current value of an explanatory variable, X, as well as q lags of X. The model also allows for a deterministic trend (t). Since the model contains p lags of Y and q lags of X we denote it by ADL(p, q).[4] In this chapter, we focus on the case where there is only one explanatory variable, X. Note, however, that we could equally allow for many explanatory variables in the analysis.

Estimation and interpretation of the ADL(p, q) model depend on whether the series, X and Y, are stationary or not. We consider these two cases separately here. Note though, that we assume throughout that X and Y have the same stationarity properties; that is, that they either must **both** be stationary or **both** have a unit root. Intuitively, regression analysis involves using X to explain Y. If X's properties differ from Y's it becomes difficult for X to explain Y. For instance, it is hard for a stationary series to explain the stochastic trend variation in a unit root series. In practice this means that, before running any time series regression, you should examine the univariate properties of the variables you plan to use. In particular, you should carry out unit root tests along the lines described in Chapter 9 for every variable in your analysis.

Time series regression when *X* and *Y* are stationary

When X and Y are stationary, OLS estimation of the ADL(p, q) regression model can be carried out in the standard way described in Chapters 4–8. Testing for the significance of variables can be done using the *t*-stats and P-values provided by computer packages like Excel. Such tests can in turn be used to select p and q, the number of lags of the dependent and explanatory variables, respectively. You should note, however, that the verbal interpretation of results is somewhat different from the standard case, as elaborated below.

In the case of the AR(p) model in Chapter 9, it proved convenient, both for OLS estimation and interpretation of results, for us to rewrite the model with ΔY as the dependent variable. Similar considerations hold for the ADL(p, q), which can be rewritten as:

(handwritten: time) *(handwritten: Some lag max of Y)*

$$\Delta Y_t = \alpha + \delta t + \rho Y_{t-1} + \gamma_1 \Delta Y_{t-1} + \ldots + \gamma_{p-1} \Delta Y_{t-p+1}$$
$$+ \theta X_t + \omega_1 \Delta X_t + \ldots + \omega_q \Delta X_{t-q+1} + e_t.$$

(handwritten: Multiplier Coefficients) *(handwritten: Some lag max of X)*

It should be emphasized that this model is the same as that in the original form of the ADL(p, q); it has merely undergone a few algebraic manipulations. Just as we had two different variants of the AR(p) model in Chapter 9, we now have two variants of the ADL(p, q) model. As before, we use new Greek letters for the coefficients in the regression to distinguish them from those in the original variant of the ADL(p, q) model.[5] This model may look complicated, but it is still nevertheless just a regression model. That is, no new mathematical techniques are required for this model, which is, after all, still based on the simple equation of a straight line.

As discussed in Chapter 9, financial time series are often highly correlated with their lags. This implies that the original form of the ADL model frequently runs into multicollinearity problems. With the rewritten form we will typically not encounter such problems. Most importantly, as we shall see, it has a further benefit, one that lies in the interpretation of the coefficients. For these reasons we will work mainly with this second variant of the ADL(p, q) model.

In Chapter 6, we discussed how to interpret regression coefficients, placing special emphasis on *ceteris paribus* conditions. Recall that we made statements of the form: "The coefficient measures the influence of lot size on the sales price of a house, *ceteris paribus*". In the ADL(p, q) model, such an interpretation can still be made, but it is not that commonly done. How then can we interpret the coefficients in the ADL model? In economics, a common way is through the concept of a **multiplier**. The use of multipliers is not that common in finance. However, we introduce the concept anyway since it relates to important concepts we will discuss later.

It is common to focus on the **long run** or **total multiplier**, which is what we will do here. To motivate this measure, suppose that X and Y are in an equilibrium or steady state, i.e. are not changing over time. All of a sudden, X changes by one unit, affecting Y, which starts to change, eventually settling down in the long run to a new equilibrium value. The difference between the old and new equilibrium values for Y can be interpreted as the long run effect of X on Y and is the long run multiplier. This multiplier is often of great interest for policymakers who want to know the eventual effects of their policy changes in various areas.

It is worth stressing that the long run multiplier measures the effect of a **permanent** change in X. That is, the story in the previous paragraph had X being at some value, then X changed permanently to a new level one unit higher than the original value. The long run multiplier measures the effect of this sort of change. In some cases, you might be interested in the effect of a temporary change in X (i.e. X starts at some original level, then increases by one unit for one period before going back to the original level the next). The long run multiplier does not measure the effect of this type of change. We can use the traditional "marginal effect" interpretation of regression coefficients for such temporary changes. The example in Chapter 8, which discussed the effect of news on the stock market, illustrates some ways of reporting the effect of a temporary change in the explanatory variable (e.g. there we were interested in the effect of news in one particular month on market capitalization. We did not discuss the effect of increasing news relating to the stock price of the company permanently as not making sense in that example).

It can be shown, (although we will not prove it here),[6] that the long run multiplier for the ADL(p, q) model is:

$$-\frac{\theta}{\rho}.$$

In other words, only the coefficients on X_t and Y_{t-1} in the rewritten ADL model matter for long run behavior. This means that we can easily obtain an estimate of the long run multiplier.

It is worth stressing that we are assuming X and Y are stationary. In Chapter 9, we discussed how $\rho = 0$ in the AR(p) model implied the existence of a unit root. The ADL model is not the same as the AR model, but to provide some rough intuition, note that if $\rho = 0$ then the long run multiplier is infinite. In fact, it can be shown that for the model to be **stable**, then we must have $\rho < 0$.[7] In practice, if X and Y are stationary, this condition will be satisfied.

Example: The effect of financial liberalization on economic growth

Researchers in the field of international finance and development are interested in whether financial factors can play an important role in encouraging growth in a developing country. The purpose of this example is to investigate this issue empirically using time series data from a single country. Data set LIBERAL.XLS contains data from Country A for 98 quarters on GDP growth and a variable reflecting financial liberalization: the expansion of the stock market. In particular, the dependent and explanatory variables are:

- Y = the percentage change in GDP.
- X = the percentage change in total stock market capitalization.

The mean of these two variables is 0.30% and 0.01% per quarter, indicating that stock markets in Country A have not expanded by much **on average**. Note, however, that this average hides wide variation. In some quarters market capitalization increased considerably, while in other quarters it decreased. Assuming that both variables are stationary, we can estimate an ADL(2, 2) model using OLS. Remember that, if the variables in a model are stationary, then the standard regression quantities (e.g. OLS estimates, P-values, confidence intervals) can be calculated in the same way as in Chapters 4–8. Table 10.1 contains the results of this procedure.

Table 10.1 ADL(2, 2) with deterministic trend model.

	Coefficient	Standard error	*t*-stat	P-value	Lower 95%	Upper 95%
Intercept	−0.028	0.041	−0.685	0.495	−0.110	0.054
Y_{t-1}	−0.120	0.013	−9.46	4.11E − 15	−0.145	−0.095
ΔY_{t-1}	0.794	0.031	25.628	7.41E − 43	0.733	0.856
X_t	0.125	0.048	2.605	0.011	0.030	0.221
ΔX_t	0.838	0.044	19.111	2.96E − 33	0.750	0.925
ΔX_{t-1}	0.002	0.022	0.103	0.918	−0.041	0.046
time	0.001	0.001	0.984	0.328	−0.001	0.002

Using the formula for the long run multiplier, we can see that its OLS estimate is −(.125/−.120) = 1.042. There are different ways of expressing this information verbally (remember that the dependent and explanatory variables are percentage changes):

1. On average, market capitalization in Country A has been increasing by 0.01% per quarter and GDP by 0.30% per quarter. If Country A's total stock market capitalization increases by 1.01% in each month (i.e. increase by one unit from 0.01 to 1.01), then in the long run its GDP should start increasing by 1.342% per quarter (i.e. the initial 0.30 plus the long run multiplier of 1.042).[8]
2. The long run multiplier effect of financial liberalization on GDP growth is 1.042%.
3. If X permanently increases by 1%, the equilibrium value of Y will increase by 1.042%.

The statistical information, though, indicates that this might not be a good model, since some of the explanatory variables are not significant (e.g. the P-values for the coefficients on ΔX_{t-1} and the time trend both imply insignificance at the 5% level). This raises the issue of lag length selection in the ADL(p, q) model. We will not discuss this topic here, other than to note that the strategy for selecting q in the regression model with lagged explanatory variables (see Chapter 8) and the strategy for selecting p in the AR(p) model (see Chapter 9) can be combined. There is no general convention about whether you should first select p, then q, then decide whether the deterministic trend should be included, or make another ordering (e.g. select q, then p then trend or select q then trend then p, etc.). As long as you are careful, you will not be led too far wrong in selecting a good model.

Exercise 10.1

Use the variables Y = percentage change in GDP growth and X = percentage change in total stock market capitalization in data set LIBERAL.XLS to decide whether the model estimated in Table 10.1 is a good one. In particular,

(a) Establish whether Y and X really do not have unit roots as was assumed in the example.
(b) Beginning with an ADL(3, 3) model with deterministic trend, perform statistical tests to choose suitable lag lengths. Were good choices for p and q made in the example? Should we have included a deterministic trend?
(c) If you found the variables do not have unit roots and made different choices for p and q than the ones in the example, calculate the long run multiplier and compare to the result in the example.

Exercise 10.2

Data set LIBERAL1.XLS contains variables of the same form as LIBERAL.XLS, however for a different country.

(a) Repeat the analysis of Exercise 10.1 using the data in LIBERAL1.XLS. That is, verify that Y and X are stationary and then test to find a suitable ADL(p, q) specification.
(b) Calculate the long run multiplier for the model estimated in (a).

Aside for Excel users

In Chapter 8 we described how to create lagged variables in Excel using copy/paste commands. Similar techniques can be used here. Note, however, that when you create ΔY_t and ΔX_t you will be using formulae. If you want to manipulate ΔY_t and ΔX_t later, e.g., to create ΔY_{t-1} and ΔX_{t-1}, you have to be careful to copy and paste the **values** in the cells and not the **formulae**. You can do so using the "Paste Special" option in Excel. You are probably noticing by now that Excel is not a very convenient software package for time series analysis. As mentioned previously, there are many other statistical software packages (e.g. Stata, E-views, MicroFit, etc.) which are much more suitable for time series analysis and you might wish to consider learning how to use one of them if you plan on doing extensive work with financial time series.

Time series regression when Y and X have unit roots: spurious regression

For the remainder of this chapter, we will assume that Y and X have unit roots. In practice, of course, you would have to test whether this was the case using the Dickey–Fuller test of the previous chapter (or any other unit root test available in your software package). We begin by focussing on the case of regression models without lags, then proceed to similar models to the ADL(p, q) model.

Suppose we are interested in estimating the following regression:

$$Y_t = \alpha + \beta X_t + e_t.$$

If Y and X contain unit roots, then OLS estimation of this regression can yield results which are completely wrong. For instance, even if the true value of β is 0, OLS can yield an estimate, $\hat{\beta}$, which is very different from zero. Statistical tests (using the t-stat or P-value) may indicate that β is not zero. Furthermore, if $\beta = 0$, then the R^2 should be zero. In fact, the R^2 will often be quite large.

To put it another way: **if Y and X have unit roots then all the usual regression results might be misleading and incorrect.** This is the so-called **spurious regression problem**. We do not have the statistical tools to prove that this problem occurs,[9] but it is important to stress the practical implication. With the one exception of cointegration that we note below, **you should never run a regression of Y on X if the variables have unit roots.**

Time series regression when Y and X have unit roots: cointegration

The one time where you do not have to worry about the spurious regression problem occurs when Y and X are **cointegrated**. This case not only surmounts the spurious regression problem, but also provides some nice financial intuition. Cointegration has received a great deal of attention recently in the financial literature and many theoretical finance models imply cointegration should occur, so it is worthwhile to discuss the topic in detail here.

Some intuition for cointegration can be obtained by considering the errors in the above regression model: $e_t = Y_t - \alpha - \beta X_t$. Written in this way, it is clear that the errors are just a linear combination of Y and X. However, X and Y both exhibit nonstationary unit root behavior such that you would expect the error to also exhibit nonstationary behavior. (After all, if you add two things with a certain property together the result generally tends to have that property.) The error does indeed usually have a unit root. Statistically, it is this unit root in the error term that causes the spurious regression problem. However, it is possible that the unit roots in Y and X "cancel each other out" and that the resulting error is stationary. In this special case, called **cointegration**, the spurious regression problem vanishes and it is valid to run a regression of Y on X. To summarize: **if Y and X have unit roots, but some linear combination of them is stationary, then we can say that Y and X are cointegrated.**[10]

The intuition behind cointegration is clearest for the case where $\alpha = 0$ and $\beta = 1$. Keep this in mind when you read the following statements. Remember also that variables with unit roots tend to exhibit trend behavior (e.g. they can be increasing steadily over time and therefore can become very large).

1. If X and Y have unit roots then they have stochastic trends. However, if they are cointegrated, the error does not have such a trend. In this case, the error will not get too large and Y and X will not diverge from one another; Y and X, in other words, will trend together. This fact motivates other jargon used to refer to cointegrated time series. You may hear them referred as either having **common trends** or **co-trending**.

2. If we are talking about a financial model involving an equilibrium concept, e is the equilibrium error. If Y and X are cointegrated then the equilibrium error stays small. However, if Y and X are not cointegrated then the equilibrium error will have a trend and departures from equilibrium become increasingly large over time. If such departures from equilibrium occur, then many would hesitate to say that the equilibrium is a meaningful one.

3. If Y and X are cointegrated then there is an equilibrium relationship between them. If they are not, then no equilibrium relationship exists. (This is essentially just a restatement of the previous point.)

4. In the real world, it is unlikely that a financial system will ever be in precise equilibrium since shocks and unexpected changes to it will always occur. However, departures from equilibrium should not be too large and there should always be a tendency to return to equilibrium after a shock occurs. Hence, if a financial model which implies an equilibrium relationship exists between Y and X is correct, then we should observe Y and X as being cointegrated.

5. If Y and X are cointegrated then their trends will cancel each other out.

To summarize: if cointegration is present, then not only do we avoid the spurious regression problem, but we also have important financial information (e.g. that an equilibrium relationship exists or that two series are trending together).

A brief mention of a few theories motivating why cointegration should occur between various financial time series should aid in understanding the importance of this concept.

Common sense tells you that, if two assets are close substitutes for one another, then their prices should not drift too far apart. After all, if one asset becomes much more expensive than a similar asset, then investors will sell the first asset in order to buy the cheaper alternative. But if many investors are selling the expensive asset, then its price should drop. And if many investors are buying the cheap asset its price would rise. Thus, the prices of the expensive and cheap assets would move closer to one another. Many financial theories formalize this intuition to imply different cointegrating relationships.

Cointegration often arises in models of the **term structure of interest rates** and the **yield curve**. A detailed discussion of these terms is beyond the scope of this book. However, the basic idea is that bonds can have different maturities or repayment periods. So you can have a bond which promises to pay a fixed interest rate for one year, or two years, or 10 years, etc. The interest rates paid on bonds of different maturities can be different since investors have different time preferences and long maturities are less flexible since they lock the investor in for a longer time period. That is, an investor could either buy a five-year bond, or a sequence of one-year bonds each year for five years. The latter strategy would be more flexible since the investor could always change her mind after each year. Hence, long-term interest rates often tend to be higher than short-term interest rates to compensate the buyer for a loss of flexibility. The exact shape of the relationship between interest rates at different maturities is called the term structure of interest rates or the yield curve (a yield is the return to holding the bond for the entire time until it matures). This provides much useful information about investor's beliefs about the future and is, thus incorporated in many financial theories some of which imply cointegrating relationships. For instance, Campbell, Lo and MacKinlay in their book *The Econometrics of Financial Markets* (Chapter 10), outline an argument where yield spreads (i.e. the difference between the yield of a bond with an N period maturity and the yield of a bond with a 1 period maturity) are stationary time series variables and show how this implies yields of different maturities should be cointegrated.

In futures markets, theories involving investors having rational expectations tend to imply cointegrating relationships. For instance, in foreign exchange markets you can buy any major currency (e.g. the $ or the £) in the conventional manner (i.e. for immediate delivery at a specified rate). For instance, at the time I am writing this I could purchase $1.90 for £1. This is referred to as the **spot exchange rate** or **spot rate**. However, it also possible to agree an exchange rate now, but carry out the actual trade at some future date (e.g. a deal might have the form "I will guarantee that one year from now, I will give you $2.00 for your £1"). Such an exchange rate, agreed now but with the actual trade to be carried out later, is called the **forward exchange rate** or **forward rate**. Similar contracts (and much more complicated ones) can be written in stock markets and, indeed, such **financial derivatives** play a huge role in modern financial markets. Many financial theories, involving market efficiency and rational expectations of investors, imply that forward rates should be good predictors of future spot rates. Empirically, as we have discussed before, it seems that prices of assets (and an exchange rate is a price of an asset) often have unit roots in them (with returns being stationary). If we combine the financial theory with this empirical regularity, it turns out that they imply that spot and forward rates should be cointegrated. In foreign exchange markets, there are many theories which imply such cointegrating relationships. We will not explain them here, but just drop a few of names such as purchasing power parity, uncovered interest parity and covered interest parity.[11]

As we have touched on previously, there are also many financial theories which come out of basic present value relationships which imply cointegration. For instance, one such theory implies that stock prices and dividends should be cointegrated. Another financial theory (the Lettau–Ludvigson paper which we mentioned above and explore below) implies that consumption (*c*), assets (*a*) and income (*y*) should be cointegrated. Such so-called cay relationships have received a great deal of attention in the recent empirical finance literature. Furthermore, theory suggests that the cointegrating error from the cay relationship plays a very important role: it should have predictive power for future stock returns.

In short, financial theory suggests cointegrating relationships between many different financial time series should exist. Hence, it is important to test whether cointegration is present (i.e. to see whether financial theory holds in practice) and, if it is present, to estimate models involving cointegrated variables (e.g. to estimate the cointegrating error from the cay relationship). Accordingly, we now address these issues, beginning with an empirical example.

Example: Cointegration between the spot and forward rates

We have discussed previously how financial theory suggests spot and forward rates should be cointegrated. As an example, FOREX.XLS contains time series data for 181 months on the spot and one-month forward exchange rates of a certain foreign currency (both variables are measured in foreign currency units per dollar).

Figure 10.1 plots these two series and provides strong visual evidence that the spot and forward rates are indeed cointegrated. That is, even though they are not identical to one another, the general trend behavior in the two variables looks quite similar.

Estimation and testing with cointegrated variables

As mentioned above, if Y and X are cointegrated, then the spurious regression problem does not apply; consequently, we can run an OLS regression of Y on X and obtain valid results. Furthermore, the coefficient from this regression is the long run multiplier. Thus, insofar as interest centers on the long run multiplier, then estimation with cointegrated variables is very easy.

Before using results from this so-called **cointegrating regression**, it is important to verify that Y and X are in fact cointegrated. Remember that if they are not cointegrated, then the spurious regression problem holds and the results you obtain can be completely meaningless. An examination of time series plots like Figure 10.1, can

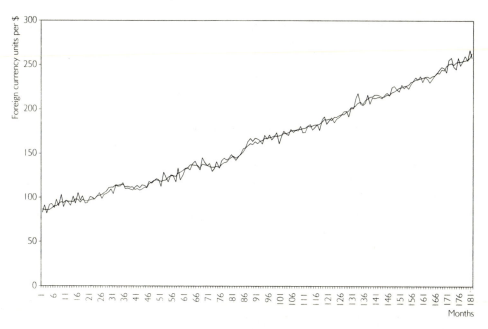

Fig. 10.1 Spot and forward rates.

be quite informative, but remember that visual examinations of graphs should not be considered substitutes for a statistical test!

Many tests for cointegration exist and some computer software packages (e.g. Stata and MicroFit) allow you to perform very sophisticated procedures at a touch of the button. We will discuss some of these in the next chapter. However, spreadsheets like Excel do not allow you to carry out these tests. Fortunately, using the regression capabilities of these spreadsheet packages coupled with some data manipulation, we can carry out at least one test for cointegration.

The test for cointegration described here is referred to as the Engle–Granger test, after the two econometricians who developed it. It is based on the regression of Y on X. Remember that, if cointegration occurs, then the errors from this regression will be stationary. Conversely, if cointegration does not occur, then the errors will have a unit root. Given the close relationship between the errors and the residuals,[12] it is reasonable to examine the properties of the residuals in order to investigate the presence of cointegration. In Chapter 9 we discussed testing for a unit root in a time series variable. Here, we test for a unit root in the *residuals* using the same techniques. In particular, the test for cointegration involves the following steps:

1. Run the regression of Y on X and save the residuals.[13]
2. Carry out a unit root test on the residuals (without including a deterministic trend).
3. If the unit root hypothesis is rejected then conclude that Y and X are cointegrated. However, if the unit root is accepted then conclude cointegration does not occur.

It is worthwhile to stress that the Engle–Granger test is based on a unit root test, so that the problems described at the end of Chapter 9 will arise. In other words, although the cointegration test is based on the *t*-statistic from a regression (in this case, one involving the residuals from a preliminary regression), you cannot use the P-value printed out by non-specialist packages like Excel. The correct critical values are published in many places (and are slightly different from the critical values for the Dickey–Fuller test). If you are going to do a great deal of work with time series data it is a good idea for you to spend the time to learn more about cointegration testing and look up these correct critical values or use a computer package such as Stata or MicroFit. However, for many purposes it is acceptable to use the same rules of thumb recommended in Chapter 9. A more sophisticated cointegration test, called the Johansen test, is described in Chapter 11. In many cases, the Johansen test performs better than the Engle–Granger test. However, the Johansen test is more complicated and cannot easily be done using a spreadsheet such as Excel.

Note that, when testing for a unit root in the residuals, it is rare to include a deterministic trend. If such a trend were included it could mean the errors could be growing steadily over time. This would violate the idea of cointegration (e.g. the idea that the system always returns to equilibrium and, hence, that errors never grow too big). Hence, we do not consider this case in this book.

In light of these considerations, when carrying out the unit root test on the residuals (see Step 2 above), use -2.89 as a critical value against which to compare the *t*-statistic. If the *t*-statistic on ρ in the unit root regression involving the residuals is more negative than -2.89, conclude that the errors do not have a unit root and hence that Y and X are cointegrated.

Note also that in the Dickey–Fuller test, we test the hypothesis that $\rho = 0$ (i.e. the null hypothesis is the unit root). In the cointegration test, we use the Dickey–Fuller methodology but cointegration is found if we reject the unit root hypothesis for the residuals. In other words, the null hypothesis in the Engle–Granger test is "no cointegration" and we conclude "cointegration is present" only if we reject this hypothesis.

It is also worth stressing that, since the Engle–Granger test is based on the Dickey–Fuller test, it suffers from the difficulties noted at the end of Chapter 9. That is, the Engle–Granger test has low power and can be misleading if structural breaks occur in the data.

Example: Cointegration between the spot and forward rates (continued from page 170)

Let us suppose that spot and forward rates both have unit roots. If we run a regression of $Y =$ the spot rate on $X =$ the forward rate using the data in FOREX.XLS we obtain the following fitted regression model:

$$\hat{Y}_i = 0.774 + 0.996 X_i.$$

The strategy above suggests that we should next carry out a unit root test on the residuals, u_t (which computer packages like Excel allow you to create) from this regression. The first step in doing this is to correctly select the lag length using the sequential strategy outlined in Chapter 9. Suppose we have done so and conclude that an AR(1) specification for the residuals is appropriate. The Dickey–Fuller strategy suggests we should regress Δu_t on u_{t-1}. The results are shown in Table 10.2.

Table 10.2 AR(1) using the errors from the cointegrating regression.

	Coefficient	Standard error	t-stat	P-value	Lower 95%	Upper 95%
Intercept	0.024	0.292	0.083	0.934	−0.552	0.600
u_{t-1}	−1.085	0.075	−14.500	5.8E − 32	−1.233	−0.938

Our rule of thumb says that we should compare the t-stat for the coefficient on u_{t-1}, which is −14.5, to a critical value of −2.89. Since the former is more negative than the latter we reject the unit root hypothesis and conclude that the residuals do not have a unit root. In other words, we conclude that the spot and forward rates are indeed cointegrated.

Since we have found cointegration we do not need to worry about the spurious regressions problem. Hence, we can proceed to an interpretation of our coefficients without worrying that the OLS estimates are meaningless. The coefficient on the forward rate is 0.996 which is very close to the value of 1 predicted by financial theory (i.e. financial theory says that spot and forward rates should on average be the same as the latter should be an optimal predictor for the former). Alternatively, we can interpret this coefficient estimate as saying that the long run multiplier is 0.996.

Exercise 10.3

Use the data in FOREX.XLS to complete the previous example. In particular,

(a) Do a Dickey–Fuller test to verify that spot and forward rates have unit roots.
(b) Do a sequential test to verify that the Dickey–Fuller test on the residuals was done correctly. That is, is an AR(1) model for the residuals appropriate?

Exercise 10.4

Use the data on Y = long-term interest rates and X = short-term interest rates in INTERESTRATES.XLS used in previous chapters.

(a) Use Dickey–Fuller tests to verify that Y and X have unit roots.
(b) Run a regression of Y on X and save the errors.
(c) Carry out a unit root test on the residuals using an AR(1) model.
(d) Carry out a unit root test on the residuals using an AR(2) model.
(e) Carry out a unit root test on the residuals using an AR(3) model.
(f) What can you conclude about the presence of cointegration between Y and X?[14]

Time series regression when Y and X are cointegrated: the error correction model

In empirical work, it is often vital to establish that Y and X are cointegrated. As emphasized above, cointegration can be related to the idea of Y and X trending together or bearing an equilibrium relationship to each other. A second important task is to estimate the long run multiplier or the long run influence of X on Y. Both cointegration testing and estimation of the long run multiplier can be done using the regression of Y on X. Accordingly, in many empirical projects you may never need to move beyond this simple regression. However, in some cases, you may be interested in understanding short run behavior in a manner that is not possible using only the regression of Y on X. In such cases, we can estimate an **error correction model** (or ECM for short).

An important theorem, known as the **Granger Representation Theorem**, says that if Y and X are cointegrated, then the relationship between them can be expressed as an ECM. In this section, we will assume Y and X are cointegrated. Error correction models have a long tradition in time series econometrics, and the Granger Representation Theorem highlights their popularity. In order to understand the properties of ECMs let us begin with the following simple version:

$$\Delta Y_t = \varphi + \lambda e_{t-1} + \omega_0 \Delta X_t + \varepsilon_t,$$

where e_{t-1} is the error obtained from the regression model with Y and X (i.e. $e_{t-1} = Y_{t-1} - \alpha - \beta X_{t-1}$) and ε_t is the error in the ECM model. Note that, if we knew e_{t-1}, then the ECM would be just a regression model (although we introduce some new Greek letters to make sure that the coefficients and error in this model do not get confused with those in other regression models). That is, ΔY_t is the dependent variable and e_{t-1} and ΔX_t are explanatory variables. Furthermore, we assume that $\lambda < 0$.[15]

To aid in interpreting the ECM, consider the implications of ΔY_t being its dependent variable. As emphasized throughout this book, the regression model attempts to use explanatory variables to explain the dependent variable. With this in mind, note that the ECM says that ΔY depends on ΔX – an intuitively sensible point (i.e. changes in X cause Y to change). In addition, ΔY_t depends on e_{t-1}. This latter aspect is unique to the ECM and gives it its name.

Remember that e can be thought of as an equilibrium error (e.g. the difference between the spot and forward rates). If it is non-zero, then the model is out of equilibrium. Consider the case where $\Delta X_t = 0$ and e_{t-1} is positive (e.g. the spot rate is higher than the forward rate). The latter implies that Y_{t-1} is too high to be in equilibrium (i.e. Y_{t-1} is above its equilibrium level of $\alpha + \beta X_{t-1}$). Since $\lambda < 0$ the term λe_{t-1} will be negative and so ΔY_t will be negative. In other words, if Y_{t-1} is above its equilibrium level, then it will start falling in the next period and the equilibrium error will be "corrected" in the model; hence the term "error correction model" (e.g. if the spot rate is too much above the forward rate, investors will find it cheap to buy forward driving up the forward rate).[16] In the case where $e_{t-1} < 0$ the opposite will hold (i.e. Y_{t-1} is below its equilibrium level, hence $\lambda e_{t-1} > 0$ which causes ΔY_t to be positive, triggering Y to rise in period t).

In sum, the ECM has both long run and short run properties built into it. The former properties are embedded in the e_{t-1} term (remember β is still the long run multiplier and the errors are from the regression involving Y and X). The short run behavior is partially captured by the equilibrium error term, which says that, if Y is out of equilibrium, it will be pulled towards it in the next period. Further aspects of short run behavior are captured by the inclusion of ΔX_t as an explanatory variable. This term implies that, if X changes, the equilibrium value of Y will also change, and that Y will also change accordingly. All in all, the ECM has some very sensible properties that are closely related to financial equilibrium concepts.

The ECM also has some nice statistical properties which mean that we do not have to worry about the spurious regression problem. Y and X both have unit roots; hence ΔY and ΔX are stationary. Furthermore, since Y and X are cointegrated, the equilibrium error is stationary. Hence, the dependent variable and all explanatory variables in the ECM are stationary. This property means that we can use OLS estimation and carry out testing using t-statistics and P-values in the standard way described in Chapter 5.

The only new statistical issue in the ECM arises due to the inclusion of e_{t-1} as an explanatory variable. Of course, the errors in a model are not directly observed. This raises the issue of how they can be used as an explanatory variable in a regression. Some sophisticated statistical techniques have been developed to estimate the ECM, but the simplest thing to do is merely to replace the unknown errors by the residuals from the regression of Y on X (i.e. replace e_{t-1} by u_{t-1}). That is, a simple technique based on two OLS regressions proceeds as follows:

Step 1. Run a regression of Y on X and save the residuals.

Step 2. Run a regression of ΔY on ΔX and the residuals from Step 1 lagged one period.

It should be emphasized that before carrying out this two-step estimation procedure for the ECM, you must verify that Y and X have unit roots and are cointegrated.

So far we have discussed the simplest error correction model. In practice, just as the ADL(p, q) model has lags of the dependent and explanatory variables, the ECM may also have lags.[17] It may also have a deterministic trend. Incorporating these features into the ECM yields:

$$\Delta Y_t = \varphi + \delta t + \lambda e_{t-1} + \gamma_1 \Delta Y_{t-1} + \ldots + \gamma_p \Delta Y_{t-p} + \omega_0 \Delta X_t + \ldots + \omega_q \Delta X_{t-q} + \varepsilon_t.$$

This expression is still in the form of a regression model and can be estimated using the two-step procedure described above. The adjustment to equilibrium intuition also holds for this model. The decisions on whether to include a deterministic trend and on which precise values for p and q are appropriate can be made using t-statistics and P-values in the same manner as for the ADL model. In fact, the ECM is closely related to the ADL model in that it is a restricted version of it.

Example: Cointegration between the spot and forward rates (continued from page 173)

In the previous part of this example, we found that the variables, Y = the spot rate and X = the forward rate, were cointegrated. This suggests that we can estimate an error correction model. To do so, we begin by running a regression of Y on X and saving the residuals (which was done in the previous part of the example). The residuals, u_t, can then be included in the following regression (in lagged form):

$$\Delta Y_t = \varphi + \lambda u_{t-1} + \omega_0 \Delta X_t + \varepsilon_t.$$

Table 10.3 gives results from OLS estimation of this model. The statistical information can be interpreted in the standard way. We can say that (with the exception of the intercept) all the coefficients are strongly statistically significant (since their P-values are much less than 0.05).

Table 10.3 Simple error correction model.

	Coefficient	Standard error	t-stat	P-value	Lower 95%	Upper 95%
Intercept	−0.023	0.342	−0.068	0.946	−0.700	0.654
u_{t-1}	−1.085	0.075	−14.458	8.69E − 32	−1.233	−0.937
ΔX_t	1.044	0.182	5.737	4.11E − 08	0.685	1.403

We noted before that $\hat{\beta} = 0.996$ and this is the estimate of the long run multiplier. The point estimates in the table of λ and ω_0 summarize the short run properties. To aid in interpretation note that all variables in the model are percentages. The coefficient on u_{t-1} of -1.085 measures how much Y responds to equilibrium errors. Since this coefficient is negative, positive errors tend to cause ΔY to be negative and hence Y to fall. In particular, an equilibrium error of one unit tends to cause the spot rate to fall by 1.085 units in the next period, *ceteris paribus*. This is a very quick adjustment to an equilibrium error! The coefficient on $\Delta X_t = 1.044$. Imagine, in other words, what would happen if the forward rate were to remain unchanged for some time ($\Delta X = 0$), but then suddenly were to change by one unit. The ECM implies that Y would instantly change by 1.044 units. In other words, the spot rate responds very quickly to changes in the forward rate.

Exercise 10.5

Use the data in FOREX.XLS to check the previous example. In particular, does the ECM have enough lags of both ΔX and ΔY?

Exercise 10.6

Use the data on Y = long-term interest rates and X = short-term interest rates in INTERESTRATES.XLS. Assume (perhaps incorrectly) that Y and X are cointegrated.

(a) Estimate an error correction model. Begin with a model containing a deterministic trend and $p = q = 4$ and then carry out statistical tests to find an appropriate ECM.
(b) Discuss your results. Pay particular attention to your estimate of λ and discuss what it tells you about the speed of adjustment to equilibrium.

Time series regression when Y and X have unit roots but are not cointegrated

You may encounter instances where unit root tests indicate that your time series have unit roots, but the Engle–Granger test indicates that the series are not cointegrated. That is, the series may not be trending together and may not have an equilibrium relationship. In these cases, you should not run a regression of Y on X due to the spurious regression problem. The presence of such characteristics suggests that you should rethink your basic model and include other explanatory variables. Instead of working with Y and X themselves, for example, you could difference them. (Remember that if Y and X have one unit root, then ΔY and ΔX should be stationary.)

In this case, you could work with the **changes** in your time series and estimate the ADL model using the techniques described at the beginning of this chapter. In other words, you may wish to estimate the original ADL model, but with changes in the variables:

$$\Delta Y_t = \alpha + \delta t + \phi_1 \Delta Y_{t-1} + \ldots + \phi_p \Delta Y_{t-p} + \beta_0 \Delta X_t + \ldots + \beta_q \Delta X_{t-q} + e_t.$$

For most time series variables, this specification should not suffer from multicollinearity problems. Alternatively, you may wish to estimate the second variant of the ADL model based on the differenced data. But if you are working with the differences of your time series and then use the variant of the ADL that involves differencing the data you end up with second differenced data:

$$\Delta^2 Y_t = \alpha + \delta t + \rho \Delta Y_{t-1} + \gamma_1 \Delta^2 Y_{t-1} + \ldots + \gamma_{p-1} \Delta^2 Y_{t-q+1}$$
$$+ \theta \Delta X_t + \omega_1 \Delta^2 X_t + \ldots + \omega_q \Delta^2 X_{t-q+1} + e_t,$$

where $\Delta^2 Y_t = \Delta Y_t - \Delta Y_{t-1}$. OLS estimation and testing can be done in either of these models in a straightforward way. Whatever route is chosen, it is important to emphasize that the interpretation of regression results will likewise change.

More specifically, let us suppose Y = exchange rates and X = interest rates. If Y and X are cointegrated, or if both are stationary, we can obtain an estimate of the long run effect of a small change in interest rates on exchange rates. If Y and X are neither stationary nor cointegrated and we estimate either of the two preceding equations, we can obtain an estimate of the long run effect of *a small change in the change of interest rates on the change in exchange rates*. This may or may not be a sensible thing to measure depending on the particular empirical exercise.

Note that, in the example at the beginning of this chapter on the effect of financial liberalization on growth, the variables were already in percentage changes. If we had begun with Y = GDP and X = total stock market capitalization we would have found they had unit roots but were not cointegrated. Hence, we would have run into the spurious regressions problem. This was why we worked with percentage changes.

Exercise 10.7

Excel data set STOCKPAB.XLS contains monthly data of the most important stock price indices in Countries A and B. The data are logged. One topic that financial researchers are interested in is whether movements in stock prices in one country can affect those in another country (e.g. bad news in one market is "contagious" and can spill over to a neighboring stock market). In light of this, you wish to investigate whether there are relationships between $Y =$ the (logged) stock price in Country A and $X =$ the (logged) stock price in Country B. In particular,

(a) Construct a time series plot of X and Y. Do they both seem to be trending? Do they seem to be trending together?
(b) Carry out unit root tests on X and Y. You should find evidence that they both have unit roots.
(c) Carry out a cointegration test on X and Y. You should find evidence that they are **not** cointegrated.
(d) Difference the data to obtain ΔX and ΔY. Repeat parts (a) and (b) with these new variables. You should find that they do not have unit roots.
(e) Specify and estimate an ADL(p, q) model using the new variables, ΔX and ΔY. Discuss your results. Note that the change in the log of a stock price index is the percentage change. That is, ΔX and ΔY can be interpreted as returns (exclusive of dividends).

Chapter summary

1. If all variables are stationary, then an ADL(p, q) model can be estimated using OLS. Statistical techniques are all standard.
2. A variant on the ADL model is often used to avoid potential multi-collinearity problems and provide a straightforward estimate of the long run multiplier.
3. If all variables are nonstationary, great care must be taken in the analysis due to the spurious regression problem.
4. If all variables are nonstationary but the regression error is stationary, then cointegration occurs.
5. If cointegration is present, the spurious regression problem does not occur.
6. Cointegration is an attractive concept for financial researchers since it implies that an equilibrium relationship exists.
7. Cointegration can be tested using the Engle–Granger test. This test is a Dickey–Fuller test on the residuals from the cointegrating regression.
8. If the variables are cointegrated then an error correction model can be used. This model captures short run behavior in a way that the cointegrating regression cannot.
9. If the variables have unit roots but are not cointegrated, you should not work with them directly. Rather you should difference them and estimate an ADL model using the differenced variables. The interpretation of these models can be awkward.

Endnotes

1. Campbell, J.Y. and Ammer, J. (1993). "What moves the stock and bond markets? A variance decomposition for long-term asset returns", *Journal of Finance*, 48, 3–37.
2. Lettau, M. and Ludvigson, S. (2001). "Consumption, aggregate wealth and expected stock returns", *Journal of Finance*, 56, 815–49.
3. Campbell, J. and Shiller, R. (1988). "Stock prices, earnings and expected dividends", *Journal of Finance*, 43, 661–76.
4. Formally, we should call this the ADL(p, q) *with **deterministic trend*** model. However, we will omit the latter phrase for the sake of simplicity. In practice, you will find that the deterministic trend is often insignificant and will be omitted from the model anyway. Note also that some textbooks abbreviate "autoregressive distributed lag" as ARDL instead of ADL.
5. The coefficients involving the lags of the dependent variable, ρ, γ_1, ..., γ_{p-1} are exactly the same functions of ϕ_1, ..., ϕ_p as in Chapter 9. The $q + 1$ coefficients θ, ω_1, ..., ω_q are similar functions of β_0, β_1, ..., β_q.
6. Deriving the long run multiplier from an ADL model is not difficult, and you should try it as an exercise. Here are some hints: assume that the model has been in equilibrium for a long time, and that equilibrium values of X and Y are given by X^* and Y^*, respectively. Now assume X is increased permanently to $X^* + 1$ and figure out what happens to Y.
7. "Stable" is a statistical term that we will not formally define in this book. It can, however, be interpreted in a common sense way: if a model is stable, it implies that the time series variables will not be exploding or stochastically trending over time. In essence, it is a very similar concept to stationarity.
8. It is worth emphasizing that 1.042 is an estimate of the long run multiplier. A confidence interval could be calculated, but this would involve derivations beyond the scope of this book.
9. You may think that the spurious regression problem occurs as a result of an omitted variable bias when lags are left out of an ADL model. But there is more to it than this. Even when no lags belong in the model, the spurious regression problem arises.
10. To motivate the word "cointegration", note that if X and Y have unit roots, then it is common jargon to say that they are **integrated**. Adding the word "co" to emphasize that the unit roots are similar or common in X and Y yields "cointegration".
11. Chapters 11 through 13 of *Quantitative Financial Economics* by Keith Cuthbertson (John Wiley & Sons, Ltd) is a good place for further reading on these topics.
12. Remember that the errors are deviations from the true regression line while residuals are deviations from the estimated regression line (see Chapter 4). Our notation for OLS residuals is u_t.
13. In Excel, you can do it by clicking on the box labeled "Residuals" and following instructions.
14. If you have done this question correctly, you will find that cointegration does seem to be present for some lag lengths, but not for others. This is a common occurrence in practical applications, so do not be dismayed by it. Financial theory and time series plots of the data definitely indicate that cointegration should occur between Y and X. But the Engle–Granger test does not consistently indicate cointegration. One possible explanation is that the Engle–Granger and Dickey–Fuller tests are known to have low power.

15. We will not formally prove why this condition must hold except to say that it is a stability condition of the sort discussed in the context of the ADL(p, q) model.

16. This intuition motivates the stability condition $\lambda < 0$, which ensures that equilibrium errors are corrected. If λ is positive then equilibrium errors will be magnified.

17. Note that we do not include more lags of e_{t-1} as explanatory variables due to an implication of the Granger Representation Theorem, which we will not discuss here.

Regression with time series variables with several equations

Chapters 8–10 developed several different regression models for time series variables. For many cases, knowledge of these models and the relevant techniques (e.g. cointegration tests) is enough to allow you to write a report and gain a good basic understanding of the properties of the data. However, in some cases, a knowledge of slightly more sophisticated methods is necessary. Fortunately, many such cases can be shown to be simple extensions of the methods learned in earlier chapters. In this chapter and the next we discuss two important such extensions. In the present chapter, we discuss methods which involve more than one equation. In the next, we discuss financial volatility. To motivate why multiple equation methods are important, we begin by discussing **Granger causality** before discussing the most popular class of multiple-equation models: so-called **Vector Autoregressive** (VAR)[1] models. VARs can be used to investigate Granger causality, but are also useful for many other things in finance. Using financial examples, we will show their importance. Furthermore, an extension of a VAR related to the concepts of cointegration and error correction is discussed in this chapter. This is called the **Vector Error Correction Model** (VECM) and it allows us to introduce another popular test for cointegration called the **Johansen test**. In Appendix 11.2, we informally introduce the concept of a **variance decomposition**. This is commonly used with financial VARs but a full understanding requires concepts beyond the scope of this book.

At the beginning of Chapter 10, we motivated the importance of regression with time series variables for financial researchers by mentioning a few papers such as one by Campbell and Ahmer called "What moves the stock and bond markets? A variance decomposition for long-term asset returns" and one by Lettau and Ludvigson called "Consumption, aggregate wealth and expected stock returns". In this chapter, we will discuss these financial examples (and several others) in more detail.

Granger causality

In this book we have referred to causality quite a bit; however, mostly through warnings about interpreting correlation and regression results as reflecting causality. For instance, in Chapter 3 we discussed an example where alcohol drinking and lung cancer rates were correlated with one another, even though alcohol drinking does not cause lung cancer. Here correlation did not imply causality. In fact, it was cigarette smoking that caused lung cancer, but a correlation between cigarette smoking and alcohol drinking produced an apparent relationship between alcohol and lung cancer.

In our discussion of regression, we were on a little firmer ground, since we attempted to use common sense in labeling one variable the dependent variable and the others the explanatory variables. In many cases, because the latter "explained" the former it was reasonable to talk about X "causing" Y. For instance, in our house price example in Chapters 4, 5, 6 and 7, the price of the house was said to be "caused" by the characteristics of the house (e.g. number of bedrooms, number of bathrooms, etc.). However, in our discussion of omitted variable bias in Chapter 6, it became clear that multiple regressions could provide a misleading interpretation of the degree of causality present if important explanatory variables were omitted. Furthermore, there are many regressions in which it is not obvious which variable causes which. For instance, in Chapter 10 (Exercise 10.7), you ran a regression of $Y =$ stock prices in Country A on $X =$ stock prices in Country B. It is possible that stock price movements in Country A cause stock markets to change in Country B (i.e. X causes Y). For instance, if Country A is a big country with an important role in the world economy (e.g. the USA), then a stock market crash in Country A could also cause panic in Country B. However, if Country A and B were neighboring countries (e.g. Thailand and Malaysia) then an event which caused panic in either country could affect both countries. In other words, the causality could run in either direction – or both! Hence, when using the word "cause" with regression or correlation results a great deal of caution has to be taken and common sense has to be used.

However, with time series data we can make slightly stronger statements about causality simply by exploiting the fact that time does not run backward! That is, if event A happens before event B, then it is possible that A is causing B. However, it is not possible that B is causing A. In other words, events in the past can cause events to happen today. Future events cannot.

These intuitive ideas can be investigated through regression models incorporating the notion of **Granger causality**. The basic idea is that a variable X **Granger causes**

Y if past values of X can help explain Y. Of course, if Granger causality holds this does not guarantee that X causes Y. This is why we say "Granger causality" rather than just "causality". Nevertheless, if past values of X have explanatory power for current values of Y, it at least suggests that X might be causing Y.

Granger causality is only relevant with time series variables. To illustrate the basic concepts we will consider Granger causality between two variables (X and Y) which are both stationary. A nonstationary case, where X and Y have unit roots but are cointegrated, will be mentioned below.

Granger causality in a simple ADL model

Since we have assumed that X and Y are stationary, the discussion of Chapter 10 suggests an ADL model is appropriate. Suppose that the following simple ADL model holds:

$$Y_t = \alpha + \phi_1 Y_{t-1} + \beta_1 X_{t-1} + e_t.$$

This model implies that last period's value of X has explanatory power for the current value of Y. The coefficient β_1 is a measure of the influence of X_{t-1} on Y_t. If $\beta_1 = 0$, then past values of X have no effect on Y and there is no way that X could Granger cause Y. In other words, if $\beta_1 = 0$ then X does not Granger cause Y. An alternative way of expressing this concept is to say that "if $\beta_1 = 0$ then past values of X have no explanatory power for Y beyond that provided by past values of Y". Since we know how to estimate the ADL and carry out hypothesis tests, it is simple to test for Granger causality. That is, OLS estimation of the above regression can be conducted using any standard spreadsheet or econometric computer package, and the P-value for the coefficient on X_{t-1} examined for significance. If β_1 is statistically significant (e.g. P-value <0.05) then we conclude that X Granger causes Y. Note that the null hypothesis being tested here is $H_0: \beta_1 = 0$ which is a hypothesis that Granger causality **does not occur**. So we should formally refer to the test of $\beta_1 = 0$ as a test of **Granger non-causality**, but we will adopt the more common informal terminology and just refer to this procedure as a **Granger causality test**.

Granger causality in an ADL model with p and q lags

Of course, the above ADL model is quite restrictive in that it incorporates only one lag of X and Y. In general, we would want to select lag lengths using the methods described in Chapter 10 to work with an ADL(p, q) model of the form:[2]

$$Y_t = \alpha + \delta t + \phi_1 Y_{t-1} + \ldots + \phi_p Y_{t-p} + \beta_1 X_{t-1} + \ldots + \beta_q X_{t-q} + e_t.$$

Here X Granger causes Y if any or all of $\beta_1, \ldots, \beta_q$ are statistically significant. In other words, if X at any time in the past has explanatory power for the current value of Y, then we say that X Granger causes Y. Since we are assuming X and Y do not contain unit roots, OLS regression analysis can be used to estimate this model. The P-values of the individual coefficients can be used to determine whether Granger causality is present. If you were using the 5% level of significance, then if any of the P-values for the coefficients $\beta_1, \ldots, \beta_q$ were less than 0.05, you would conclude that Granger causality is present. If none of the P-values is less than 0.05 then you would conclude that Granger causality is not present.

The strategy outlined above is a useful one that can be carried out quite simply in Excel or any other statistical software package. You are likely to obtain reliable evidence about whether X Granger causes Y by following it. Note, however, that there is formally a more correct – also more complicated – way of carrying out this test. Recall that the null hypothesis tested is formally one of Granger non-causality. That is, X does not Granger cause Y if past values of X have no explanatory power for the current value of Y. Appropriately, then, we want to test the hypothesis H_0: $\beta_1 = \beta_2 = \ldots = \beta_q = 0$ and conclude that X Granger causes Y only if the hypothesis is rejected. Note that this test is slightly different from the one proposed in the previous paragraph. That is, a joint test of $\beta_1 = \beta_2 = \ldots = \beta_q = 0$ is not exactly the same as q individual tests of $\beta_i = 0$ for $i = 1, \ldots, q$. We have not discussed how to carry out tests to determine whether several coefficients are jointly equal to zero. For readers interested in such joint tests, Appendix 11.1 offers some practical advice.

However, if you choose to follow the simpler strategy outlined above then you should note the following:

If you find any or all of the coefficients $\beta_1, \ldots, \beta_q$ to be significant using t-statistics or the P-values of individual coefficients, you may safely conclude that X Granger causes Y. If none of these coefficients is significant, it is probably the case that X does not Granger cause Y. However, you are more likely to be wrong if you conclude the latter than if you had used the correct joint test of Granger non-causality.

Example: Do stock price movements in Country A Granger cause stock price movements in Country B?

Monthly data on logged stock prices for Countries A and B is located in data set STOCKPAB.XLS, introduced in Exercise 10.7. If you have done that exercise, you will recall that stock prices in both countries appear to have unit roots, but are not cointegrated. However, the differences of these series are stationary and can be nicely interpreted as stock market returns (exclusive of dividends). We will use these differenced variables to investigate whether stock returns in Country A Granger cause those in Country B.

Table 11.1 contains results from OLS estimation of the regression of $\Delta Y =$ stock returns in Country A on four lags of itself, four lags of $\Delta X =$ stock returns in Country B and a deterministic trend.

Table 11.1 ADL model using stock returns in Country A as the dependent variable.

	Coefficient	Standard error	t-stat	P-value	Lower 95%	Upper 95%
Intercept	−0.751	0.710	−1.058	0.292	−2.156	0.654
ΔY_{t-1}	0.822	0.170	4.850	3.81E − 6	0.486	1.158
ΔY_{t-2}	−0.041	0.186	−0.222	0.825	−0.409	0.326
ΔY_{t-3}	0.142	0.186	0.762	0.448	−0.227	0.511
ΔY_{t-4}	−0.181	0.175	−1.035	0.303	−0.526	0.165
ΔX_{t-1}	−0.016	0.143	−0.114	0.909	−0.299	0.267
ΔX_{t-2}	−0.118	0.143	−0.823	0.412	−0.402	0.166
ΔX_{t-3}	−0.042	0.143	−0.292	0.771	−0.324	0.241
ΔX_{t-4}	0.038	0.142	0.266	0.791	−0.244	0.319
Time	0.030	0.011	2.669	0.009	0.0077	0.052

An examination of the P-values in Table 11.1 indicates that only the deterministic trend and last period's stock returns in Country A have explanatory power for present stock returns in Country A. All of the coefficients on the lags of stock returns in Country B are insignificant. Stock returns in Country B do not seem to Granger cause stock returns in Country A.[3]

Causality in both directions

In many cases, it is not obvious which way causality should run. For instance, should stock markets in Country A affect markets in Country B or should the reverse hold? In such cases, when causality may be in either direction, it is important that you check for it. If Y and X are the two variables under study, in addition to running a regression of Y on lags of itself and lags of X (as above), you should also run a regression of X on lags of itself and lags of Y. In other words, you should work with two separate equations: one with Y being the dependent variable and one with X being the dependent variable. This is a simple example of a regression model with more than one equation.

Note that it is possible to find that Y Granger causes X and that X Granger causes Y. In the case of complicated models, such bi-directional causality is quite common and even reasonable. Think, for instance, of the relationship between interest rates and exchange rates. It is not unreasonable that interest rate policy may affect future exchange rates. However, it is also equally reasonable to think that exchange rates may also affect future interest rate policy (e.g. if the exchange rate is perceived to be too high now the central bank may be led to decrease interest rates in the future).

Example: Do stock price movements in Country B Granger cause stock price movements in Country A?

In the previous example we used data set STOCKPAB.XLS to investigate whether stock returns in Country B Granger caused stock returns in Country A. We found that they did not. However, it is possible that causality runs in the opposite direction: from Country A to Country B.

Table 11.2 contains results from OLS estimation of the regression of $\Delta X =$ stock returns in Country B on four lags of itself, four lags of $\Delta Y =$ stock returns in Country A and a deterministic trend.

Here we do find evidence that stock returns in Country A Granger cause stock returns in Country B. In particular, the coefficient on ΔY_{t-1} is highly significant, indicating that last month's stock returns in Country A has strong explanatory power for stock returns in Country B.

Table 11.2   ADL model using stock returns in Country B as the dependent variable.

	Coefficient	Standard error	t-stat	P-value	Lower 95%	Upper 95%
Intercept	−0.609	0.835	−0.730	0.467	−2.262	1.044
ΔX_{t-1}	0.053	0.168	0.312	0.755	−0.280	0.386
ΔX_{t-2}	−0.040	0.169	−0.235	0.814	−0.374	0.294
ΔX_{t-3}	−0.058	0.168	−0.348	0.728	−0.391	0.274
ΔX_{t-4}	0.036	0.167	0.215	0.830	−0.295	0.367
ΔY_{t-1}	0.854	0.200	4.280	3.83E − 5	0.459	1.249
ΔY_{t-2}	−0.217	0.218	−0.993	0.323	−0.649	0.215
ΔY_{t-3}	0.234	0.219	1.067	0.288	−0.200	0.668
ΔY_{t-4}	−0.272	0.205	−1.323	0.188	−0.678	0.135
Time	0.046	0.013	3.514	0.001	0.020	0.072

Exercise 11.1

In the previous examples using the data set STOCKPAB.XLS, we have set $p = q = 4$ (i.e. four lags of stock returns in both countries). Using County A as the dependent variable and the sequential testing procedure outlined in Chapter 10 select optimal values for p and q. Discuss whether stock returns in Country B Granger cause stock returns in Country A using the ADL(p, q) model you have selected. Repeat the analysis using Country B as the dependent variable.

Exercise 11.2

Excel file LONGGDP.XLS contains annual data on real GDP per capita for four of the world's largest English-speaking countries (USA, UK, Canada and Australia) for the years 1870–1993.

(a) Take differences to obtain time series of the growth in GDP per capita for each of the four countries.

(b) Investigate where GDP growth in any country Granger causes GDP growth in any other country. For instance, does GDP growth in the USA Granger cause GDP growth in the UK? Does it in Canada?

This brief discussion of Granger causality has focussed on two variables, X and Y. However, there is no reason why these basic techniques cannot be extended to the case of many variables. For instance, if we had three variables, X, Y and Z, and were interested in investigating whether X or Z Granger cause Y, we would simply regress Y on lags of Y, lags of X and lags of Z. If, say, the lags of Z were found to be significant and the lags of X not, then we could say that Z Granger causes Y, but X does not.

Granger causality with cointegrated variables

Testing for Granger causality among cointegrated variables is very similar to the method outlined above. Remember that, if variables are found to be cointegrated (something which should be investigated using unit root and cointegration tests), then you should work with an error correction model (ECM) involving these variables. In the case where you have two variables, this is given by:

$$\Delta Y_t = \varphi + \delta t + \lambda e_{t-1} + \gamma_1 \Delta Y_{t-1} + \ldots + \gamma_p \Delta Y_{t-p} + \omega_1 \Delta X_{t-1} + \ldots + \omega_q \Delta X_{t-q} + \varepsilon_t.$$

As noted in Chapter 10, this is essentially an ADL model except for the presence of the term λe_{t-1}. Remember that $e_{t-1} = Y_{t-1} - \alpha - \beta X_{t-1}$, an estimate of which can be obtained by running a regression of Y on X and saving the residuals. Intuitively, X Granger causes Y if past values of X have explanatory power for current values of Y. Applying this intuition to the ECM, we can see that past values of X appear in the terms $\Delta X_{t-1}, \ldots, \Delta X_{t-q}$ and e_{t-1}. This implies that X does not Granger cause Y if $\omega_1 = \ldots = \omega_q = \lambda = 0$. Chapter 10 discussed how we can use two OLS regressions to estimate ECMs, and then use their P-values or confidence intervals to test for causality. Thus, t-statistics and P-values can be used to test for Granger causality in the same way as the stationary case. Also, the F-tests described in Appendix 11.1 can be used to carry out a formal test of H_0: $\omega_1 = \ldots = \omega_q = \lambda = 0$.

In the previous paragraph we described how to test whether X Granger causes Y. Testing whether Y Granger causes X is achieved by reversing the roles that X and Y play in the ECM. One interesting consequence of the Granger Representation Theorem is worth noting here (without the proof). If X and Y are cointegrated then some form of Granger causality must occur. That is, either X must Granger cause Y or Y must Granger cause X (or both).

Exercise 11.3

Use the data on Y = long-term interest rates and X = short term-interest rates in INTERESTRATES.XLS. Assume (perhaps incorrectly in light of Exercise 10.4) that Y and X are cointegrated. Test whether Y Granger causes X. Test whether X Granger causes Y.

Vector autoregressions

Our discussion of Granger causality naturally leads us to an interest in models with several equations and the topic of Vector Autoregressions or VARs. Before discussing their popularity and estimation, we will first define what a VAR is. Initially, we will assume that all variables are stationary. If the original variables have unit roots, then we assume that differences have been taken such that the model includes the changes in the original variables (which do not have unit roots). The end of this section will consider the extension of this case to that of cointegration.

In previous chapters, we used an Excel spreadsheet to produce empirical results. However, even with the single-equation time series models of Chapters 8–10, spreadsheets are somewhat awkward (e.g. creating lagged variables involves extensive copying and pasting of data). When we are working with several equations, it becomes even more difficult. And some of the features introduced (e.g. variance decompositions and impulse responses), are extremely difficult to produce using a spreadsheet. In the following chapter, when considering financial volatility, it becomes yet more difficult to work with a spreadsheet. Accordingly, in the remainder of this book, empirical results will be produced using the computer package Stata. This has good capabilities for working with time series. There are many other good computer packages with similar capabilities (e.g. MicroFit, E-views, etc.). If you plan on working extensively with financial time series, it is a good idea to leave the world of spreadsheets and work with one of these.

When we investigated Granger causality between X and Y, we began with a restricted version of an ADL(p, q) model with Y as the dependent variable. We used it to investigate if X Granger caused Y. We then went on to consider causality in the other direction, which involved switching the roles of X and Y in the ADL;

in particular, X became the dependent variable. We can write the two equations as follows:

$$Y_t = \alpha_1 + \delta_1 t + \phi_{11} Y_{t-1} + \ldots + \phi_{1p} Y_{t-p} + \beta_{11} X_{t-1} + \ldots + \beta_{1q} X_{t-q} + e_{1t},$$

and

$$X_t = \alpha_2 + \delta_2 t + \phi_{21} Y_{t-1} + \ldots + \phi_{2p} Y_{t-p} + \beta_{21} X_{t-1} + \ldots + \beta_{2q} X_{t-q} + e_{2t}.$$

The first of these equations tests whether X Granger causes Y; the second, whether Y Granger causes X. Note that now the coefficients have subscripts indicating which equation they are in. For instance, α_1 is the intercept in the first equation, and α_2 the intercept in the second. Furthermore, the errors now have subscripts to denote the fact that they will be different in the two equations.

These two equations comprise a VAR. A VAR is the extension of the autoregressive (AR) model to the case in which there is more than one variable under study. Remember that the AR model introduced in Chapter 9 involved one dependent variable, Y_t, which depended only on lags of itself (and possibly a deterministic trend). A VAR has more than one dependent variable (e.g. Y and X) and, thus, has more than one equation (e.g. one where Y_t is the dependent variable and one where X_t is). Each equation uses as its explanatory variables lags of *all the variables under study* (and possibly a deterministic trend).

The two equations above constitute a VAR with two variables. For instance, you can see that in the first equation Y depends on p lags of itself and on q lags of X. The lag lengths, p and q, can be selected using the sequential testing methods discussed in Chapters 8 through 10. However, especially if the VAR has more than two variables, many different lag lengths need to be selected (i.e. one for each variable in each equation). In light of this, it is common to set $p = q$ and use the same lag length for every variable in every equation. The resulting model is known as a VAR(p) model. The following VAR(p) has three variables, Y, X and Z:

$$Y_t = \alpha_1 + \delta_1 t + \phi_{11} Y_{t-1} + \ldots + \phi_{1p} Y_{t-p} + \beta_{11} X_{t-1} + \ldots + \beta_{1p} X_{t-p}$$
$$+ \delta_{11} Z_{t-1} + \ldots + \delta_{1p} Z_{t-p} + e_{1t},$$

$$X_t = \alpha_2 + \delta_2 t + \phi_{21} Y_{t-1} + \ldots + \phi_{2p} Y_{t-p} + \beta_{21} X_{t-1} + \ldots + \beta_{2p} X_{t-p}$$
$$+ \delta_{21} Z_{t-1} + \ldots + \delta_{2p} Z_{t-p} + e_{2t},$$

$$Z_t = \alpha_3 + \delta_3 t + \phi_{31} Y_{t-1} + \ldots + \phi_{3p} Y_{t-p} + \beta_{31} X_{t-1} + \ldots + \beta_{3p} X_{t-p}$$
$$+ \delta_{31} Z_{t-1} + \ldots + \delta_{3p} Z_{t-p} + e_{3t}.$$

Note that, in addition to an intercept and deterministic trend, each equation contains p lags of all variables in study. VAR(p) models with more than three variables can be obtained in an analogous manner.

Since we assume that all the variables in the VAR(p) are stationary, estimation and testing can be carried out in the standard way. That is, you can obtain estimates of coefficients in each equation using OLS. P-values or t-statistics will then allow you to ascertain whether individual coefficients are significant. You can also use the material covered in Appendix 11.1 to carry out more complicated F-tests. However, as we have stressed above, there are many software packages that allow you to work with VARs in an easier fashion (e.g. Stata, MicroFit or E-views) than any spreadsheet.

VARs are, then, easy to use (especially if you have an appropriate computer software package). However, you may be wondering why we would want to work with such models. One reason has to be Granger causality testing. That is, VARs provide a framework for testing for Granger causality between each set of variables. However, there are many other reasons for why we would want to use them that we should also mention. For instance, a point which we will discuss below is that VARs are often used for forecasting. However, financial researchers also use VARs in many other contexts. This is not a book that discusses financial theory, so exact derivations of the financial theories motivating use of VARs will not be provided. But models involving so-called present value relationships often work with VARs using the (log) dividend-price ratio and dividend growth. VARs have been used to investigate issues relating to the term structure of interest rates (using interest rates of various maturities, interest rate spreads, etc.), intertemporal asset allocation (using returns on various risky assets), the rational valuation formula (using the dividend-price ratio and returns), the interaction of bond and equity markets (using stock and bond return data), etc. Even if you do not understand details of the previous sentences, the point to note is that VARs have been used in a wide variety of financial problems. In the following material, we work through one particularly popular financial VAR.

Example: What moves the stock and bond markets?

An influential paper in the *Journal of Finance* in 1991 ("What moves the stock and bond markets? A variance decomposition for long-term asset returns" by Campbell and Ammer) investigated the factors which influenced the stock and bond markets in the long run. Without going into the theoretical derivations, suffice it to note here that the authors develop a model where, at a given point in time, unexpected movements in excess stock returns should depend on changes in expectations (i.e. news) about future dividend flows, future excess stock returns and future real interest rates. Similarly, current unexpected movements in excess bond returns should depend on changes in expectations (i.e. news) about future inflation, future interest rates and future excess bond returns. The question of interest is which of these various factors is most important in driving the stock and bond markets. The authors conclude that news about future excess stock returns is the most important factor in driving the stock market and news about future inflation is the most important factor in driving the bond market.

A key part of this model (and many similar models) is that the researcher has to distinguish between "expected" and "unexpected" values of variables. To show how this distinction is operationalized, let er_t be the excess return on the stock market at time t. Consider the investor at time $t - 1$ trying to make investment decisions. At time $t - 1$, she will not know exactly what er_t will be. However, she will have some expectation about what it might be. Let us denote the expectation at time $t - 1$ of what the excess stock return at time t will be by $E_{t-1}(er_t)$. (We remind the reader that expected values were defined and discussed at the end of Chapter 2. Please refer back to this material if you have forgotten what an expected value is.) As discussed in the previous paragraph, unexpected movements in stock and bond markets are crucial to the underlying financial theory. These are defined as $er_t - E_{t-1}(er_t)$ (i.e. unexpected things are defined as the difference between what actually happened and what was expected).

Even though we have not spelled out all the details, we hope the previous paragraph has motivated why expectations such $E_{t-1}(er_t)$ appear in financial models. VARs are frequently used to model such expectations. That is, since the right-hand side of an equation in a VAR only contains variables dated $t - 1$ or earlier, it can be thought of as reflecting information available to the investor at time $t - 1$. So if we have an equation where er_t is the dependent variable we can use the fitted value from this regression (see Chapter 4 for a discussion of fitted values) as an estimate of $E_{t-1}(er_t)$. Using this informal motivation for why VARs are useful, and noting that some variables (e.g. dividend-price ratios) have been found useful for long-run prediction of stock and bond markets, the authors of the paper end up working with a VAR involving the following six variables:[4]

1. er is the excess stock return.
2. r is the real interest rate.
3. dy is the change in the return on a short-term bond.
4. s is the yield spread (difference in yields between a 10-year and a two-month bond).
5. dp is the log of the dividend-price ratio.
6. rb is the relative bill rate (a return on a short-term bond relative to the average returns over the last year).

Monthly observations from December 1947 through February 1987 on all of these variables are available in the data set VAR.XLS.

We should mention that the authors did extensive testing to confirm that all of these variables are stationary. In general, before carrying out an analysis using time series data, you must conduct unit root tests. Remember that, if unit roots are present but cointegration does not occur, then the spurious regression problem exists. In this case, you should work with differenced data. Alternatively, if unit roots exist and cointegration does occur, then you will have important information that the series are trending together. In the present case, tests indicate that we can accept the hypothesis that all variables are stationary.

Exercise 11.4

Use the data on all the variables in VAR.XLS. Test for unit roots in each of the variables.

Table 11.3 presents results from estimation of a VAR(1). Note that this table is in a slightly different format from previous ones. Since there are six variables in our VAR (i.e. er, r, dy, s, dp and rb), there are six equations to estimate. We have put results for all equations in one table. Each equation regresses a dependent variable on one lag of all the variables in the VAR. To save space, we have included only the OLS estimate and P-value of each coefficient with the P-value being in parentheses below the estimate.

If we examine the significant coefficients (i.e. those with P-value less than 0.05), some interesting patterns emerge. There are not too many significant coefficients – it is often hard to predict financial variables. However, it can be seen

Table 11.3 Estimates from a VAR(1) with er, r, dy, s, dp and rb as dependent variables (P-values in parentheses).

	Dependent variable					
	er_t	r_t	dy_t	s_t	dp_t	rb_t
Interc.	−1.593	0.678	0.116	0.066	−0.007	0.082
	(0.053)	(0.354)	(0.362)	(0.562)	(0.635)	(0.516)
er_{t-1}	−0.018	−0.099	0.013	−0.004	−0.043	0.014
	(0.696)	(0.041)	(0.064)	(0.573)	(0.000)	(0.042)
r_{t-1}	0.033	0.473	−0.012	0.007	−0.0004	−0.011
	(0.466)	(0.000)	(0.089)	(0.237)	(0.608)	(0.104)
dy_{t-1}	−0.640	0.416	0.067	−0.045	0.003	0.096
	(0.056)	(0.161)	(0.196)	(0.326)	(0.585)	(0.062)
s_{t-1}	0.318	0.215	0.075	0.862	0.004	0.100
	(0.173)	(0.299)	(0.037)	(0.000)	(0.407)	(0.006)
dp_{t-1}	0.425	−0.087	−0.048	0.026	1.005	−0.049
	(0.012)	(0.561)	(0.066)	(0.261)	(0.000)	(0.061)
rb_{t-1}	−0.357	0.064	−0.011	−0.017	1.56	0.888
	(0.174)	(0.783)	(0.778)	(0.643)	(0.119)	(0.000)

that there are some significant explanatory variables. For instance, the last month's dividend-price ratio does have significant explanatory power for excess stock returns this month. Last month's yield spread does have explanatory power for the change in short-term bond returns.

Some financial researchers would simply report the results from the VAR as shedding light on the inter-relationships between key financial variables. However, others would use results from this VAR as a first step in an analysis of what moves the stock and bond markets. A common method of doing this is through something called a **variance decomposition**. It is difficult to explain variance decompositions without using concepts beyond the scope of this book. The interested reader will find an informal discussion of variance decompositions in Appendix 11.2 at the end of this chapter. To give the reader a little flavor of the kinds of questions variance decompositions can answer, note that, in the Campbell and Ammer paper, the authors use them to make statements such that it "attributes only 15% of the variance of stock returns to the variance of news about future dividends, and 70% to news about future excess returns".

Lag length selection in VARs

The results in the previous example are based on a VAR(1). That is, we set $p = 1$ and used one lag of each variable to explain the dependent variable. In general, of course, we might want to set p to values other than one. The literature on lag length selection in VARs is voluminous and most of the criteria suggested are too complicated to be easily calculated using a spreadsheet such as Excel. However, more sophisticated statistical packages do automatically calculate many criteria for lag length. For instance, Stata calculates several **information criteria** with names like **Akaike's information criterion (AIC)**, the **Schwarz Bayes information criterion (SBIC)** and the **Hannan–Quinn information criterion (HQIC)**. A full explanation of these would require concepts beyond those covered in this book. However, for use in practice, all you need to know is that these can be calculated for VARs for every lag length up to p_{max} (the maximum possible lag length that is reasonable). You then select the lag length which yields the smallest value for your information criterion.[5]

In addition, the *t*-stats and P-values we have used throughout this book provide useful information on lag length.

If we estimate VAR(p) models for $p = 1, 2, 3$ and 4 using the data in VAR.XLS we obtain the results shown in Table 11.4.

Note that the SBIC and HQIC select VAR(2)'s since the smallest values for these criteria occur at this lag length. However, the AIC selects a VAR(4). This is the kind of conflict which often occurs in empirical practice: one criterion (or hypothesis test) indicates one thing whereas another similar criterion indicates something else. There is nothing you can do when this happens other than honestly report that this has occurred. There are statistical reasons (which we will not discuss) for thinking that

Table 11.4 Information criteria for VAR(p) for different
lag lengths.

Lag length	AIC	SBIC	HQIC
$p = 1$	8.121	8.267	8.492
$p = 2$	7.084	7.355	7.774
$p = 3$	7.026	7.424	8.037
$p = 4$	6.934	7.458	8.266

the AIC might tend to choose too long a lag length. Accordingly, most researchers, facing the results in the tables, would be inclined to simply work with a VAR(2). For the sake of brevity, we will not present coefficients for the VAR(2) as this model would involve six equations with each equation having 13 explanatory variables (e.g. two lags of each of six variables plus the intercept). To present all these estimates would require a large table.

Exercise 11.5

Estimate a VAR(2) using the data in VAR.XLS. Which explanatory variables are significant? Discuss Granger causality among all the variables in the model.

Exercise 11.6

Excel file LONGGDP.XLS, as you will recall, contains annual data on real GDP per capita for four of the largest English-speaking countries (USA, UK, Canada and Australia) for the years 1870–1993. Take differences to obtain time series of the growth in GDP per capita for each of the four countries. Construct a VAR using this data.

Forecasting with VARs

We have said relatively little in the book so far about forecasting, despite the fact that this is an important activity of financial researchers. There are two main reasons for omitting the topic. First, the field of forecasting is enormous. Given the huge volume of research and issues to consider, it is impossible to do justice to the field in a book like this.[6] Second, basic forecasting using the computer is either very easy or very hard, depending on what computer software you have. To be precise, many computer packages (e.g. Stata or MicroFit) have forecasting facilities that are simple to use. Once you have estimated a model (e.g. a VAR or an AR), you can forecast simply by adding an appropriate option to an estimation command. In other words, many computer packages can allow you to undertake basic forecasting without a deep knowledge of the topic. However, spreadsheets such as Excel typically do not have forecasting capabilities for the models used in this book. It is possible to calculate forecasts, but it is awkward, involving extensive typing of formulae.

In light of these issues, we will offer only a brief introduction to some of the practical issues and intuitive ideas relating to forecasting. All our discussion will relate to forecasting with VARs but it is worth noting that the ideas also relate to forecasting with univariate time series models. After all, an AR model is just a VAR with only one equation.

Forecasting is usually done using time series variables. The idea is that you use your observed data to predict what you expect to happen in the future. In more technical terms, you use data for periods $t = 1, \ldots, T$ to forecast periods $T + 1$, $T + 2$, etc.

To provide some intuition for how forecasting is done, consider a VAR(1) involving two variables, Y and X:

$$Y_t = \alpha_1 + \delta_1 t + \phi_{11} Y_{t-1} + \beta_{11} X_{t-1} + e_{1t},$$

and

$$X_t = \alpha_2 + \delta_2 t + \phi_{21} Y_{t-1} + \beta_{21} X_{t-1} + e_{2t}.$$

You cannot observe Y_{T+1} but you want to make a guess of what it is likely to be. Using the first equation of the VAR and setting $t = T + 1$, we obtain an expression for Y_{T+1}:

$$Y_{T+1} = \alpha_1 + \delta_1 (T+1) + \phi_{11} Y_T + \beta_{11} X_T + e_{1T+1}.$$

This equation cannot be directly used to obtain Y_{T+1} since we don't know what e_{1T+1} is. In words, we don't know what unpredictable shock or surprise will hit the economy next period. Furthermore, we do not know what the coefficients are. However, if we ignore the error term (which cannot be forecast since it is unpredictable) and replace the coefficients by their estimates we obtain a forecast which we denote as $\hat{Y}_{T+1}$:

$$\hat{Y}_{T+1} = \hat{\alpha}_1 + \hat{\delta}_1 (T+1) + \hat{\phi}_{11} Y_T + \hat{\beta}_{11} X_T.$$

If you are working in a spreadsheet such as Excel, note that everything in the formula for $\hat{Y}_{T+1}$ can be taken from either the original data or from the output from the regression command. It is conceptually easy just to plug in all the individual numbers (i.e. the estimates of the coefficients and Y_T, X_T and $T + 1$) into a formula to calculate $\hat{Y}_{T+1}$. A similar strategy can be used to obtain $\hat{X}_{T+1}$. You can see how, in practice, calculating these forecasts in this way can be awkward and time consuming. Hence, if you plan on doing more forecasting, we stress that it is preferable to avoid spreadsheets such as Excel and work with specialized statistical packages such as Stata or MicroFit.

The previous paragraph described how to forecast one period into the future. We can use the same strategy for two periods, provided that we make one extension. In the one period case, we used X_T and Y_T to create $\hat{Y}_{T+1}$ and $\hat{X}_{T+1}$. In the two period case, $\hat{Y}_{T+2}$ and $\hat{X}_{T+2}$ depend on Y_{T+1} and X_{T+1}. But since our data only runs until period T, we do not know what Y_{T+1} and X_{T+1} are. Consequently, we replace Y_{T+1} and X_{T+1} by $\hat{Y}_{T+1}$ and $\hat{X}_{T+1}$. That is, use the relevant equation from the VAR, ignore the error, replace the coefficients by their estimates and replace past values of the variables that we do not observe by their forecasts. In a formula:

$$\hat{Y}_{T+2} = \hat{\alpha}_1 + \hat{\delta}_1(T+2) + \hat{\phi}_{11}\hat{Y}_{T+1} + \hat{\beta}_{11}\hat{X}_{T+1}.$$

The above equation can be calculated in a spreadsheet, although somewhat awkwardly. $\hat{X}_{T+2}$ can be calculated in a similar manner using the formula:

$$\hat{X}_{T+2} = \hat{\alpha}_2 + \hat{\delta}_2(T+2) + \hat{\phi}_{21}\hat{Y}_{T+1} + \hat{\beta}_{21}\hat{X}_{T+1}.$$

We can use the general strategy of ignoring the error, replacing coefficients by their estimates and replacing lagged values of variables that are unobserved by forecasts, to obtain forecasts for any number of periods in the future for any VAR(p).

The previous discussion demonstrated how to calculate point estimates of forecasts. Of course, in reality, what actually happens is rarely identical to your forecast. In Chapter 5, we discussed a similar issue. There we pointed out that OLS provides estimates only of coefficients, and that these will not be precisely correct. For this reason, in addition to estimates, we also recommended that you present confidence intervals. These reflect the level of uncertainty about the coefficient estimate. When forecasting, confidence intervals can also be calculated, and these can be quite informative. It is increasingly common for government agencies, for instance, to present confidence intervals for their forecasts. For instance, the Bank of England can be heard on occasion to make statements of the form: "Our forecast of inflation next year is 1.8%. We are 95% confident that it will be between 1.45% and 2.15%". Many computer packages automatically provide confidence intervals and, thus, you do not need to know their precise formula when forecasting. If you are using a spreadsheet, the formula is fairly complicated and it would be awkward to calculate, which is why we do not present it here.

Exercise 11.7

It is recommended that you do this question and others involving forecasting only if you have access to a computer package that is capable of doing forecasts. If you are working with a spreadsheet such as Excel this question will be difficult.

Use the variables *er*, *r*, *dy*, *s*, *dp* and *rb* from VAR.XLS which contains data until February 1987.

(a) Using data through December 1986 and a VAR(p) for various values of p (e.g. p = 1, 3, 4) construct forecasts for all variables for January and

February 1987. Are these forecasts close to the actual values of these variables in these months?

(b) In part (a), data from December 1947 through December 1986 was used to estimate the VAR, which was then used to forecast January and February 1987. Try forecasting for longer and longer periods. For instance, try using data through the end of 1985 to forecast 1986 and 1987 data. Now try using data through the end of 1984 to forecast 1985, 1986 and 1987 data, etc. Discuss your results. Do your results suggest that VARs are better at forecasting a short period ahead than a long period?

Exercise 11.8

Using the data in Exercise 11.6 and the VAR constructed therein, carry out a forecasting exercise for GDP growth for the four included countries. Experiment with various forecast horizons. Does the VAR forecast well?

Vector autoregressions with cointegrated variables

In the preceding discussion of VARs we assumed that all variables are stationary. If some of the original variables have unit roots and are **not** cointegrated, then the ones with unit roots should be differenced and the resulting stationary variables should be used in the VAR. This covers every case except the one where the variables have unit roots and are cointegrated.

Recall that in this case in the discussion of Granger causality, we recommended that you work with an ECM. The same strategy can be employed here. In particular, instead of working with a vector autoregression (VAR), you should work with a vector error correction model (VECM). Like the VAR, the VECM will have one equation for each variable in the model. In the case of two variables, Y and X, the VECM is:

$$\Delta Y_t = \varphi_1 + \delta_1 t + \lambda_1 e_{t-1} + \gamma_{11}\Delta Y_{t-1} + \ldots + \gamma_{1p}\Delta Y_{t-p} + \omega_{11}\Delta X_{t-1} + \ldots + \omega_{1q}\Delta X_{t-q} + \varepsilon_{1t}$$

and

$$\Delta X_t = \varphi_2 + \delta_2 t + \lambda_2 e_{t-1} + \gamma_{21}\Delta Y_{t-1} + \ldots + \gamma_{2p}\Delta Y_{t-p}$$
$$+ \omega_{21}\Delta X_{t-1} + \ldots + \omega_{2q}\Delta X_{t-q} + \varepsilon_{2t}.$$

As before, $e_{t-1} = Y_{t-1} - \alpha - \beta X_{t-1}$. Note that the VECM is the same as a VAR with differenced variables, except for the term e_{t-1}. An estimate of this error correction variable can be obtained by running an OLS regression of Y on X and saving the residuals. We can then use OLS to estimate ECMs, and P-values and confidence intervals can be obtained. Lag length selection and forecasting can be done in a similar fashion to the VAR, with the slight added complication that forecasts of the error correction term, e_t, must be calculated. However, this is simple using OLS estimates of α and β and replacing the error, e_t, by the residual u_t. Furthermore, many computer packages such as Stata or MicroFit will do estimation, testing and forecasting in VECMs automatically. We have mentioned many financial examples where cointegration occurs (see Chapter 10) and will not repeat this material here. However, we will go through an extended example shortly.

Of course, as with any of the models used in this chapter, you should always do unit root tests to see if your variables are stationary or not. If your variables have unit roots, then it is additionally worthwhile to test for cointegration. In the previous chapter, we introduced a test for cointegration based on checking whether there is a unit root in the residuals from the cointegrating regression. However, there is a more popular cointegration test called the **Johansen test**. To explain this test would require a discussion of concepts beyond the scope of this book. However, if you have a software package (e.g. Stata) which does the Johansen test, then you can use it in practice. Accordingly, we offer a brief intuitive description of this test.

The first thing to note is that it is possible for more than one cointegrating relationship to exist if you are working with several time series variables (all of which you have tested and found to have unit roots). To be precise, if you are working with M variables, then it is possible to have up to $M - 1$ cointegrating relationships (and, thus, up to $M - 1$ cointegrating residuals included in the VECM). For instance, in Chapter 10 we mentioned a financial theory arguing that the cay variables (consumption, assets and income) are cointegrated. As we shall see below, there probably is just one cointegrating relationship between these variables. That is, c, a and y all have unit roots, but $c_t - \alpha - \beta_1 a_t - \beta_2 y_t$ is stationary. However, in theory it would have been possible for there to be two cointegrating relationships (e.g. if $c_t - y_t$ and $a_t - y_t$ were both stationary). Thus, it is often of interest to test, not simply for whether cointegrating is present or not, but for the number of cointegrating relationships.

The Johansen test can be used to test for the number of cointegrating relationships using VECMs. For reasons we will not explain, the "number of cointegrating relationships" is referred to as the "cointegrating rank". The details of the Johansen test statistic are quite complicated. However, like any hypothesis test, you can compare the test statistic to a critical value and, if the test statistic is greater than the critical value, you reject the hypothesis being tested. Fortunately, many software packages (e.g. Stata) will calculate all these numbers for you. We will see how this works in the following example.

Before working through this example, note that when you do the Johansen test you have to specify the lag length and the deterministic trend term. The former we have discussed before. That is, lag length can be selected using information criteria as described above. With VECMs it is possible simply to put an intercept and/or deterministic trend in the model (as we have done in the equations above – see the terms with coefficients φ and δ on them). However, it is also possible to put an intercept and/or deterministic trend actually in the cointegrating residual (e.g. if you say $c_t - \alpha$

$- \beta_1 a_t - \beta_2 y_t$ is the cointegrating residual you are putting an intercept into it). The Johansen test varies slightly depending on the exact configuration of deterministic terms you use, so you will be asked to specify these before doing the Johansen test.

Example: Consumption, aggregate wealth and expected stock returns

In an influential paper in the *Journal of Finance* in 2001, "Consumption, aggregate wealth and expected stock returns", Lettau and Ludvigson present financial theory arguing that the cay variables should be cointegrated and the cointegrating residual should be able to predict excess stock returns. They then present empirical evidence in favor of their theory. In a subsequent paper ("Understanding trend and cycle in asset values: Reevaluating the wealth effect on consumption" in the *American Economic Review* in 2004), using the cay data, they build on this argument using VECMs and present variance decompositions which shed light on their theory (we will discuss the variance decomposition in Appendix 11.2).

We will not repeat the theory (nor will we consider the forecasting aspect of their paper). However, we stress that their work uses all the tools we have been developing in this chapter: testing for cointegration, estimation of a VECM and variance decompositions. We will investigate the presence of cointegration here using US data from 1951Q4 through 2003Q1 on c which is consumption (formally it is the log of real per capita expenditures on nondurables and services excluding shoes and clothing); a which is our measure of assets (formally it is the log of a measure of real per capita household net worth including all financial and household wealth as well as consumer durables); and y which is the log of after-tax labor income. This data is available in CAY.XLS.

Unit root tests indicate that all of these variables have unit roots. If we do the Johansen test using a lag length of one and restricting the deterministic term to allow for intercepts only (i.e. no deterministic trends such as those with coefficients δ in the previous equations are allowed for), we get the results in Table (using Stata).

Table 11.5 Johansen test for cointegration using cay data.

Rank	Trace statistic	5% Critical value
0	37.27	29.68
1	6.93	15.41
2	0.95	3.76

How should you interpret this table? Note first that "Trace statistic" is the name of the test statistic used in the Johansen test and "Rank" indicates the number of cointegrating relationships with Rank = 0 indicating cointegration is not present. With the Johansen test, the hypothesis being tested is always a certain cointegrating rank with the alternative hypothesis being that cointegrating rank is greater than hypothesis being tested.

If we compare the Trace statistic to its critical value we can see, for Rank = 0, that the test statistic is greater than the 5% critical value. This means we can reject the hypotheses that Rank = 0 at the 5% level of significance (in favor of the hypothesis that Rank ≥ 1). Thus, the Johansen test indicates that cointegration is present. However, if we look at the row with Rank = 1 we see that the test statistic is less than the critical value. Thus, we can accept that hypothesis that Rank = 1 (and are not finding evidence in favor of Rank ≥ 2). Thus, we are finding evidence that Rank = 1 (with this evidence, the information in the last row of the table is not relevant). As expected by Lettau and Ludvigson, we are finding evidence that one cointegrating relationship exists in this data set.

Armed with the information that one cointegrating relationship seems to exist, you can then (following Lettau and Ludvigson) calculate the cointegrating residual and investigate whether this has predictive power for expected stock returns. Alternatively, you could use this information to specify a VECM with one cointegrating relationship (and, thus, one error correction term). Following Lettau and Ludvigson, you could then do a variance decomposition to investigate further issues in financial economics (see Appendix 11.2 for more details).

Exercise 11.9

For this question, use the data on spot and forward exchange rates in FOREX.XLS.

(a) Starting with $p_{max} = 4$, select a lag length for the VECM and estimate the VECM.
(b) Using the VECM from part (a), carry out a forecasting exercise. Experiment with various forecast horizons. Does the VECM forecast well?

Exercise 11.10

Use the data on Y = long-term interest rates and X = short-term interest rates in INTERESTRATES.XLS.

(a) Assume (perhaps incorrectly in light of Exercise 10.4) that Y and X are cointegrated. Repeat the steps in Exercise 11.9 to carry out a forecasting exercise.

(b) Now assume that Y and X have unit roots but are not cointegrated. Construct a VAR using differenced data (i.e. ΔY and ΔX) and carry out a forecasting exercise.

(c) Compare results from part (a) and (b). What effect does assuming (possibly incorrectly) cointegration have on forecasting performance?

Exercise 11.11

Use the data from CAY.XLS.

(a) Test for unit roots in all the variables in this data set.

(b) Test for cointegration in these variables using the Engle–Granger test from Chapter 10. Does this test yield the same finding as the Johansen test?

(c) In Table 11.5, the Johansen test was done with one lag. Does the finding of the Johansen test differ if you use two lags? Three lags? Four lags?

(d) Discuss the issue of lag length selection in this data set using information criteria.

Chapter summary

1. X Granger causes Y if past values of X have explanatory power for Y.
2. If X and Y are stationary, standard statistical methods based on an ADL model can be used to test for Granger causality.
3. If X and Y have unit roots and are cointegrated, statistical methods based on an ECM can be used to test for Granger causality.
4. Vector autoregressions, or VARs, have one equation for each variable being studied. Each equation chooses one variable as the dependent variable. The explanatory variables are lags of all the variables under study.
5. VARs are useful for forecasting, testing for Granger causality or, more generally, understanding the relationships between several series.
6. If all the variables in the VAR are stationary, OLS can be used to estimate each equation and standard statistical methods can be employed (e.g. P-values and t-statistics can be used to test for significance of variables).
7. If the variables under study have unit roots and are cointegrated, a variant on the VAR called the Vector Error Correction Model, or VECM, should be used.
8. The Johansen test is a very popular test for cointegration included in many software packages.

Appendix 11.1: Hypothesis tests involving more than one coefficient

In Chapters 5 and 6 we discussed the F-statistic, which was used for testing the hypothesis $R^2 = 0$ in the multiple regression model:

$$Y = \alpha + \beta_1 X_1 + \beta_2 X_2 + \ldots + \beta_k X_k + e.$$

We discussed how this was equivalent to testing $H_0 : \beta_1 = \ldots = \beta_k = 0$ (i.e. whether all the regression coefficients are jointly equal to zero). We also discussed testing the significance of individual coefficients using t-statistics or P-values.

However, we have no tools for testing intermediate cases (e.g. in the case $k = 4$, we might be interested in testing $H_0 : \beta_1 = \beta_2 = 0$). Such cases arose in our discussion of Granger causality (e.g. we had a regression model with four lags of stock returns in Country A, four lags of stock returns in Country B and a deterministic trend and we were interested in testing whether the coefficients on the four lags of stock returns in Country B were all zero). The purpose of this appendix is to describe a procedure and a rough rule of thumb for carrying out these kind of tests.

The F-statistic described in Chapter 5 is more properly referred to as **an** F-statistic since it is only one of an enormous class of test statistics that take their critical values from statistical tables for the F-distribution. In this book, as you know by now, we have provided little statistical theory, and do not describe how to use statistical tables. However, if you plan to do much work in Granger causality testing, you are well-advised to study a basic statistics or econometrics book to learn more about the statistical underpinnings of hypothesis testing.

To understand the basic F-testing procedure we introduce a distinction between **unrestricted** and **restricted** regression models. That is, most hypotheses you would want to test place restrictions on the model. Hence, we can distinguish between the regression with the restrictions imposed and the regression without. For instance, if the unrestricted regression model is:

$$Y = \alpha + \beta_1 X_1 + \beta_2 X_2 + \beta_3 X_3 + \beta_4 X_4 + e,$$

and you wish to test the hypothesis $H_0 : \beta_2 = \beta_4 = 0$, then the restricted regression model is:

$$Y = \alpha + \beta_1 X_1 + \beta_3 X_3 + e.$$

The general strategy of hypothesis testing is that a test statistic is first calculated and then compared to a critical value. If the test statistic is greater than the critical value then you reject the hypothesis; otherwise, you accept the hypothesis. In short, there are always two components to a hypothesis testing procedure: a test statistic and a critical value.

Here the test statistic is usually called the F-statistic and is given by:

$$f = \frac{\left(R_U^2 - R_R^2\right)/J}{R_U^2/(T-k)},$$

where R_U^2 and R_R^2 are the R^2s from the unrestricted and restricted regression models, respectively. J is the number of restrictions (e.g. $J = 2$ in our example since $\beta_2 = 0$ and $\beta_4 = 0$ are two restrictions). T is the number of observations and k is the number of explanatory variables in the unrestricted regression (including the intercept).

Note that the F-statistic can be obtained by running the unrestricted and restricted regressions (e.g. regress Y on X_1, X_2, X_3 and X_4 to get R_U^2, then regress Y on X_1 and X_3 to get R_R^2) and then calculating the above formula using a spreadsheet or calculator. Many specialist statistics packages (e.g. Stata or MicroFit) will calculate the F-statistic for you automatically if you specify the hypothesis being tested.

Obtaining the critical value with which to compare the F-statistic is a more problematic procedure (although some software packages will provide a P-value automatically). Formally, the critical value depends on $T - k$ and J. Most econometrics or statistics textbooks will contain statistical tables for the F-distribution which will provide the relevant critical values. Table 11.6 contains critical values which you may use as a rough rule of thumb if $T - k$ is large.

For instance, if you have a large number of observations, are testing $J = 2$ restrictions (i.e. $\beta_2 = 0$ and $\beta_4 = 0$), and you want to use the 5% level of significance, then you will use a critical value of 3.00 with which to compare the F-statistic.

To aid in interpretation, note that the case $J = 1$ has not been included since testing only one restriction is something that the t-statistic already does. Note also that the critical values always get smaller as the number of restrictions increases. This fact can be used to approximate critical values for values of J that are not included in Table 11.6.

For instance, the critical value for testing $J = 7$ restrictions will lie somewhere between the critical values for the restrictions $J = 5$ and $J = 10$ given in Table 11.6. In many cases, knowing that the correct critical value lies between two numbers will be enough for you to decide whether to accept or reject the hypothesis. Consequently, even though Table 11.6 does not include every possible value for J, you may be able to use it if J differs from those above.

Formally, the critical values in the previous table are correct if $T - k$ is equal to infinity. The correct critical values for $T - k > 100$ are quite close to these. To give

Table 11.6 Critical values for F-test if $T - k$ is large.

Significance level	$J = 2$	$J = 3$	$J = 4$	$J = 5$	$J = 10$	$J = 20$
5%	3.00	2.60	2.37	2.21	1.83	1.57
1%	4.61	3.78	3.32	3.02	2.32	1.88

Table 11.7   Critical values for *F*-test if $T - k$ is 40.

Significance level	$J = 2$	$J = 3$	$J = 4$	$J = 5$	$J = 10$	$J = 20$
5%	3.23	2.92	2.69	2.53	2.08	1.84
1%	5.18	4.31	3.83	3.51	2.80	2.37

you an idea of how bad an error may be made if $T - k < 100$, examine Table 11.7, which gives the correct critical values if $T - k = 40$.

As you can see, these critical values are all somewhat larger than those given in the table for $T - k$ equal to infinity. You may want to use these if your value for $T - k$ is about 40. However, we also report them here to get some idea of the error that may result if you use the large sample critical values. For instance, if $J = 2$, $T - k = 40$ and you obtain an *F*-statistic of 4 then using either table is fine: both state that the hypothesis should be rejected at the 5% level of significance. However, if the *F*-statistic were 3.1 you would incorrectly reject it using the large sample table.

In summary, you can safely use the methods and tables given in this appendix in the following cases:

1. If your sample size is large relative to the number of explanatory variables (e.g. $T - k > 100$) the large sample table above is fine.
2. If $T - k$ is approximately 40 the $T - k = 40$ table is a safe choice.
3. If $T - k$ is neither large, nor approximately 40, you are still safe using $T - k = 40$ table, provided your test statistic is not close to the critical value and provided $T - k$ is not extremely small (e.g. $T - k < 10$).

Generally speaking, so long as you have either a large number of data points or your data does not fall into one of these "borderline" cases, you should not be led astray by using the methods outlined in this appendix.

Example: Do stock returns in Country A Granger cause stock returns in Country B? (continued from page 187)

In the body of this chapter, we carried out Granger causality tests using stock returns in two countries. We found that stock returns in Country B did not Granger cause stock returns in Country A, but that stock returns in Country A did Granger cause stock returns in Country B. Here, we will investigate whether these conclusions still hold by carrying out the correct *F*-tests for Granger causality.

Consider first whether stock returns in Country B Granger cause stock returns in Country A. In the body of the chapter we use the following unrestricted model where Y = stock returns in Country A and X = stock returns in Country B:

$$Y_t = \alpha + \delta t + \phi_1 Y_{t-1} + \ldots + \phi_4 Y_{t-4} + \beta_1 X_{t-1} + \ldots + \beta_4 X_{t-4} + e_t.$$

$T = 128$[7] and $k = 10$ (i.e. $p = q = 4$ plus we have the deterministic trend in the model). OLS estimation of this model yields $R_U^2 = 0.616$.

The hypothesis that Granger causality does not occur is $H_0 : \beta_1 = \ldots = \beta_4 = 0$ which involves 4 restrictions; hence $J = 4$. The restricted regression model is:

$$Y_t = \alpha + \delta t + \phi_1 Y_{t-1} + \ldots + \phi_4 Y_{t-4} + e_t.$$

OLS estimation of this model yields $R_R^2 = 0.613$.

Using these numbers we calculate that the F-statistic is 0.145. Since $T - k = 118$ and is large, we can compare 0.145 to a critical value of 2.37. Since 0.145 < 2.37 we cannot reject the hypothesis at the 5% level of significance. Accordingly, we accept the hypothesis that stock returns in Country B do not Granger cause stock returns in Country A.

To test whether stock returns in Country A Granger cause stock returns in Country B we repeat the steps above except that now the dependent variable refers to Country B and the explanatory variable refers to Country A. If we use OLS to estimate the restricted and unrestricted regressions, we obtain $R_U^2 = 0.605$ and $R_R^2 = 0.532$. Note that the other elements in the formula for the F-statistic do not change. Plugging these numbers into the equation for the F-statistic yields $f = 33.412$, which is much larger than either the 1% or 5% critical values. In this case, we can safely reject the hypothesis that $\beta_1 = \ldots = \beta_4 = 0$ and conclude that stock returns in Country A do Granger cause stock returns in Country B.

Note that the findings that stock returns in Country B do not Granger cause stock returns in Country A but that stock returns in Country A do Granger cause stock returns in Country B, are exactly the same as given in the body of the chapter. In general, however, the results from joint hypothesis testing may differ from individually testing each hypothesis.

Appendix 11.2: Variance decompositions

As the examples in this chapter have shown, variance decompositions are popular in finance. To fully understand what they are would require concepts beyond the scope of this book (e.g. matrix algebra). However, some statistical software packages allow you to calculate variance decompositions in a fairly straightforward manner. Accordingly, with a good software package, some intuition and a thorough understanding of the financial problem you are working on, it should be possible for you to do variance decompositions in practice even without matrix algebra. Furthermore, some intuition should help you to read and understand empirical results presented in many papers in finance. The purpose of this appendix is to provide such intuition about variance decompositions.

In the example "What moves the stock and bond markets?" discussed in the body of the chapter, recall that the underlying paper developed a model where unexpected movements in excess stock returns should depend on changes in expectations about future dividend flows and future excess stock returns (among other things). A key question was which of these various factors is most important in driving the stock markets. The authors' model is much more sophisticated, but a simplified version could be written as:

$$uer = newsd + newser$$

where *uer* is the component capturing unexpected movements in expected returns, *newsd* is the component reflecting future news about dividends and *newser* is the component reflecting future news about expected returns. Do not worry where these components come from other than to note that they can be calculated using the data and the VAR coefficients.

Financial researchers are interested in the relative roles played by *newsd* and *newser* in explaining *uer*. One way of measuring this is through variances. Remember (see Chapter 2) that, as its name suggests, the variance is a measure of the variability in a variable. We motivated the regression R^2 (see Chapter 4) as measuring the proportion of the variability in the dependent variable that could be explained by the explanatory variables. Here we can do something similar. That is, we can measure the proportion of the variability of *uer* that can be explained by *newsd* (or *newser*) and use this as a measure of the role played by *newsd* (or *newser*) in explaining *uer*. This is a simple example of a variance decomposition.

Formally, if *newsd* and *newser* are independent of one another[8] we have:

$$var(uer) = var(newsd) + var(newser).$$

If we divide both side of this equation by var(*uer*) then we get:

$$1 = \frac{var(newsd)}{var(uer)} + \frac{var(newser)}{var(uer)}.$$

The two terms on the right-hand side of this equation can be interpreted as measures of the relative roles of news about dividends and news about excess returns. For instance, the first of them can be interpreted as: "The proportion of the variability in unexpected excess returns that can be explained by news about future dividends is var(*newsd*)/var(*uer*)" and it can be calculated using the VAR.

The Lettau and Ludgvigson example using the cay data allows us to describe another common sort of variance decomposition. The empirical puzzle this paper is investigating is why the huge swings in stock markets over the last decade (e.g. the dot.com boom followed by the bust) did not have larger effects on consumption. The VECM they estimate, along with a variance decomposition, indicates a sensible story: that many fluctuations in the stock market were treated by households as being transitory and these did not have large effects on their consumption. Only permanent changes in wealth affected consumption. This kind of variance decomposition is a so-called "permanent-transitory decomposition".

Remember (see Chapter 9) that unit root variables have a long memory property. Errors in unit root variables tend to have permanent effects. However, the cointegrating error is, by definition, stationary. This can be interpreted as implying the cointegrating error will have only a transitory effect on any of the variables. In a VECM, our variables have unit roots in them, but the cointegrating error is stationary. Thus, it has some errors which have permanent effects and others which have transitory effects. Using the VECM, you can figure out these permanent and transitory components and do a variance decomposition in the same way as described above.

That is, a simplified version of such a model would imply:

$$a = permanent + transitory,$$

where *permanent* and *transitory* are the permanent and transitory components of assets (denoted by a, which includes stock market investments). As before we can take variances of both sides of the equation, divide by the variance of assets to get:

$$1 = \frac{var(permanent)}{var(a)} + \frac{var(transitory)}{var(a)},$$

and then use $var(permanent)/var(a)$ as a measure of the role of permanent shocks in driving fluctuations in assets.

These two examples are meant to give you an intuition about what variance decompositions are all about and how they are used in practice. To develop a deeper understanding, you will have to do additional reading in a textbook which uses more sophisticated mathematics than this one. For instance, *Quantitative Financial Economics* (Second edition) by Cuthbertson and Nitzsche (published by John Wiley & Sons, Ltd) has a discussion of variance decompositions on pages 296–302.

Endnotes

1. The notation "VAR" for "Vector Autoregression" is the standard one in financial econometrics. However, some financial analysts use VAR to denote "value-at-risk" which is a different concept altogether.
2. Note that the variable X_t has been omitted from this ADL(p, q) model. The reason is because Granger causality tests seek to determine whether past – not current – values of X can explain Y. If we were to include X_t we would be allowing for contemporaneous causality and all the difficulties noted previously in this book about interpreting both cor-

relations and regressions as reflecting causality would hold. You may also be wondering why we are using this ADL(p, q) model as opposed to the variant in which ΔY_t is the dependent variable (see Chapter 10). The reason is that it is easier to interpret Granger causality in this basic ADL(p, q) model as implying coefficients are equal to zero. We could have covered all the material in this section using our previous ADL(p, q) variant, but it would have led to some messy hypothesis tests.

3. This conclusion is based on an examination of the individual P-values for each coefficient. The joint test of $\beta_1 = \ldots = \beta_4 = 0$ is detailed in Appendix 11.1 and supports the conclusion that stock returns in Country B do not Granger cause stock returns in Country A.

4. Precise data sources and definitions are given in the original paper. To illustrate VAR techniques, the definitions provided here are adequate.

5. This statement is true in Stata (and most financial econometrics textbooks and software packages). However, confusingly, some statisticians define information criteria as being the negative of that used by Stata. With this definition, you would select the lag length which yields the largest value for the information criterion. So please be careful when using information criteria and read the manual or help facilities of your computer software.

6. One introductory text is Philip Hans Franses, *Time Series Models for Business Economics and Forecasting*, Cambridge University Press.

7. Remember that differencing variables and including lagged variables in a regression decreases the number of observations, which is why $T = 128$ rather than $T = 133$.

8. If news about dividends and excess returns are correlated then the covariance between the two will enter this formula.

CHAPTER 12

Financial volatility

Chapters 8–11 developed several different regression models for time series variables. Throughout, we were always interested in the variables themselves. For instance, we were interested in explaining stock or bond returns, exchange rates and yield spreads. However, there are many cases where we are not interested in the variables themselves, but in their volatility (measured by the variance). For instance, in Chapter 4 we introduced the capital asset pricing model (CAPM) and discussed how risk was important for investment decisions. The risk of investing in the stock of a company was related to the volatility of its share price (and other factors).

Another very important field of research relates to the pricing of financial derivatives (e.g. options and other securities whose payoff is derived from the price of an underlying asset). If you have studied the theory of finance, you may be aware of the Black–Scholes option price formula and other similar derivative pricing methods. In this book, we will not derive such formulae. We note only that, in these formulae, the volatility of the price of the underlying asset plays a crucial role. The methods introduced in this chapter are commonly used to provide estimates of this volatility.

We begin our discussion of volatility in asset prices informally, staying with familiar regression methods. We then discuss a very popular method for estimating financial volatility called **autoregressive conditional heteroskedasticity (ARCH)**. The ARCH model shares a great deal of intuition with the regression model (including the AR model), but is not exactly the same as a regression model. Accordingly, methods like OLS cannot be used with ARCH. However, many computer software packages (e.g. Stata, E-views, MicroFit, etc.) can estimate ARCH models. So the fact that the theory underlying the estimation of ARCH models is difficult need not preclude your using them in practice. This chapter also discusses some extensions of ARCH models.

Volatility in asset prices: Introduction

To provide some intuition, recall our discussion of the random walk model in Chapter 9. We defined the model as:

$$Y_t = Y_{t-1} + e_t$$

or

$$\Delta Y_t = e_t.$$

We then noted that there were good reasons for believing that such a model might be appropriate for measuring economic phenomena like stock prices or exchange rate. In other words, the stock return (exclusive of dividends) was unpredictable.

The simple random walk model is a little unreasonable as a description of stock price behavior since stocks do appreciate in value over time. A slightly more realistic model is:

$$\Delta Y_t = \alpha + e_t.$$

This model can be interpreted as implying that stock prices, on average, increase by α per period, but are otherwise unpredictable. Known as the **random walk with drift** model, it adds an intercept to the random walk model, thus allowing stock prices to "drift" upwards over time (if $\alpha > 0$). Equivalently, stock returns are on average α but are otherwise unpredictable.

In the rest of this section, we will assume that the random walk model for an asset price is the correct one. That is, we will assume that either the asset price follows a pure random walk or that it follows a random walk with drift, and that we have taken deviations from the mean. To avoid confusion, we will let Δy_t indicate the series with deviations from means taken (i.e. $\Delta y_t = \Delta Y_t - \Delta \overline{Y}$, where $\Delta \overline{Y} = \Sigma \Delta Y_t / T$). Remember that taking deviations from the mean implies that there is no intercept in the model (see Appendix 4.1). Thus, even if the asset price is drifting upwards over time we can ignore the drift term and simply write, $\Delta y_t = e_t$.

Although the ARCH model provides a better definition for volatility, it is possible to simply use Δy_t^2 as an estimate of volatility at time t. To motivate this choice, note that high volatility is associated with big changes, either in a positive or in a negative direction. Since any number squared becomes positive, large rises or large falls in the price of an asset will imply Δy_t^2 is positive and large. In contrast, in stable times the asset price will not be changing much and Δy_t^2 will be small. Hence, our measure of volatility will be small in stable times and large in chaotic times.

An alternative motivation for our measure of volatility can be obtained by recalling some material from Chapter 2. There we stressed that variance is a measure of the volatility of a variable. In general, it is common practice to equate the two and use variance as a measure of volatility. But using the variance as a measure of volatility presents problems in the present context. A key point here is that we want to allow the volatility of an asset to change over time. The volatility at time t might be different from that at time $t - 1$ or $t + 1$, etc. In Chapter 2, we used all observations to provide one estimate of the variance. Here we can use only the observation at time t to provide an estimate of the variance at time t. (In other words, it makes no sense to use data at time $t + 1$ to estimate the variance at time t since the variance might be different in the two periods.)

If you: (i) note that we can only use one observation to estimate the variance; (ii) note that we have assumed the data is in deviations from mean form and, hence, has mean zero; and (iii) use the formula for the variance from Chapter 2, then you obtain Δy_t^2 as an estimate of the variance.[1]

You can calculate this measure of volatility of an asset price quite easily in any spreadsheet or statistical computer package simply by differencing the stock price data, taking deviations from means and then squaring it. Once this is done, you will have a new time series variable – volatility – which you can then analyze using the tools introduced earlier.

Autoregressive models are commonly used to model "clustering in volatility", which is often present in financial time series data. Consider, for instance, an AR(1) model that uses volatility as the time series variable of interest:

$$\Delta y_t^2 = \alpha + \phi \Delta y_{t-1}^2 + e_t.$$

This model has volatility in a period depending on volatility in a previous period. If, for instance, $\phi > 0$ then if volatility was unusually high last period (e.g. Δy_{t-1}^2 was very large), it will also tend to be unusually high this period. Alternatively, if volatility was unusually low last period (e.g. Δy_{t-1}^2 was near zero) then this period's volatility will also tend to be low. In other words, if the volatility is low it will tend to stay low, if it is high it will tend to stay high. Of course, the presence of the error, e_t, means that there can be exceptions to this pattern. But, in general, this model implies that we will tend to observe intervals or clusters in time where volatility is low and intervals where it is high. In empirical studies of asset prices, such a pattern is very common. As an example, recall that in Chapter 2, we plotted the £/$ exchange rate (see Figure 2.1). If you look back at this figure, you can see long spells when the exchange rate changed very little (e.g. 1949–1967 and 1993–1996) and other, longer spells (e.g. 1985–1992) where it was more volatile.

The previous discussion refers to the AR(1) model, but it can be extended to the AR(p) model. All of the intuition given in Chapter 9 is relevant here. The only difference is that the interpretation relates to the volatility of the series rather than to the series itself. Furthermore, all of the statistical techniques we described in Chapter 9 are relevant here. Provided the series is stationary (e.g. $|\phi| < 1$ in the AR(1) case), then OLS estimates and P-values can be interpreted in the standard way. Testing for a unit root can be conducted using a Dickey–Fuller test. In short, there is nothing statistically new here.

Example: Volatility in stock prices

Excel worksheet STOCK.XLS contains data on $Y =$ the stock price of a company collected each week for four years (i.e. $T = 208$). The data has been logged. Figure 12.1 provides a time series plot of this data.

You can see that the price of this stock has tended to increase over time, although there are several periods when it also fell. The price of the stock was £24.53 per share in the first month, increasing to £30.14 in the 208th month.[2]

Figure 12.2 plots ΔY, the percentage change in Y. Since $100 \times [\ln(Y_t) - \ln(Y_{t-1})]$ is the percentage change in the stock price, we multiply the first difference of the data used to create Figure 12.1 by 100.

An examination of Figure 12.2 indicates that the change in stock price in any given week was usually positive, but that there were some weeks when the price fell. In the middle of the period of study (i.e. roughly weeks 90–110), there were many large changes (both in a positive and a negative direction). For instance, in weeks 94 and 96 the stock price increased by over 1.5%. This is a huge increase in one week. If increases of this magnitude were to keep on occurring for a year, the price of the stock would more than double (i.e. a weekly return of 1.5% becomes an annualized return of over 100%). However, in weeks 92, 93 and 95, stock prices fell by almost as much. All in all, the stock price in this middle period was much more volatile than in others.

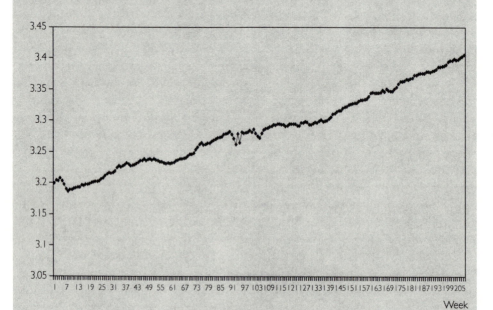

Fig. 12.1 Log of stock price.

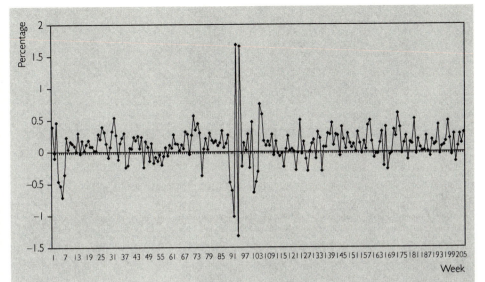

Fig. 12.2 Percentage change in stock price.

Table 12.1 AR(1) model using volatility as variable of interest.

	Coefficient	Standard error	t-Stat	P-value	Lower 95%	Upper 95%
Intercept	0.024	0.015	1.624	0.106	−0.005	0.053
Δy_{t-1}^2	0.737	0.047	15.552	1.74E − 36	0.643	0.830

In order to investigate the volatility properties of stock price in more depth we take deviations from the mean for the observations of the differenced data used to create Figure 12.2 and then square them. That is, we: (i) calculate the average change in stock price, 0.099%; (ii) subtract this number from every stock price change; and (iii) square the result. Figure 12.3 plots the resulting series which is our measure of volatility.

Note that volatility is the **square** of the stock price and hence cannot be negative. The pattern most evident in Figure 12.3 is the large increase in volatility in weeks 90–97 and, to a lesser extent, in weeks 4–8 and 101–107. This provides visual evidence that the volatility of this stock does indeed seem to vary over time.

More formal evidence on the pattern of volatility can be found by building an AR(p) model using the techniques of Chapter 9 and volatility as the variable of interest. The sequential testing procedure suggested in that chapter yields the AR(1) model shown in Table 12.1.

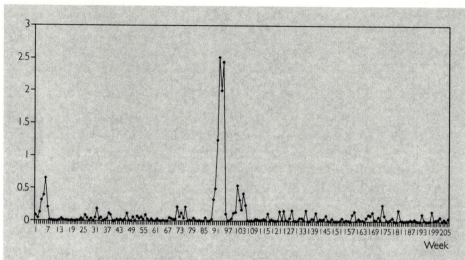

Fig. 12.3 Volatility of stock price.

It can be seen that last week's volatility has strong explanatory power for this week's volatility, since its coefficient is strongly statistically significant. Furthermore, $R^2 = 0.54$, indicating that 54% of the variation in volatility can be explained by last period's volatility. Consequently, it does seem as if volatility clusters are present. If volatility is high one period, it will also tend to be high the next period.

This information might be of great interest to an investor wishing to purchase this stock. Suppose an investor has just observed that $\Delta y_{t-1} = 0$ and therefore that $\Delta y_{t-1}^2 = 0$. In other words, the stock price changed by its average amount in period $t-1$. The investor is interested in predicting volatility in period t in order to judge the likely risk involved in purchasing the stock. Since the error is unpredictable, the investor ignores it (i.e. it is just as likely to be positive as negative). Below is the fitted AR(1) model:

$$\Delta \hat{y}_t^2 = 0.024 + 0.737 \Delta y_{t-1}^2.$$

Since $\Delta y_{t-1}^2 = 0$, the investor predicts volatility in period t to be 0.024. However, had he observed $\Delta y_{t-1}^2 = 1$, he would have predicted volatility in period t to be 0.761 (i.e. 0.024 + 0.737). This kind of information can be incorporated into financial models of investor behavior.

Exercise 12.1

NYSE.XLS contains data on ΔY = the percentage change in stock prices each month from 1952 through 1995 on the New York Stock Exchange (NYSE). For those interested in precise details, the data are value-weighted stock returns exclusive of dividends deflated using the Consumer Price Index. Note that this data is already in differenced form but deviations from the mean have not been taken, i.e. it is ΔY not Y or Δy.

(a) Make a time series plot of this data and comment on any patterns you observe.

(b) Using the techniques discussed in Chapter 9, comment on the univariate time series properties of ΔY. What does its autocorrelation function look like? If you build an $AR(p)$ model using this data what is p? Is ΔY stationary? Are stock returns on the NYSE predictable (i.e. can past stock returns help you to predict current values)?

(c) Assume that the original series, Y, follows a random walk such that an $AR(0)$ model for ΔY is appropriate (possibly with an intercept). Calculate the volatility of this variable as described in this chapter.

(d) Plot the volatility of this series. Does it appear that volatility clustering is present?

(e) Construct an $AR(p)$ model for the volatility series and discuss its properties. Can past values of volatility on the stock market help you to predict current volatility?

Autoregressive conditional heteroskedasticity (ARCH)

The class of ARCH models (including extensions) is probably the most popular one for working with financial volatility. It is most compactly explained by working with the familiar regression model:

$$Y_t = \alpha + \beta_1 X_{1t} + \beta_2 X_{2t} + \ldots + \beta_k X_{kt} + e_t.$$

Note that this general model contains many of the other models we have been working with. For instance, if $X_{jt} = Y_{t-j}$ (i.e. the explanatory variables are lags of the dependent variable) then this is an AR model. Another interesting case we will focus on below occurs if there are no explanatory variables at all (i.e. $\alpha = \beta_1 = \ldots = \beta_k = 0$) in which case the ARCH model we will describe shortly simply relates to the dependent variable itself. If we set this dependent variable to be the demeaned stock returns (i.e. $\Delta y_t = \Delta Y_t - \Delta \overline{Y}$), then we will be working with a model of financial volatility analogous to that used in the first half of this chapter.

The ARCH model relates to the variance (or volatility) of the error, e_t. You may wish to review the material at the end of Chapter 2 if you have forgotten the properties of variances. To simplify notation (and adopt a very common notation in financial econometrics), we will let:

$$\sigma_t^2 = \text{var}(e_t).$$

In other words, σ_t^2 will be our notation for volatility. It is this which is crucial in many financial applications. Note that we are allowing volatility to vary over time – which is quite important in light of our previous discussion of clustering of volatility.

The ARCH model with p lags (denoted by ARCH(p)) assumes that today's volatility is an average of past errors squared:

$$\sigma_t^2 = \gamma_0 + \gamma_1 e_{t-1}^2 + \ldots + \gamma_p e_{t-p}^2,$$

where $\gamma_1, \ldots, \gamma_p$ are coefficients that can be estimated in many statistical software packages. In the case where we have no explanatory variables and the dependent variable is Δy_t, we have

$$\sigma_t^2 = \gamma_0 + \gamma_1 \Delta y_{t-1}^2 + \ldots + \gamma_p \Delta y_{t-p}^2,$$

and the ARCH volatility depends on recent values of Δy_t^2 – the metric for volatility we were using in the first half of this chapter. This model is closely related to the autoregressive model (which accounts for the "AR" part of the name ARCH) and ARCH models have similar properties to AR models – except that these properties relate to the volatility of the series.

Example: Volatility in stock prices (continued from page 216)

With ARCH models we do not need to worry about subtracting the mean from stock returns as we did in the first half of the chapter (by simply including an intercept in the regression model we are allowing for a random walk with drift). Accordingly, we use the logged stock price data from STOCK.XLS and simply take the first different to create the variable ΔY_t. If we estimate an ARCH(1) model with ΔY_t as the dependent variable and an intercept in the regression equation, our computer software package produces a table similar to Table 12.2.

Table 12.2   ARCH(1) model using stock returns data.

	Coefficient	P-value	Lower 95%	Upper 95%
ΔY_t				
Intercept	0.105	0.000	0.081	0.129
ARCH				
Lag 1	0.660	0.000	0.302	1.018
Intercept	0.024	0.000	0.016	0.032

The upper part of Table 12.2 refers to the coefficients in the regression equation. In this case, we have only included an intercept (labeled α in the regression equation). The lower part of the table refers to the ARCH equation. Since we are working with an ARCH(1) model, the equation includes an intercept (labeled γ_0 in the ARCH equation) and one lag of the errors squares (labeled γ_1 in the ARCH equation and "Lag 1" in the table). The numbers in the table can be read in the same manner as in the tables we have reported in earlier regression chapters. That is, the numbers in the column labeled "Coefficient" are estimates of the coefficients (although, in this case, they are not OLS estimates, but rather more sophisticated estimates designed for ARCH models). The numbers in the columns labeled "P-value" are P-values for testing the hypothesis that the corresponding coefficient equals zero. In this case, since the P-values are all less than 0.05, we can conclude all the variables (in the regression equation and the ARCH equation) are statistically significant at the 5% level. The final two columns are lower and upper bounds for a 95% confidence interval.

The estimate of γ_1 (i.e. the coefficient on the lagged errors squared in the ARCH equation) is 0.660, indicating that volatility this month depends strongly on the errors squared last month. This shows that there is persistence in volatility of a similar degree to that found using the simpler methods in the first half of this chapter. Remember that we previously found that the AR(1) coefficient in a regression involving Δy_t^2 was estimated to be 0.737.

Lag length selection in ARCH models can be done in the same manner as with any time series model. That is, you can use an information criterion (see Chapter 11) to select a model, or simply look at P-values for whether coefficients equal zero (and, if they do seem to be zero, then variables can be dropped). For instance, if we estimate an ARCH(2) model using the stock return data we obtain Table 12.3.

Table 12.3 ARCH(2) model using stock returns data.

	Coefficient	P-value	Lower 95%	Upper 95%
ΔY_t				
Intercept	0.109	0.000	0.087	0.131
ARCH				
Lag 1	0.717	0.000	0.328	1.107
Lag 2	−0.043	0.487	−0.165	0.079
Intercept	0.025	0.000	0.016	0.033

The coefficient estimates in Table 12.3 are very similar to those for the ARCH(1) model. However, the coefficient on "Lag 2" (i.e. γ_2) is not significant, since its P-value is greater than 0.05. Thus, we have evidence that an ARCH(1) model is adequate and the second lag added by the ARCH(2) model does not add significant explanatory power to the model.

For many purposes (e.g. pricing financial derivatives), an estimate of σ_t^2 is required for every time period. We will not discuss how software packages produce this, but note only that this is provided by them.

There are many extensions of the ARCH model that are used by financial analysts. For instance, Stata lists seven different variants of the ARCH model with acronyms like GARCH, SAARCH, TARCH, AARCH, NARCH and NARCHK. Another popular alternative model, which is not in the ARCH class is called **stochastic volatility**. If you are doing a great deal of work on financial volatility, you should do further study to learn more about these models. Here we will only introduce the most popular of these extensions: Generalized ARCH or GARCH. This takes the ARCH model and adds on lags of the volatility measure itself (instead of just adding lags of squared errors). Thus, a GARCH model with (p, q) lags is denoted by GARCH(p, q) and has a volatility equation of:

$$\sigma_t^2 = \gamma_0 + \gamma_1 e_{t-1}^2 + \ldots + \gamma_p e_{t-p}^2 + \lambda_1 \sigma_{t-1}^2 + \ldots + \lambda_q \sigma_{t-q}^2.$$

The properties of the GARCH model are similar to the ARCH model. For instance, the coefficients can be interpreted in a similar fashion to AR coefficients and related to the degree of persistence in volatility. However, it can be shown that the GARCH model is much more flexible, much more capable of matching a wide variety of patterns of financial volatility.

Example: Volatility in stock prices (continued from page 219)

If we estimate a GARCH(1, 1) model with our stock return data, we obtain the results in Table 12.4.

Table 12.4   GARCH(1, 1) model using stock returns data.

	Coefficient	P-value	Lower 95%	Upper 95%
ΔY_t				
Intercept	0.109	0.000	0.087	0.131
ARCH				
ARCH lag 1	0.714	0.000	0.327	1.101
GARCH lag 1	−0.063	0.457	−0.231	0.104
Intercept	0.026	0.000	0.015	0.038

The numbers in this table can be interpreted in the same manner as for the ARCH tables. Here, however, we have an extra row labeled "GARCH lag 1" which contains results for λ_1 (i.e. the lagged volatility). It can be seen that this coefficient is insignificant, since its P-value is greater than 0.05. Thus, for this data set, the extension to a GARCH(1, 1) model does not seem necessary. The ARCH(1) model does perfectly well.

Exercise 12.2

NYSE.XLS contains data on ΔY = the percentage change in stock prices each month from 1952 through 1995 on the New York Stock Exchange (NYSE).

(a) Estimate ARCH(p) models for various values of p. Is there volatility clustering in this data (i.e. does an ARCH model beat a simpler model where there is constant volatility which means $\gamma_1 = \ldots = \gamma_p = 0$)? Which value of p is preferable?

(b) For your preferred choice of p, make a time series plot of volatility (i.e. plot a graph of σ_t^2).

(c) Repeat parts (a) and (b) using a GARCH(p, q). Does your graph of volatility look the same with ARCH and GARCH models?

Exercise 12.3

This exercise is a substantive empirical project and uses the data from the book *Nonlinear Time Series Models in Empirical Finance* by Philip Hans Franses and Dick van Dijk (Cambridge University Press). The data is available at http://www.few.eur.nl/few/people/djvandijk/nltsmef/nltsmef.htm. This data set was used in Exercise 9.9 and more details are provided there. It contains stock price indices from Amsterdam (EOE), Frankfurt (DAX), Hong Kong (Hang Seng), London (FTSE100), New York, (S&P500), Paris (CAC40), Singapore (Singapore All Shares) and Tokyo (Nikkei). It also has exchange rates for the Australian dollar, British pound, Canadian dollar, German DeutschMark, Dutch guilder, French franc, Japanese yen and the Swiss franc, all expressed as number of units of the foreign currency per US dollar. The sample period for the stock indexes runs from 6 January 1986 until 31 December 1997, whereas for the exchange rates the sample covers the period from 2 January 1980 until 31 December 1997.

Investigate financial volatility using this data with ARCH and GARCH models. Do stock returns appear to exhibit volatility? Do exchange rates?

An issue much studied by financial researchers is whether volatility in financial markets differs depending on the frequency a financial market is observed. For instance, stock markets might be more volatile when observed every day than when observed monthly. Investigate this issue using this data set. Note that it is available at a daily frequency. When you work with weekly data you can use data every Wednesday. For monthly frequency use the last day of each month.

Chapter summary

1. Many time series variables, particularly asset prices, seem to exhibit random walk behavior. For this reason, it is hard to predict how they will change in the future. However, such variables often do exhibit predictable patterns of volatility.
2. The square of the change in an asset price is a measure of its volatility.
3. Standard time series methods can be used to model the patterns of volatility in asset prices. The only difference is that volatility of the asset price is used as the dependent variable.
4. ARCH models are a more formal way of measuring volatility. They contain two equations. One is a standard regression equation. The second is a volatility equation, where volatility is defined as being the (time varying) variance of the regression error.
5. ARCH models share similarities with AR models, except that the "AR" part relates to the volatility equation.
6. There are many extensions of ARCH, of which GARCH is the most popular.
7. ARCH and GARCH models can be estimated using many common statistical software packages (but are hard to work with using a spreadsheet).

Endnotes

1. In deriving this result we have ignored the $N-1$ term in the denominator in the formula introduced in Chapter 2. You should simply note that it is not important here. In some formulas for the variance, $N-1$ is replaced by N. Here, $N=1$ so we can just ignore it.
2. This follows from the fact that $\ln(24.53)$ is 3.200 and $\ln(30.14)$ is 3.406.

Writing an empirical project

This appendix offers general guidelines on writing an empirical paper or project. Chapter 2 discusses many data sources should you wish to collect your own data for your project. Alternatively, the website associated with this book contains all the data used in the empirical illustrations in this book. If you are interested in working with cross-sectional data, EQUITY.XLS could form the basis for a good project (see Exercise 7.7). If you are interested in time series data, then Exercise 9.9 could form the basis for an empirical project. If you are interested in financial volatility then Exercise 12.3 is a good place to start.

Description of a typical empirical project

Financial analysts are engaged in research in a wide variety of areas today. Undergraduate and graduate students, academics, financial advisors, investment advisors working in the private sector, policymakers working in the civil service and central banks – may all need to write reports that involve analyzing financial data. Depending on the topic and intended audience, the form of these reports can vary widely, so that there is no one correct format for an empirical paper. With this in mind, we provide an outline that a financial report below as a guideline for future empirical work. Note, however, that, in the context of your own undergraduate projects or careers, it may not be necessary for you to include all of these elements in your report(s).

1. **Introduction.** Most reports begin with an introduction that briefly motivates and describes the issue being studied and summarizes the main empirical findings. The

introduction should be written in simple non-technical language, with statistical and financial jargon kept to a minimum. A reader who is not an expert in the field should be able to read and understand the general issues and findings of the report or paper.

2. **Literature review.** This should summarize related work that others have done. It should list and very briefly describe other papers and findings that relate to yours.

3. **Financial theory.** If the report is academic in nature and involves a formal theoretical model, then it is often described in this section. Outside of academia, you may not need to include a formal model, but this section allows you to describe the financial or institutional issues of your work in more detail. This section can be more technical than the preceding ones and will typically include some mathematics and financial jargon. In short, you can address this section solely to an audience of experts in your field.

4. **Data.** In this section you should describe your data, including a detailed discussion of its sources.

5. **The model to be estimated.** In this section you should discuss how you use the data to investigate the financial theory outlined in section 3. The exact form of this section might vary considerably, depending on the topic and on the intended audience. For instance, you may want to argue that a particular regression is of interest for the study, that a certain variable will be the dependent variable and that other variables will be the explanatory variables. Similarly, in a time series exercise, you may wish to argue that your financial theory implies that your variables should be cointegrated and that, for this reason, a test of cointegration will be carried out. Or, if you are interested in pricing financial derivatives, you can use this to motivate a particular model of financial volatility. In short, it is in this section that you should justify the techniques used in the next section.

6. **Empirical results.** This section is typically the heart of any report. At this stage you should describe your empirical findings and discuss how they relate to the financial issue(s) under investigation. It should contain both statistical and financial information. By "financial" information we refer, for example, to coefficient estimates or to a finding of cointegration between two variables, and what these findings may imply for financial theory. In contrast, "statistical" information may include: results from hypothesis tests that show how coefficient estimates are significant; a justification for choice of lag length; an explanation for deleting insignificant explanatory variables; a discussion of model fit (e.g. the R^2 or outliers); etc. Much of this information can be presented in charts or graphs. It is not uncommon for papers to begin with some simple graphs (e.g. a time series plot of the data) and then follow with a table of descriptive statistics (e.g. the mean, standard deviation, and minimum/maximum of each variable, and a correlation matrix). Another table might include results from a more formal statistical analysis, such as OLS coefficient estimates, together with t-statistics (or P-values), R^2s and F-statistics for testing the significance of the regression as a whole.

7. **Conclusion.** This should briefly summarize the issues addressed in the paper, specifically, its most important empirical findings.

General considerations

The following contains a discussion of a few of the issues that you should keep foremost in your mind while carrying out an empirical project. In particular, it discusses what constitutes good empirical science and how you should present your results.

The first thing worth stressing is that there are no right or wrong empirical results. *Empirical results are what they are and you should not be disappointed if they do not show what you had hoped they would.* In an ideal world, a researcher comes up with a new theory then carries out empirical work that supports this new theory in a statistically significant way. *The real world very rarely approaches this ideal.*

In the real world, explanatory variables that you expect to be statistically significant often aren't significant. Variables you expect to be cointegrated often aren't cointegrated. Coefficients you expect to be positive often turn out to be negative. These results are obtained all the time – even in the most sophisticated of studies. They should not discourage you! Instead, you should always keep an open mind. *A finding that a theory does not seem to work is just as scientifically valid as a finding that a theory does work.*

Furthermore, empirical results are often unclear or confusing. For instance, one statistical test might indicate one thing while another the opposite. Likewise, an explanatory variable that is significant in one regression might be insignificant in another regression. There is nothing you can do about this, except to report your results honestly and try (if possible) to understand why such conflicts or confusions are occurring.

It would be rare for a researcher to completely falsify her results. Often, however, she may be tempted to do slightly dishonest things in order to show that results are indeed as financial reasoning anticipated. For instance, it is common for a researcher to run a large number of regressions with many different explanatory variables. On the whole, this is a very wise thing; a sign that the researcher is exploring the data in detail and from a number of angles. However, if the researcher presents only the regression that supports a particular theory and not the other regressions that discredit it, she is intentionally misleading the reader. Always avoid this temptation to misrepresent your results!

On the issue of how results should be presented, I cannot stress enough the importance of clarity and brevity. Whether it is a good thing or a bad thing, it is undoubtedly the case that university lecturers, readers of investment advice, civil servants, policymakers and employers are busy people who do not want to spend a lot of time reading long, poorly organized and verbose reports.

One key skill that writers of good reports show is selectivity. For example, you may have many different coefficient results and tests statistics from your various regression runs. An important part of any report is to decide what information is important and what is unimportant to your readership. Select only the most important information for inclusion in your report and – as always – report honestly and openly the results that you obtain.

APPENDIX B

Data directory

Data file	Content	Data type	Chapter
ADVERT.XLS	Sales and advertising expenditure	Cross-sectional, $N = 84$ companies	Chapter 5
BADNEWS.XLS	Market cap. and oil price	Time Series, $T = 60$ months	Chapter 8
CAPM.XLS	Excess returns for Company A and the stock market	Time series, $T = 120$ months	Chapters 4, 5 and 6
CAY.XLS	Consumption, assets and income	Time series, $T = 206$ quarters	Chapter 11
CORMAT.XLS	Artificial variables labeled Y, X and Z	Cross-sectional, $N = 20$	Chapter 3
EQUITY.XLS	Firm share value, debt, sales, income, assets, SEO dummy	Cross-sectional, $N = 309$ companies	Chapters 3, 4, 5 and 7
EX34.XLS	Artificial variables labeled Y, X_1, X_2 and X_3	Cross-sectional, $N = 20$	Chapter 3
EX46.XLS	Artificial variables labeled Y and X	Cross-sectional, $N = 50$	Chapter 4
EXECUTIVE.XLS	Executive compensation, profits, changes in sales and change in debts	Cross-sectional, $N = 70$ companies	Chapters 2, 3, 4, 5 and 6
EXRUK.XLS	UK pound/US dollar exchange rate	Time series, January 1947 through October, 1996, $T = 598$ months	Chapter 2

Data file	Content	Data type	Chapter
FIG51.XLS	Artificial variables labeled X and Y	Cross-sectional, $N = 5$	Chapter 5
FIG52.XLS	Artificial variables labeled X and Y	Cross-sectional, $N = 100$	Chapter 5
FIG53.XLS	Artificial variables labeled X and Y	Cross-sectional, $N = 100$	Chapter 5
FIG54.XLS	Artificial variables labeled X and Y	Cross-sectional, $N = 100$	Chapter 5
FIG95.XLS	Artificial variable created with $\phi = 0$	Time series, $T = 100$	Chapter 9
FIG96.XLS	Artificial variable created with $\phi = 0.8$	Time series, $T = 100$	Chapter 9
FIG97.XLS	Artificial variable created with $\phi = 1$	Time series, $T = 100$	Chapter 9
FIG98.XLS	Trend stationary artificial variable	Time series, $T = 100$	Chapter 9
FOREX.XLS	Spot and forward exchange rates	Time series, $T = 181$ months	Chapters 10 and 11
GDPPC.XLS	Real GDP per capita	Cross-sectional, $N = 90$ countries	Chapters 2 and 5
HPRICE.XLS	Housing prices and housing characteristics (e.g. lot size, number of bedrooms)	Cross-sectional, $N = 546$ houses	Chapters 3, 5, 6 and 7
INTERESTRATES. XLS	Long- and short-term interest rates	Time series, 1954Q1 through 1994Q4, $T = 164$ quarters	Chapters 2, 9, 10 and 11
LIBERAL.XLS	Growth in GDP and market cap.	Time series, $T = 98$ months	Chapter 10
LIBERAL1.XLS	Growth in GDP and market cap.	Time series, $T = 98$ months	Chapter 10
LONGGDP.XLS	Real GDP per capita for Australia, USA, UK, Canada	Time series, 1870 through 1993, $T = 124$ years	Chapter 11
LONGRUN.XLS	Stock return and dividend-price ratio	Time series, $T = 1200$ months	Chapter 8
NYSE.XLS	NYSE stock price index	Time series, January 1952 through December 1995, $T = 528$ months	Chapters 9 and 12
STOCK.XLS	Logged stock price data	Time series, $T = 208$ weeks	Chapter 12
STOCKPAB.XLS	Stock prices in two countries	Time series, $T = 131$ months	Chapters 10 and 11
VAR.XLS	Variables used in Campbell–Ammer paper	Time series, $T = 471$ months	Chapter 11

User Note: The website accompanying this book http://www.wiley.com/go/koopafd contains all these data sets in Excel file format (".xls"). Most computer software packages will read Excel files. If your package does not, you can use the "Save As" option in Excel to save the files in other formats (e.g. as ASCII text files).

Index

CPSIA information can be obtained at www.ICGtesting.com
Printed in the USA
BVOW07s2049200713

326399BV00001B/2/P

9 780470 013212